DANCING WITH THE DEVIL

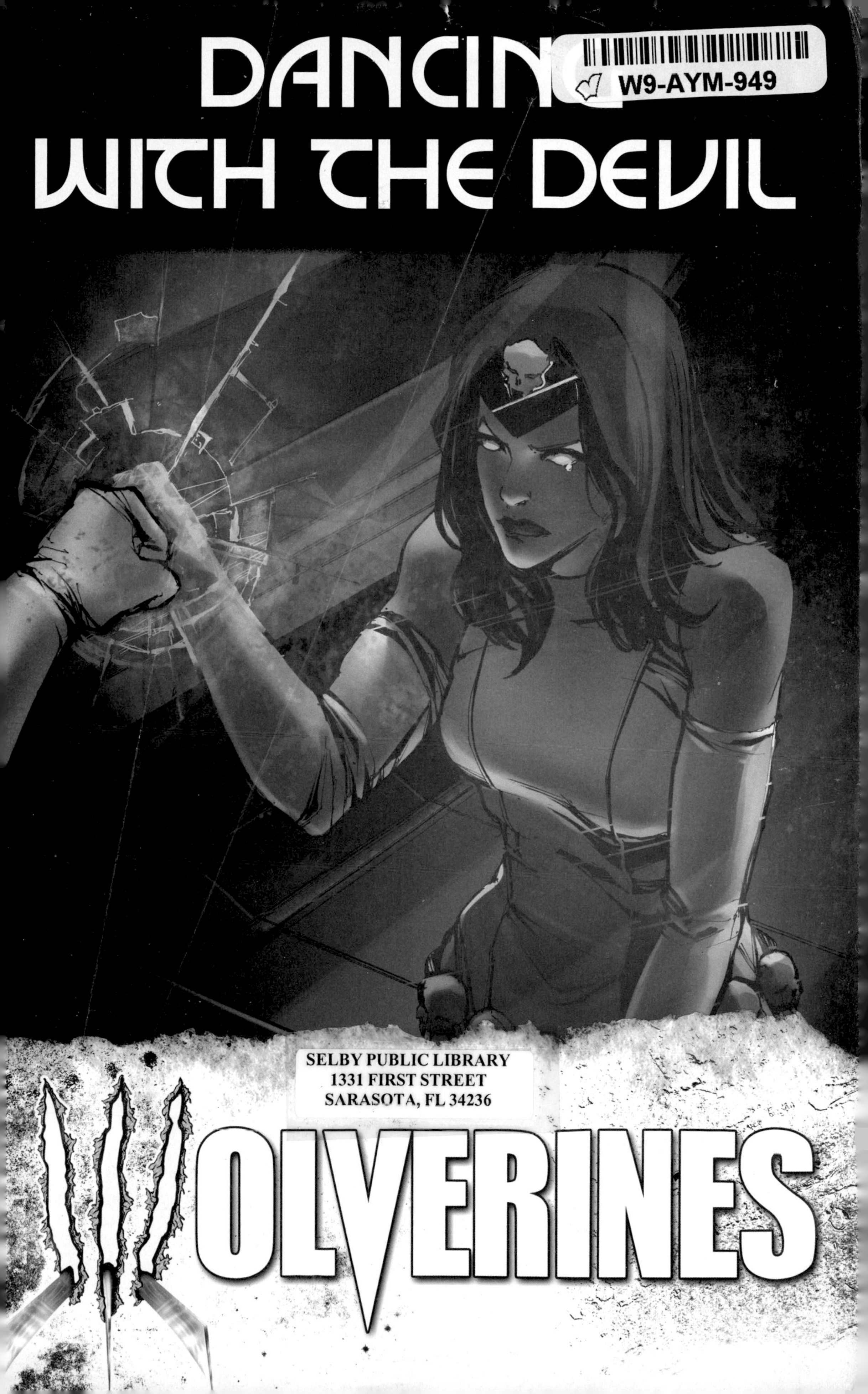

WOLVERINES

WRITERS

CHARLES SOULE (#1, #3, #5) &
RAY FAWKES (#2, #4)

COLORISTS

FCO PLASCENCIA (#1), ISRAEL SILVA &
BRETT SMITH (#2), SONIA OBACK (#4)
AND LEE LOUGHRIDGE (#5)

ARTISTS

NICK BRADSHAW & WALDEN WONG (#1),
ALISSON BORGES (#2), JUAN DOE (#3),
ARIELA KRISTANTINA (#1, PGS. 17-18 & #4) AND
JONATHAN MARKS (#5)

LETTERER

VC'S CORY PETIT

COVER ART

NICK BRADSHAW &
FCO PLASCENCIA (#1-2, #5) AND
ANDY CLARKE & MARTE GRACIA (#3-4)

EDITORS

KATIE KUBERT &
MIKE MARTS

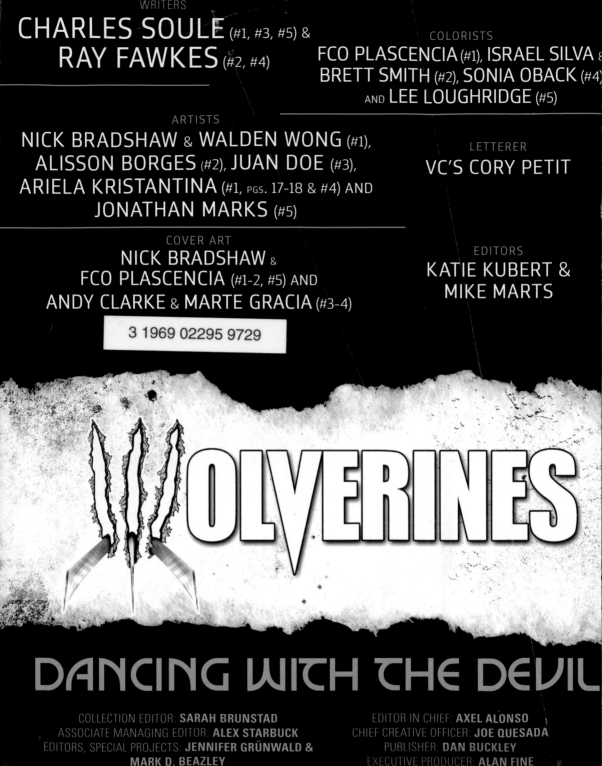

WOLVERINES

DANCING WITH THE DEVIL

COLLECTION EDITOR: **SARAH BRUNSTAD**
ASSOCIATE MANAGING EDITOR: **ALEX STARBUCK**
EDITORS, SPECIAL PROJECTS: **JENNIFER GRÜNWALD & MARK D. BEAZLEY**
SENIOR EDITOR, SPECIAL PROJECTS: **JEFF YOUNGQUIST**
SVP PRINT, SALES & MARKETING: **DAVID GABRIEL**

EDITOR IN CHIEF: **AXEL ALONSO**
CHIEF CREATIVE OFFICER: **JOE QUESADA**
PUBLISHER: **DAN BUCKLEY**
EXECUTIVE PRODUCER: **ALAN FINE**

WOLVERINES VOL. 1: DANCING WITH THE DEVIL. Contains material originally published in magazine form as WOLVERINES #1-5. First printing 2015. ISBN# 978-0-7851-9286-2. Published by MARVEL WORLDWIDE, INC., a subsidiary of MARVEL ENTERTAINMENT, LLC. OFFICE OF PUBLICATION: 135 West 50th Street, New York, NY 10020. **Printed in Canada.** ALAN FINE, EVP - Office of the President, Marvel Worldwide, Inc. and EVP & CMO Marvel Characters B.V.; DAN BUCKLEY, Publisher & President - Print, Animation & Digital Division; JOE QUESADA, Chief Creative Officer; TOM BREVOORT, SVP of Publishing; DAVID BOGART, SVP of Operations & Procurement, Publishing; C.B. CEBULSKI, SVP of Creator & Content Development; DAVID GABRIEL, SVP Print, Sales & Marketing; JIM O'KEEFE, VP of Operations & Logistics; DAN CARR, Executive Director of Publishing Technology; SUSAN CRESPI, Editorial Operations Manager; ALEX MORALES, Publishing Operations Manager; STAN LEE, Chairman Emeritus. For information regarding advertising in Marvel Comics or on Marvel.com, please contact Niza Disla, Director of Marvel Partnerships, at ndisla@marvel.com. For Marvel subscription inquiries, please call 800-217-9158. **Manufactured between 2/27/2015 and 4/6/2015 by SOLISCO PRINTERS, SCOTT, QC, CANADA.**

10 9 8 7 6 5 4 3 2 1

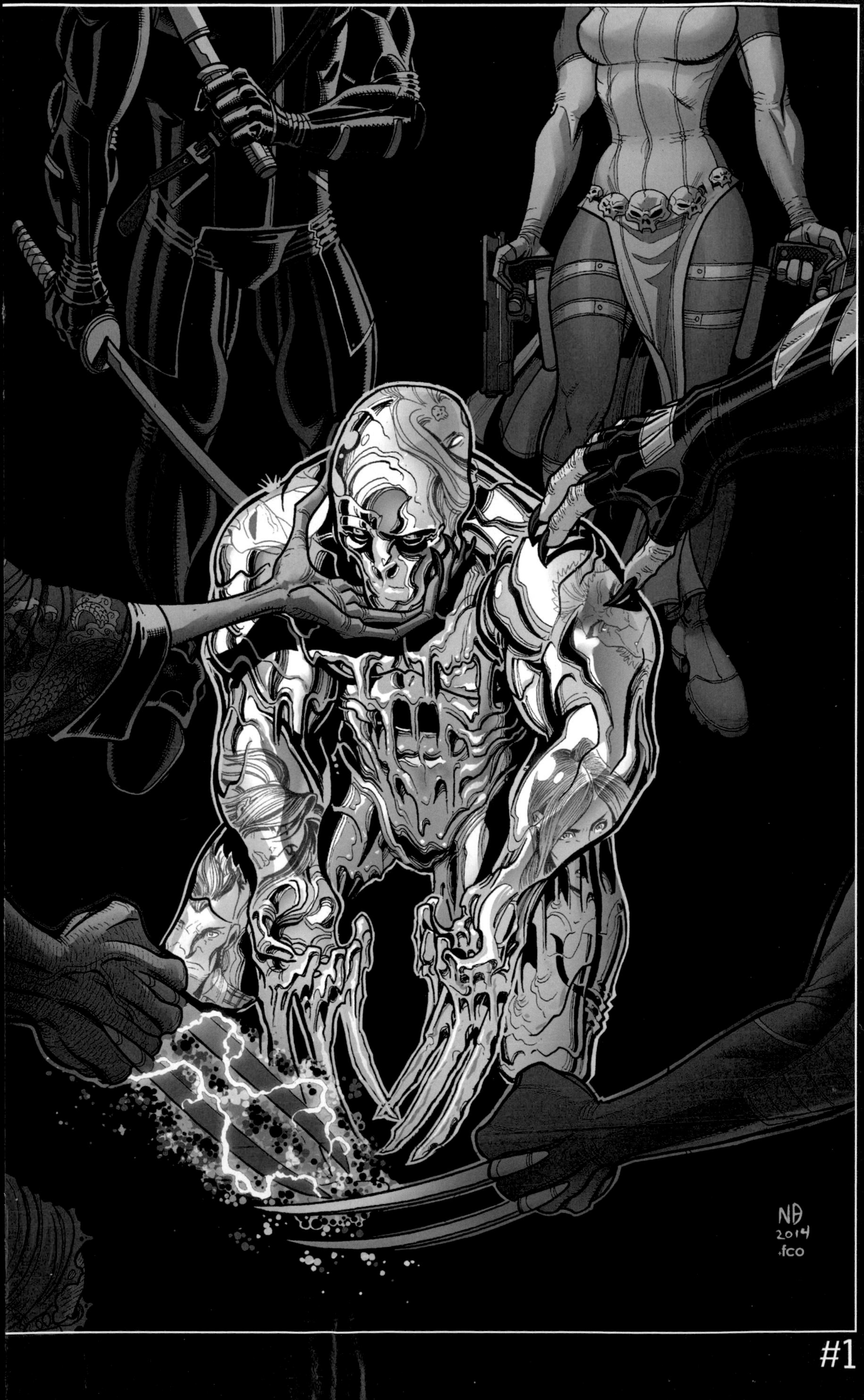
NB
2014
.fco

#1

THE WOLVERINE IS DEAD.
HIS LEGACY REMAINS.

LOGAN MET HIS END WHILE DESTROYING A REVAMPED VERSION OF THE WEAPON X PROJEC
LOCATED IN A FACILITY KNOWN AS PARADISE, LED BY DR. ABRAHAM CORNELIUS – THE MA
RESPONSIBLE FOR INFUSING WOLVERINE'S BODY WITH THE UNBREAKABLE ADAMANTIU.
THAT COATED HIS SKELETON AND CLAWS.

LOGAN COULD NOT ESCAPE, BUT OTHERS DID – FIVE OF CORNELIUS' TEST SUBJECTS, AI
GRANTED STRANGE NEW POWERS – SHOGUN, EX-SOLDIER FUSED WITH THE SPIRIT OF TH
DEADLY DEMON NINJA OGUN; NEURO, BRILLIANT PSYCHOPATH; ENDO, TROUBLED SPEEDSTEI
SKEL, IMMENSELY STRONG BUT PHYSICALLY ADDICTED TO VIOLENCE; AND JUNK – WIT
ABILITIES RELATED TO ANIMAL TRAITS ACTIVATED IN HIS GENES. NONE WERE EVER INTENDE
TO SURVIVE OUTSIDE PARADISE, AND HAVE BEEN INFUSED WITH A TICKING CLOCK IN THEI
DNA THAT WILL KILL THEM UNLESS IT CAN BE DEACTIVATED.

THESE LOST WEAPONS KIDNAPPED A GROUP OF FIVE OF WOLVERINE'S DEADLIEST ASSOCIATE
INCLUDING MYSTIQUE, SABRETOOTH, LADY DEATHSTRIKE, DAKEN AND X-23, IN THE HOF
THAT THEIR HEALING FACTORS MIGHT HOLD THE KEY TO SAVING THE TEST SUBJECTS' LIVE
THE REFUGEES FROM PARADISE HOLD SIGNIFICANT LEVERAGE OVER THE FIVE KILLERS – SECRE
"CONTROL WORDS" THAT CAN MANIPULATE, SEDATE OR EVEN KILL EACH OF THEM.

A DEAL WAS STRUCK, WITH THE TEST SUBJECTS AGREEING TO RELEASE MYSTIQUE AND THE OTHERS I
EXCHANGE FOR THEIR HELP – BUT FIRST, THE TWO TEAMS UNDERTAKE A MISSION TOWARDS A GOA
THAT COULD SAVE BOTH GROUPS FROM EXTINCTION...

PARADISE

THE WOLVERINES

WOLVERINES

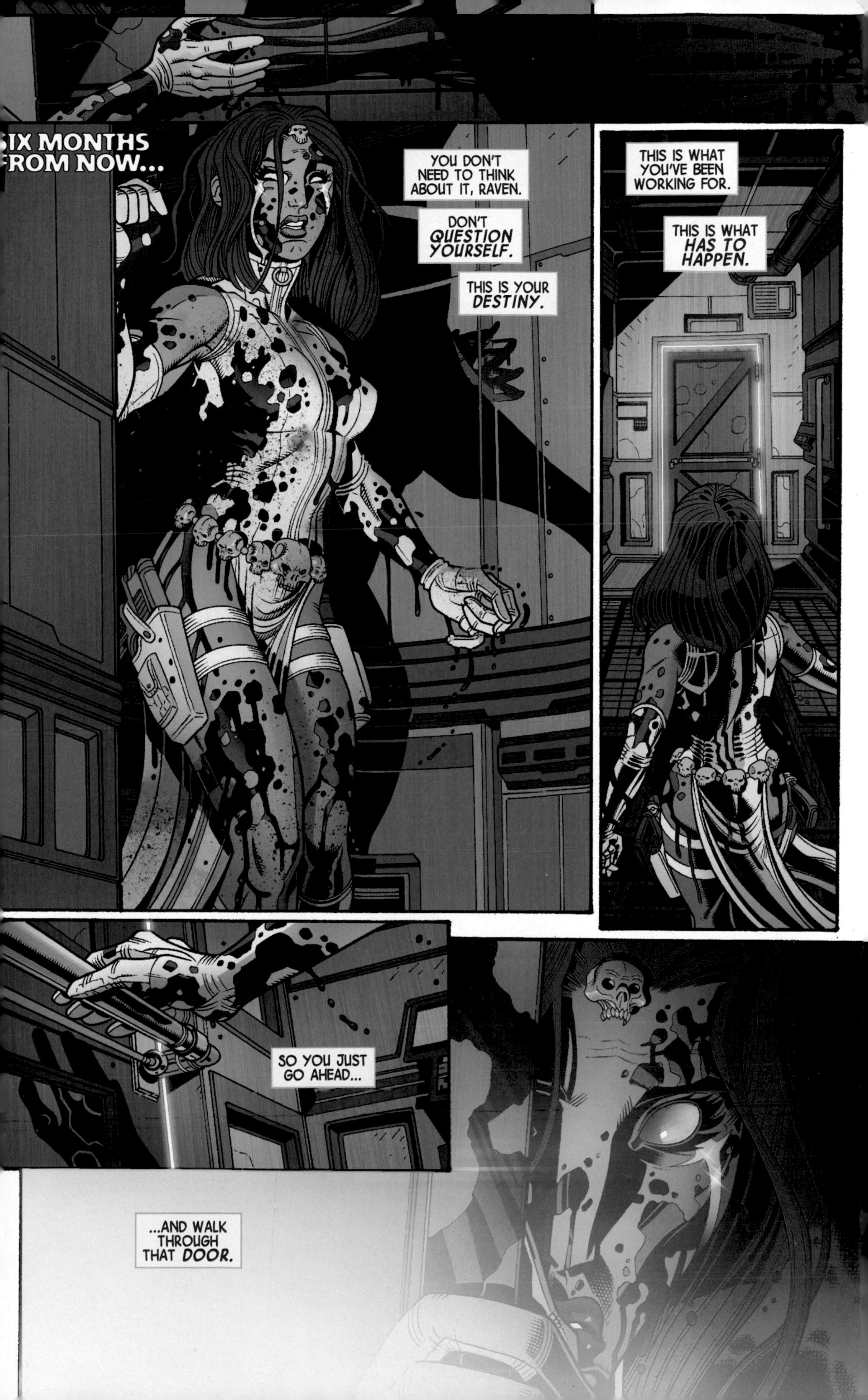
SIX MONTHS
FROM NOW...
YOU DON'T NEED TO THINK ABOUT IT, RAVEN.
DON'T QUESTION YOURSELF.
THIS IS YOUR DESTINY.
THIS IS WHAT YOU'VE BEEN WORKING FOR.
THIS IS WHAT HAS TO HAPPEN.
SO YOU JUST GO AHEAD...
...AND WALK THROUGH THAT DOOR.

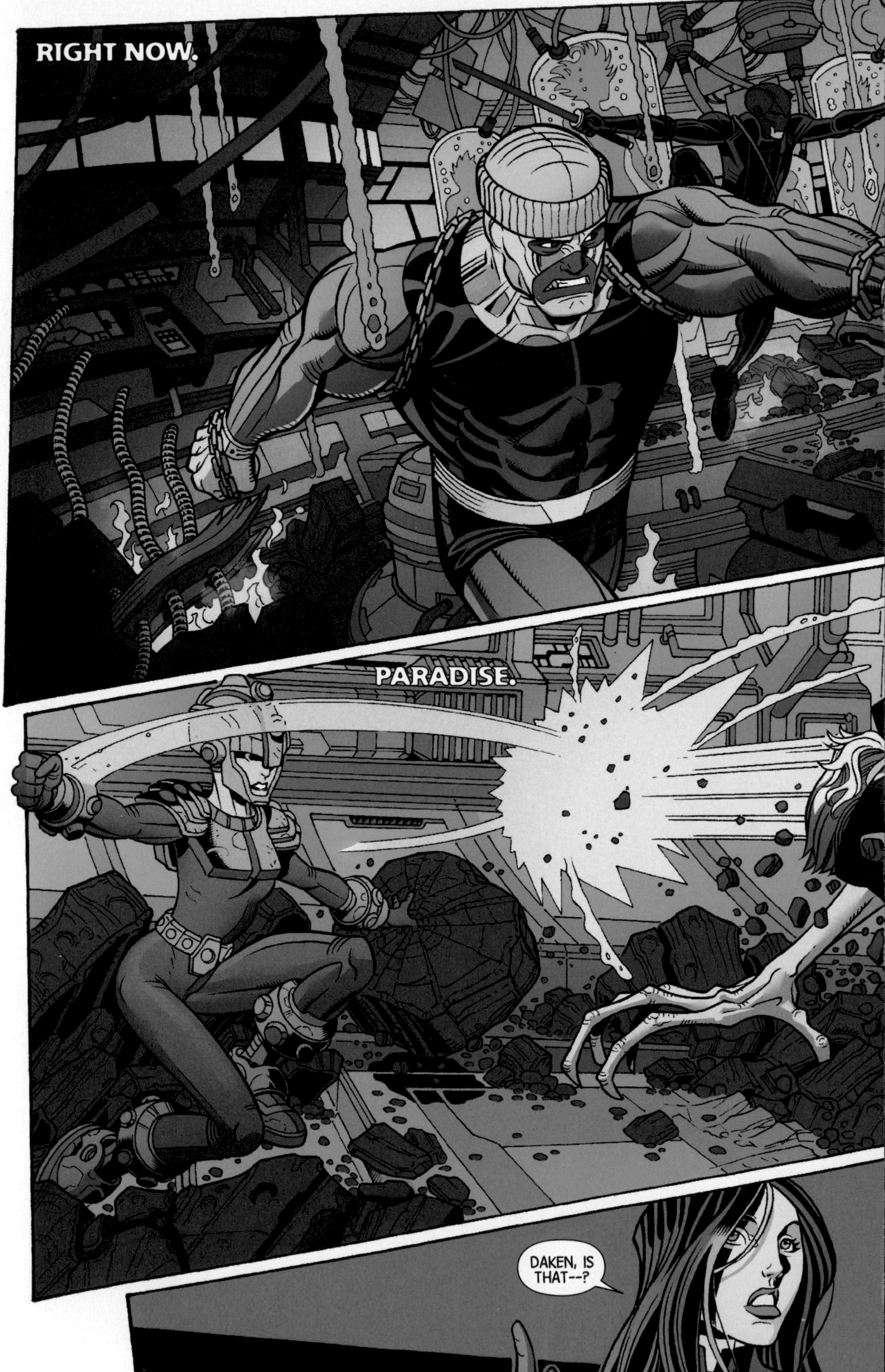
RIGHT NOW.
PARADISE.
DAKEN, IS THAT--?

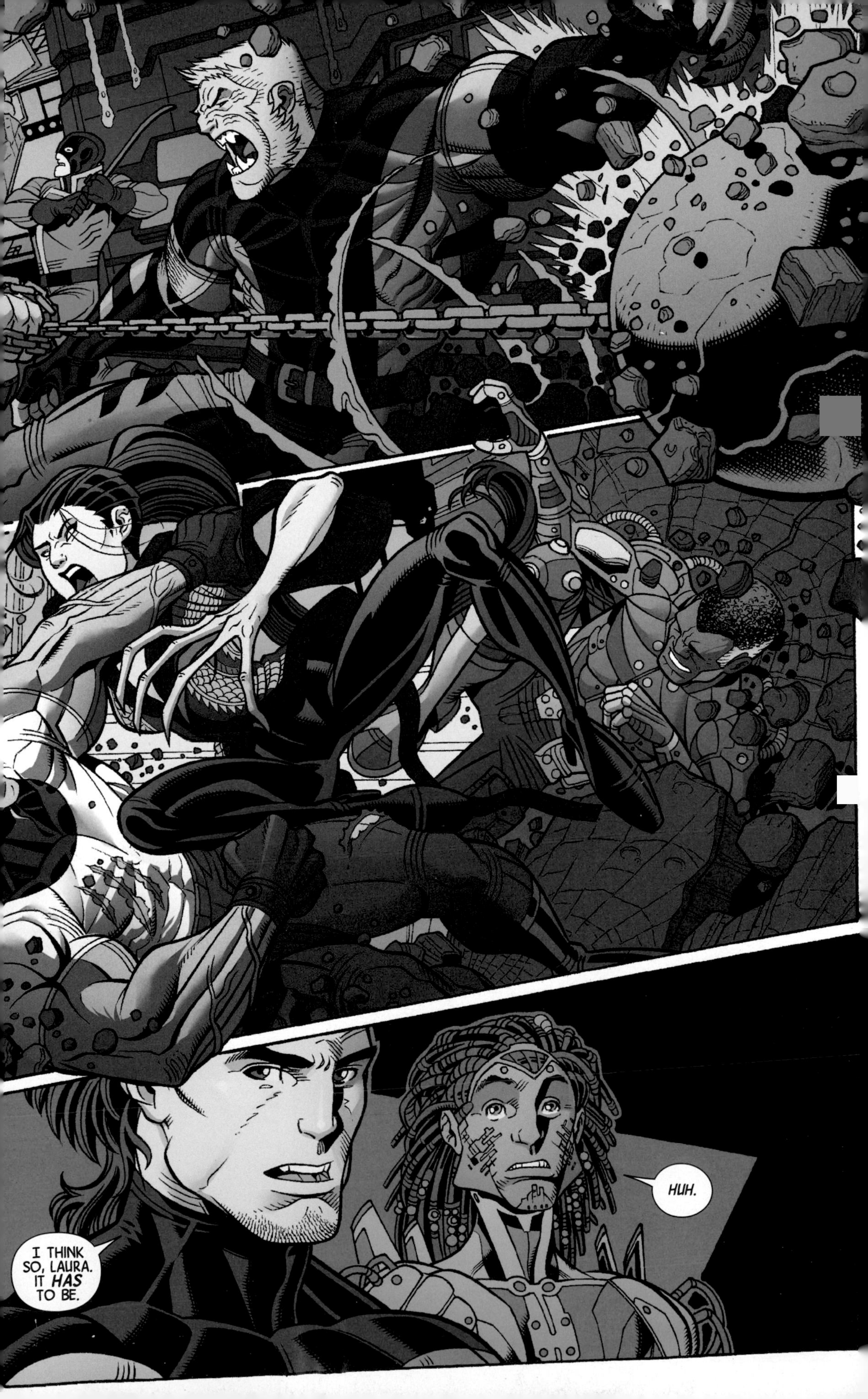
HUH.
I THINK SO, LAURA. IT *HAS* TO BE.

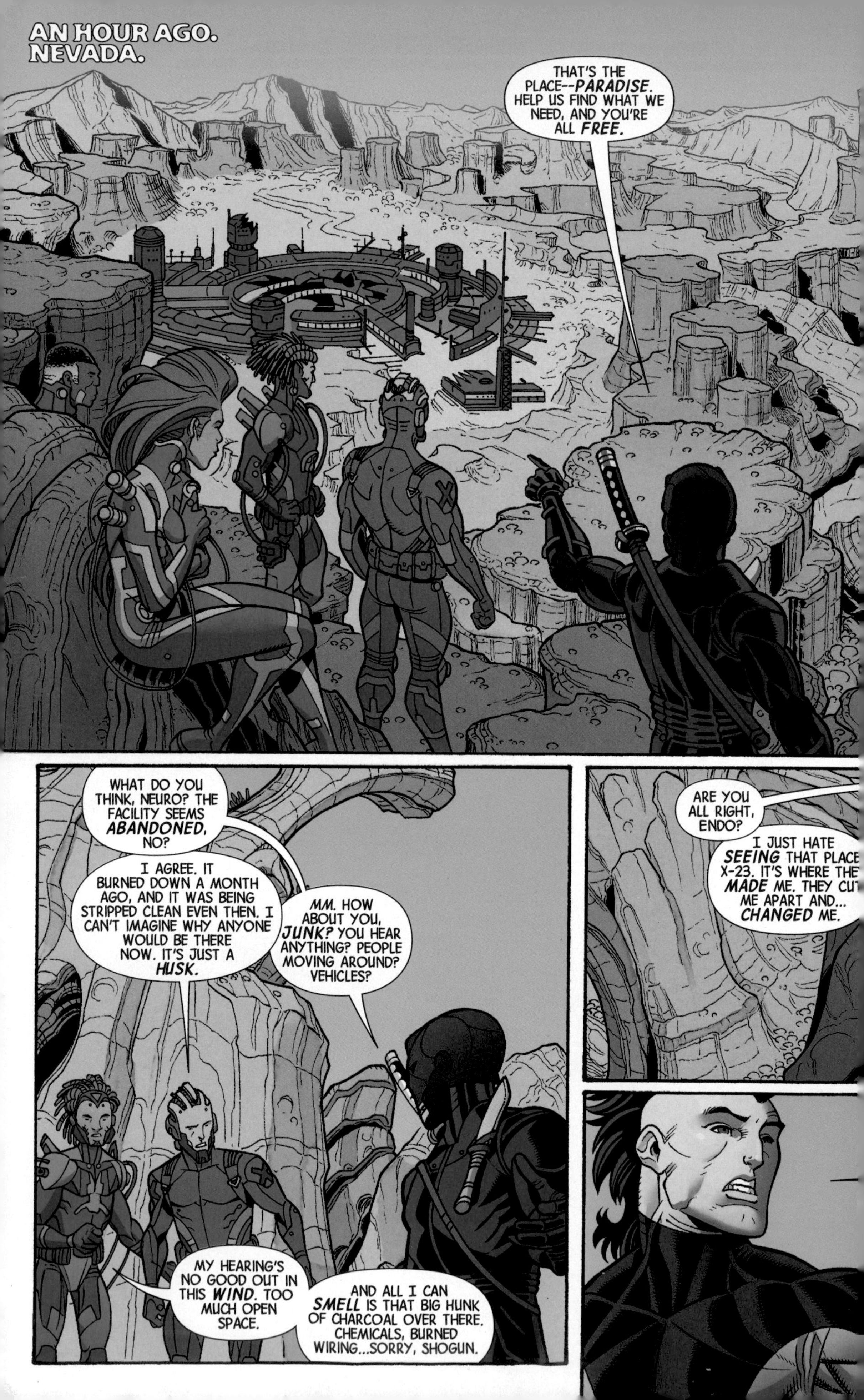
AN HOUR AGO. NEVADA.
THAT'S THE PLACE--PARADISE. HELP US FIND WHAT WE NEED, AND YOU'RE ALL FREE.
WHAT DO YOU THINK, NEURO? THE FACILITY SEEMS ABANDONED, NO?
I AGREE. IT BURNED DOWN A MONTH AGO, AND IT WAS BEING STRIPPED CLEAN EVEN THEN. I CAN'T IMAGINE WHY ANYONE WOULD BE THERE NOW. IT'S JUST A HUSK.
MM. HOW ABOUT YOU, JUNK? YOU HEAR ANYTHING? PEOPLE MOVING AROUND? VEHICLES?
MY HEARING'S NO GOOD OUT IN THIS WIND. TOO MUCH OPEN SPACE.
AND ALL I CAN SMELL IS THAT BIG HUNK OF CHARCOAL OVER THERE. CHEMICALS, BURNED WIRING...SORRY, SHOGUN.
ARE YOU ALL RIGHT, ENDO?
I JUST HATE SEEING THAT PLACE X-23. IT'S WHERE THE MADE ME. THEY CUT ME APART AND... CHANGED ME.

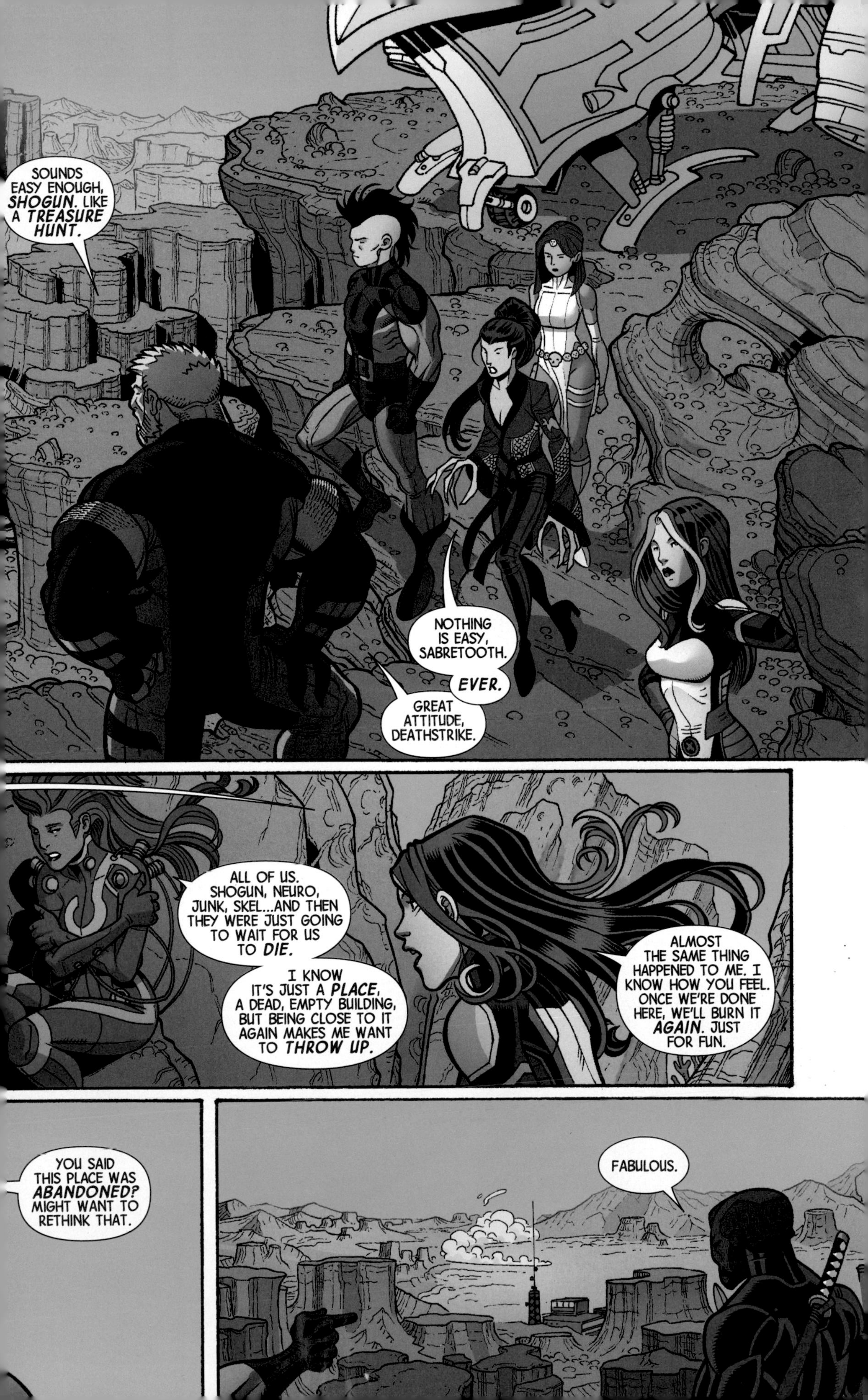
SOUNDS EASY ENOUGH, SHOGUN. LIKE A TREASURE HUNT.
NOTHING IS EASY, SABRETOOTH.
EVER.
GREAT ATTITUDE, DEATHSTRIKE.
ALL OF US. SHOGUN, NEURO, JUNK, SKEL...AND THEN THEY WERE JUST GOING TO WAIT FOR US TO DIE.
I KNOW IT'S JUST A PLACE, A DEAD, EMPTY BUILDING, BUT BEING CLOSE TO IT AGAIN MAKES ME WANT TO THROW UP.
ALMOST THE SAME THING HAPPENED TO ME. I KNOW HOW YOU FEEL. ONCE WE'RE DONE HERE, WE'LL BURN IT AGAIN. JUST FOR FUN.
YOU SAID THIS PLACE WAS ABANDONED? MIGHT WANT TO RETHINK THAT.
FABULOUS.

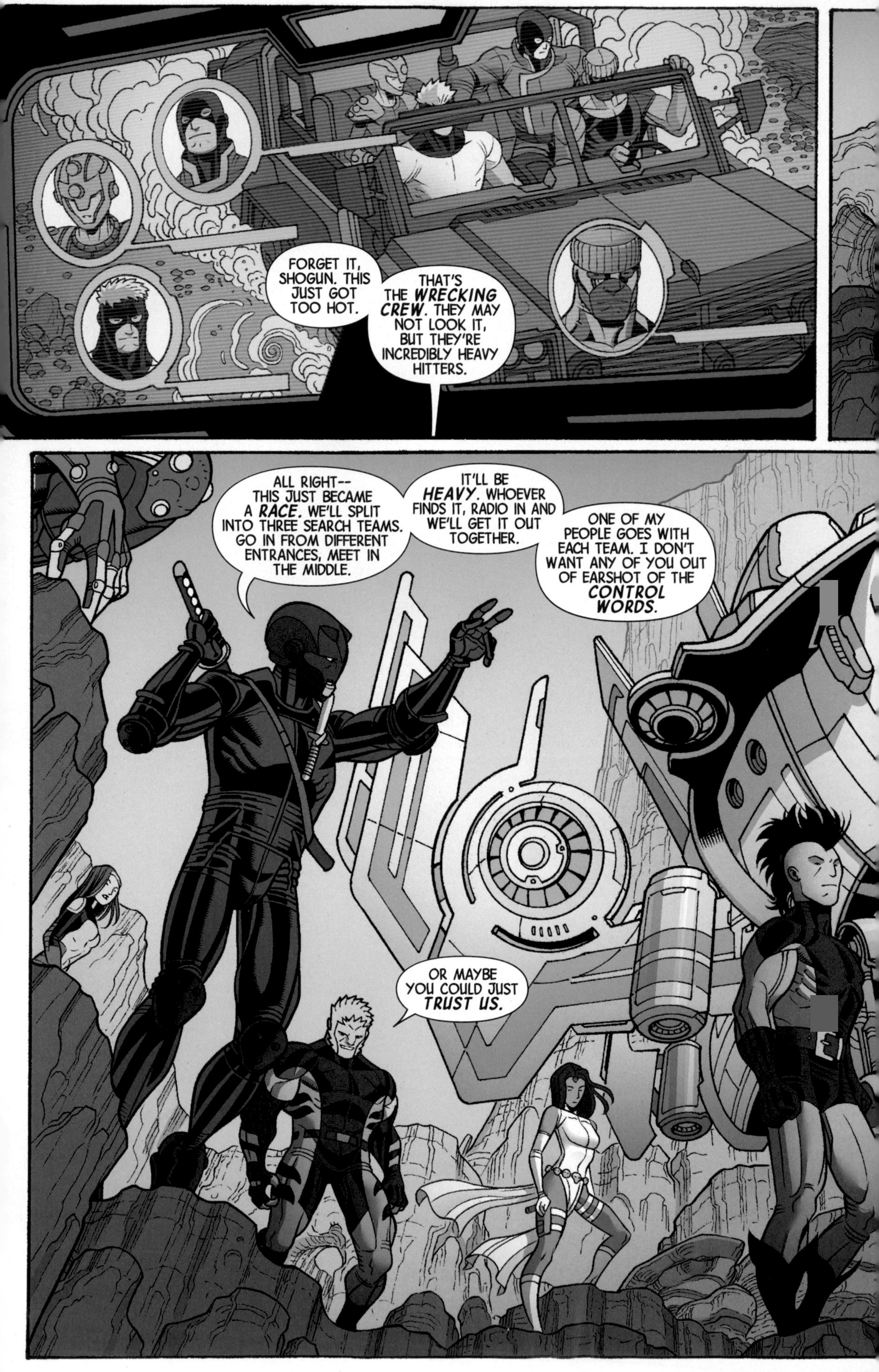

FORGET IT, SHOGUN. THIS JUST GOT TOO HOT.
THAT'S THE *WRECKING CREW*. THEY MAY NOT LOOK IT, BUT THEY'RE INCREDIBLY HEAVY HITTERS.
ALL RIGHT-- THIS JUST BECAME A *RACE.* WE'LL SPLIT INTO THREE SEARCH TEAMS. GO IN FROM DIFFERENT ENTRANCES, MEET IN THE MIDDLE.
IT'LL BE *HEAVY*. WHOEVER FINDS IT, RADIO IN AND WE'LL GET IT OUT TOGETHER.
ONE OF MY PEOPLE GOES WITH EACH TEAM. I DON'T WANT ANY OF YOU OUT OF EARSHOT OF THE *CONTROL WORDS*.
OR MAYBE YOU COULD JUST *TRUST US.*

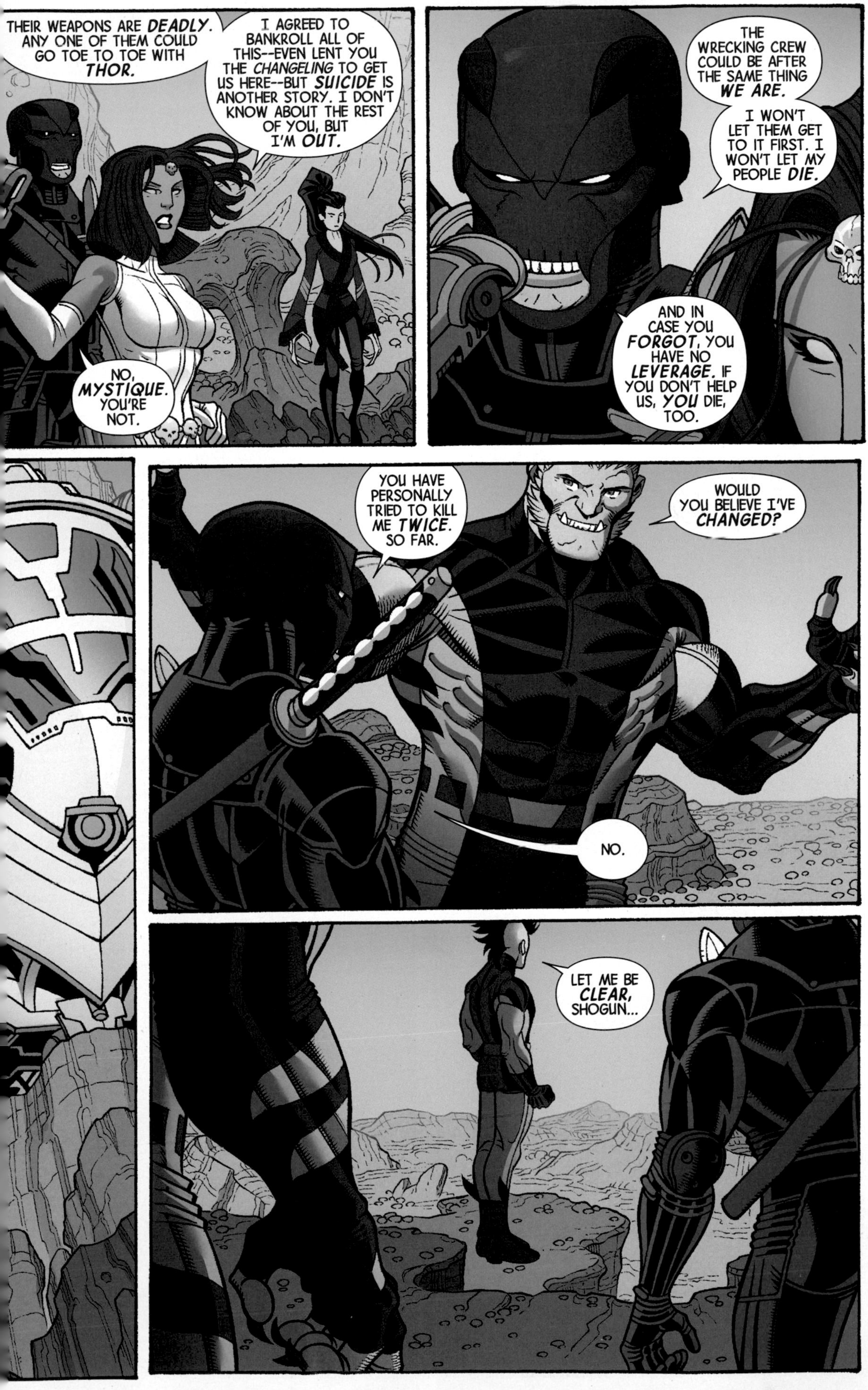
THEIR WEAPONS ARE DEADLY. ANY ONE OF THEM COULD GO TOE TO TOE WITH THOR.
I AGREED TO BANKROLL ALL OF THIS--EVEN LENT YOU THE CHANGELING TO GET US HERE--BUT SUICIDE IS ANOTHER STORY. I DON'T KNOW ABOUT THE REST OF YOU, BUT I'M OUT.
NO, MYSTIQUE. YOU'RE NOT.
THE WRECKING CREW COULD BE AFTER THE SAME THING WE ARE.
I WON'T LET THEM GET TO IT FIRST. I WON'T LET MY PEOPLE DIE.
AND IN CASE YOU FORGOT, YOU HAVE NO LEVERAGE. IF YOU DON'T HELP US, YOU DIE, TOO.
YOU HAVE PERSONALLY TRIED TO KILL ME TWICE. SO FAR.
WOULD YOU BELIEVE I'VE CHANGED?
NO.
LET ME BE CLEAR, SHOGUN...

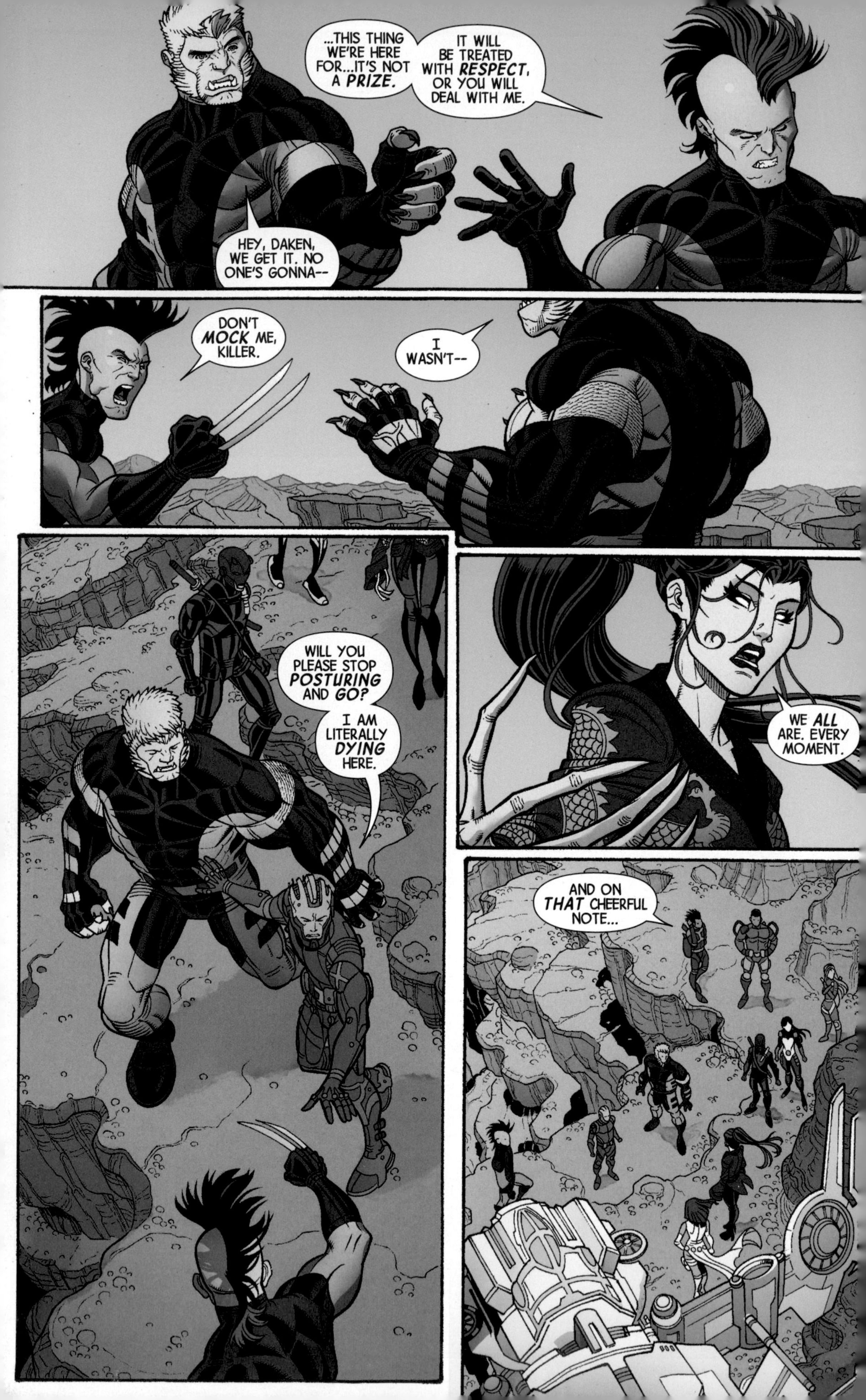
...THIS THING WE'RE HERE FOR...IT'S NOT A PRIZE.
IT WILL BE TREATED WITH RESPECT, OR YOU WILL DEAL WITH ME.
HEY, DAKEN, WE GET IT. NO ONE'S GONNA--
DON'T MOCK ME, KILLER.
I WASN'T--
WILL YOU PLEASE STOP POSTURING AND GO?
I AM LITERALLY DYING HERE.
WE ALL ARE. EVERY MOMENT.
AND ON THAT CHEERFUL NOTE...

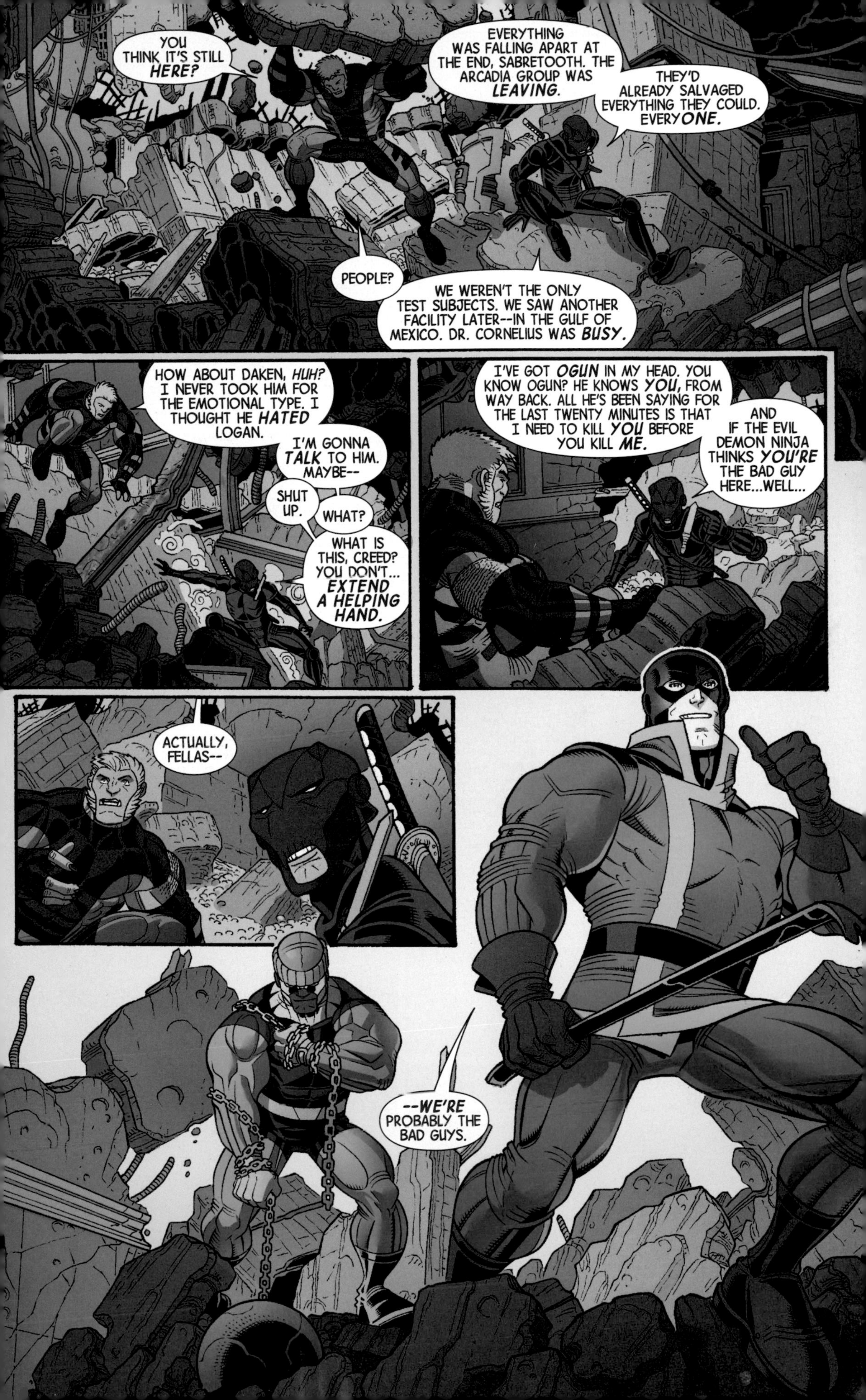
YOU THINK IT'S STILL HERE?
EVERYTHING WAS FALLING APART AT THE END, SABRETOOTH. THE ARCADIA GROUP WAS LEAVING.
THEY'D ALREADY SALVAGED EVERYTHING THEY COULD. EVERYONE.
PEOPLE?
WE WEREN'T THE ONLY TEST SUBJECTS. WE SAW ANOTHER FACILITY LATER--IN THE GULF OF MEXICO. DR. CORNELIUS WAS BUSY.
HOW ABOUT DAKEN, HUH? I NEVER TOOK HIM FOR THE EMOTIONAL TYPE. I THOUGHT HE HATED LOGAN.
I'M GONNA TALK TO HIM. MAYBE--
SHUT UP.
WHAT?
WHAT IS THIS, CREED? YOU DON'T... EXTEND A HELPING HAND.
I'VE GOT OGUN IN MY HEAD. YOU KNOW OGUN? HE KNOWS YOU, FROM WAY BACK. ALL HE'S BEEN SAYING FOR THE LAST TWENTY MINUTES IS THAT I NEED TO KILL YOU BEFORE YOU KILL ME.
AND IF THE EVIL DEMON NINJA THINKS YOU'RE THE BAD GUY HERE...WELL...
ACTUALLY, FELLAS--
--WE'RE PROBABLY THE BAD GUYS.

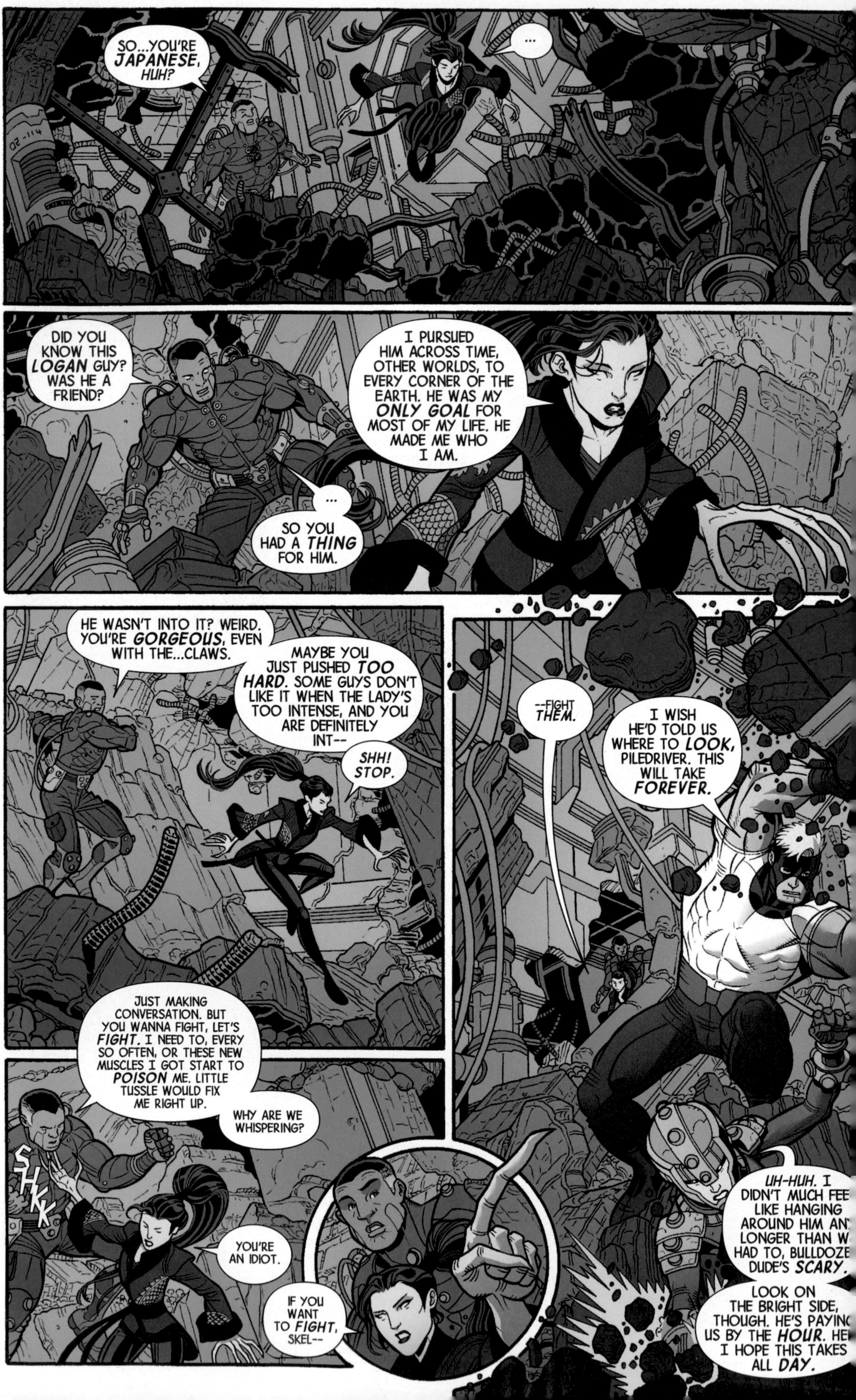

SO...YOU'RE JAPANESE, HUH?
...
DID YOU KNOW THIS LOGAN GUY? WAS HE A FRIEND?
I PURSUED HIM ACROSS TIME, OTHER WORLDS, TO EVERY CORNER OF THE EARTH. HE WAS MY ONLY GOAL FOR MOST OF MY LIFE. HE MADE ME WHO I AM.
...
SO YOU HAD A THING FOR HIM.
HE WASN'T INTO IT? WEIRD. YOU'RE GORGEOUS, EVEN WITH THE...CLAWS.
MAYBE YOU JUST PUSHED TOO HARD. SOME GUYS DON'T LIKE IT WHEN THE LADY'S TOO INTENSE, AND YOU ARE DEFINITELY INT--
SHH! STOP.
JUST MAKING CONVERSATION. BUT YOU WANNA FIGHT, LET'S FIGHT. I NEED TO, EVERY SO OFTEN, OR THESE NEW MUSCLES I GOT START TO POISON ME. LITTLE TUSSLE WOULD FIX ME RIGHT UP.
WHY ARE WE WHISPERING?
SHKK
YOU'RE AN IDIOT.
IF YOU WANT TO FIGHT, SKEL--
--FIGHT THEM.
I WISH HE'D TOLD US WHERE TO LOOK, PILEDRIVER. THIS WILL TAKE FOREVER.
UH-HUH. I DIDN'T MUCH FEE LIKE HANGING AROUND HIM AN LONGER THAN W HAD TO, BULLDOZE DUDE'S SCARY.
LOOK ON THE BRIGHT SIDE, THOUGH. HE'S PAYIN US BY THE HOUR. HE I HOPE THIS TAKES ALL DAY.

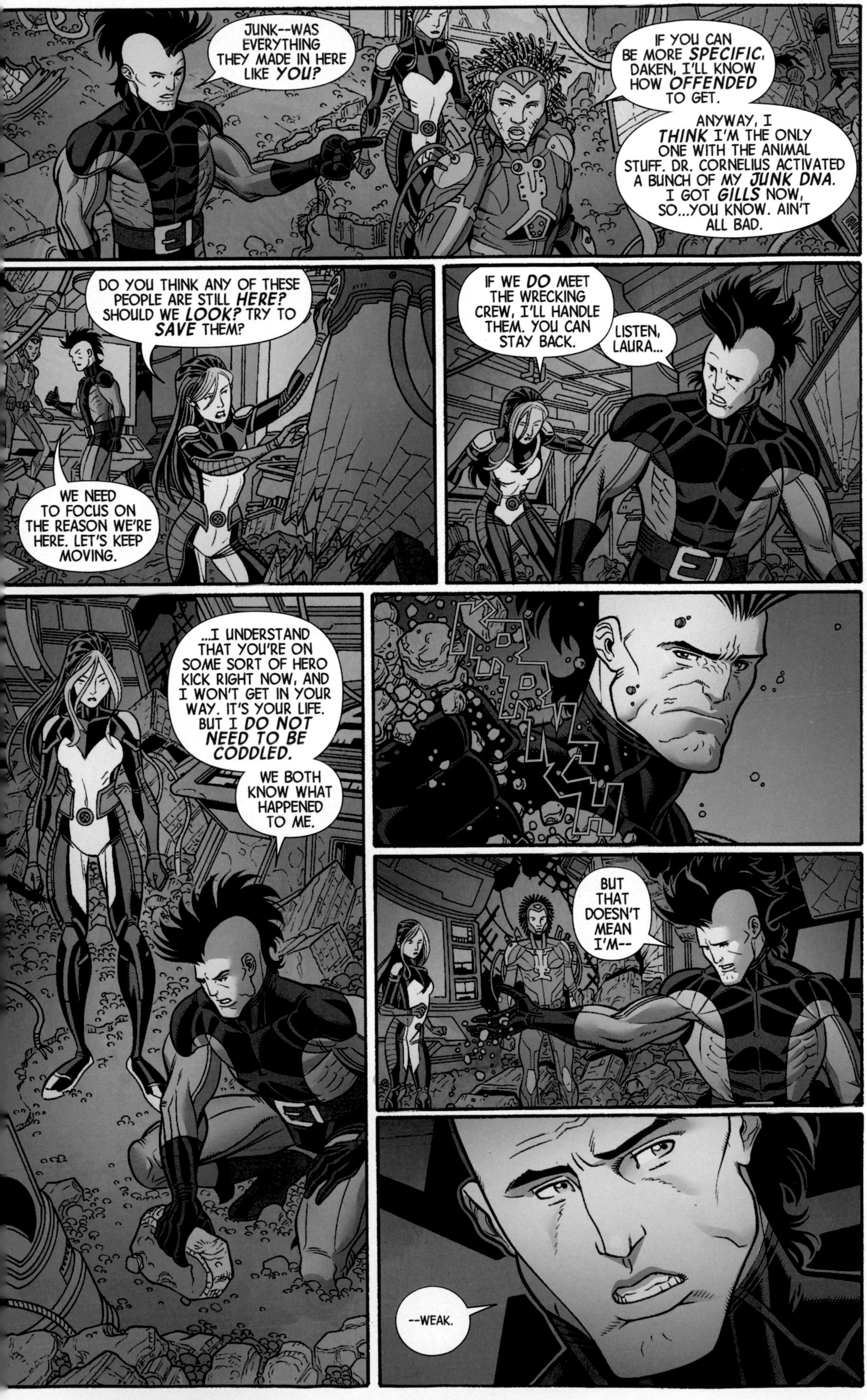
JUNK--WAS EVERYTHING THEY MADE IN HERE LIKE YOU?
IF YOU CAN BE MORE SPECIFIC, DAKEN, I'LL KNOW HOW OFFENDED TO GET.
ANYWAY, I THINK I'M THE ONLY ONE WITH THE ANIMAL STUFF. DR. CORNELIUS ACTIVATED A BUNCH OF MY JUNK DNA. I GOT GILLS NOW, SO...YOU KNOW. AIN'T ALL BAD.
DO YOU THINK ANY OF THESE PEOPLE ARE STILL HERE? SHOULD WE LOOK? TRY TO SAVE THEM?
WE NEED TO FOCUS ON THE REASON WE'RE HERE. LET'S KEEP MOVING.
IF WE DO MEET THE WRECKING CREW, I'LL HANDLE THEM. YOU CAN STAY BACK.
LISTEN, LAURA...
...I UNDERSTAND THAT YOU'RE ON SOME SORT OF HERO KICK RIGHT NOW, AND I WON'T GET IN YOUR WAY. IT'S YOUR LIFE. BUT I DO NOT NEED TO BE CODDLED.
WE BOTH KNOW WHAT HAPPENED TO ME.
KRRUNCH
BUT THAT DOESN'T MEAN I'M--
--WEAK.

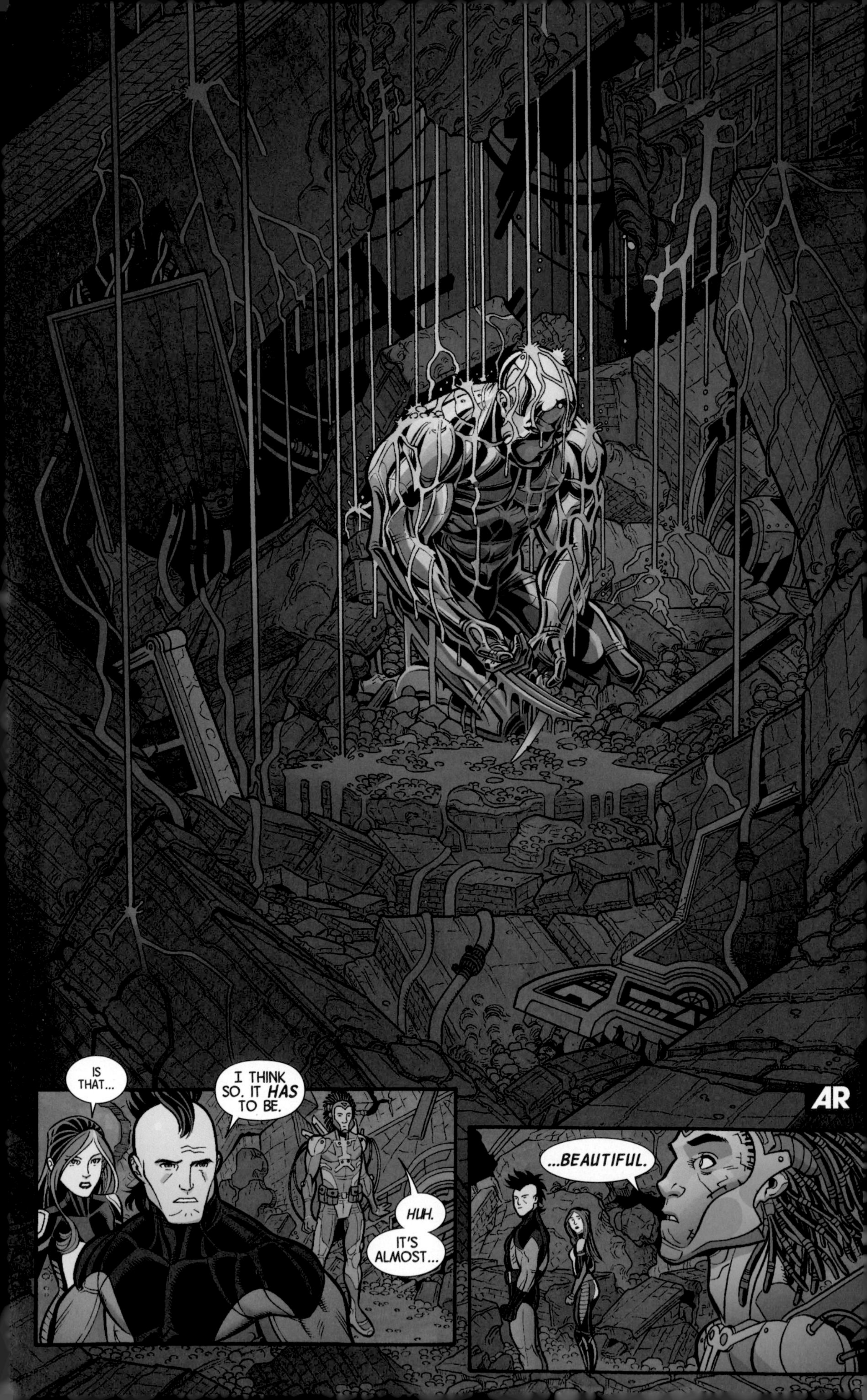
IS THAT...
I THINK SO. IT HAS TO BE.
HUH.
IT'S ALMOST...
...BEAUTIFUL.
AR

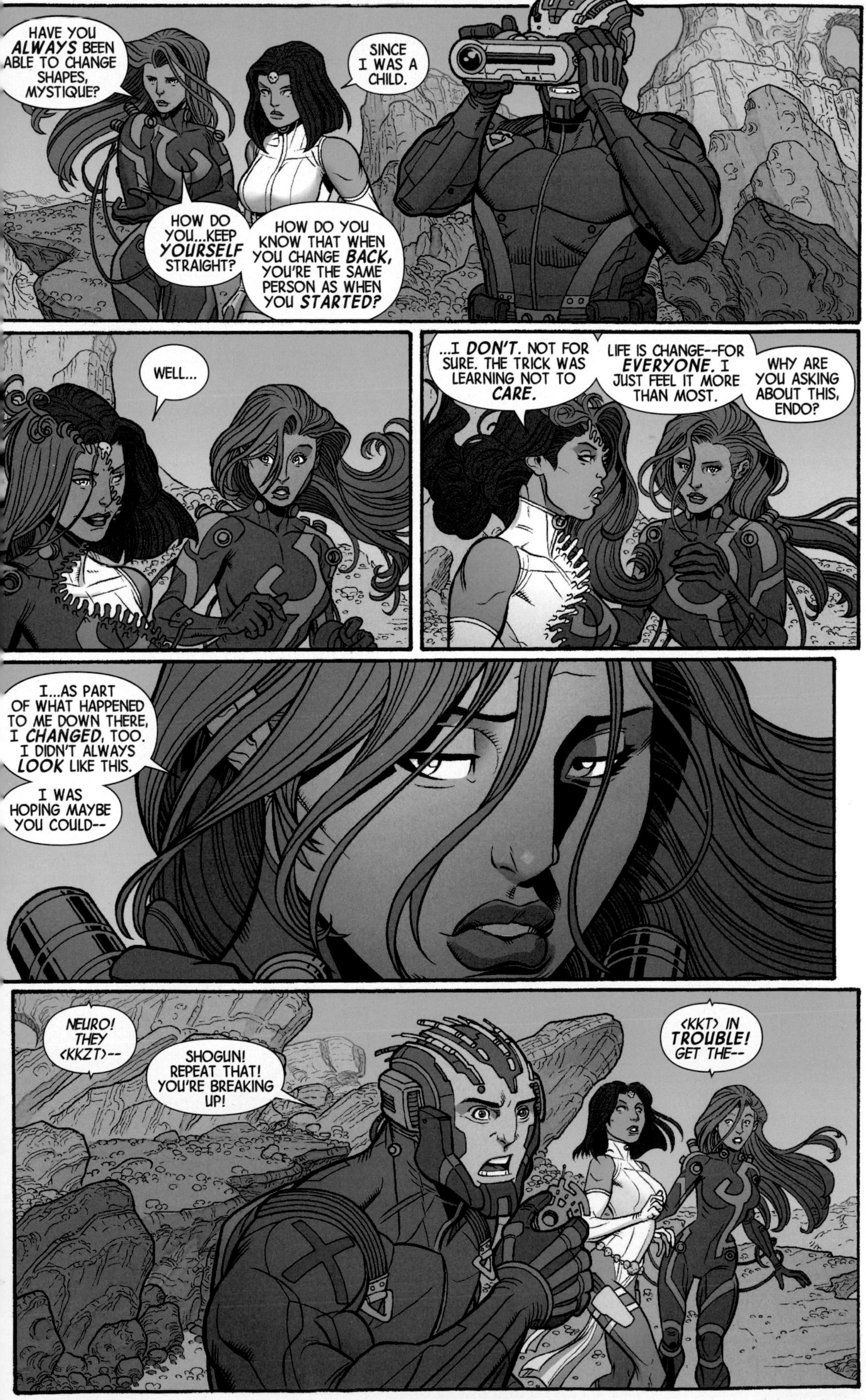
HAVE YOU ALWAYS BEEN ABLE TO CHANGE SHAPES, MYSTIQUE?
SINCE I WAS A CHILD.
HOW DO YOU...KEEP YOURSELF STRAIGHT?
HOW DO YOU KNOW THAT WHEN YOU CHANGE BACK, YOU'RE THE SAME PERSON AS WHEN YOU STARTED?
WELL...
...I DON'T. NOT FOR SURE. THE TRICK WAS LEARNING NOT TO CARE.
LIFE IS CHANGE--FOR EVERYONE. I JUST FEEL IT MORE THAN MOST.
WHY ARE YOU ASKING ABOUT THIS, ENDO?
I...AS PART OF WHAT HAPPENED TO ME DOWN THERE, I CHANGED, TOO. I DIDN'T ALWAYS LOOK LIKE THIS.
I WAS HOPING MAYBE YOU COULD--
NEURO! THEY <KKZT>--
SHOGUN! REPEAT THAT! YOU'RE BREAKING UP!
<KKT> IN TROUBLE! GET THE--

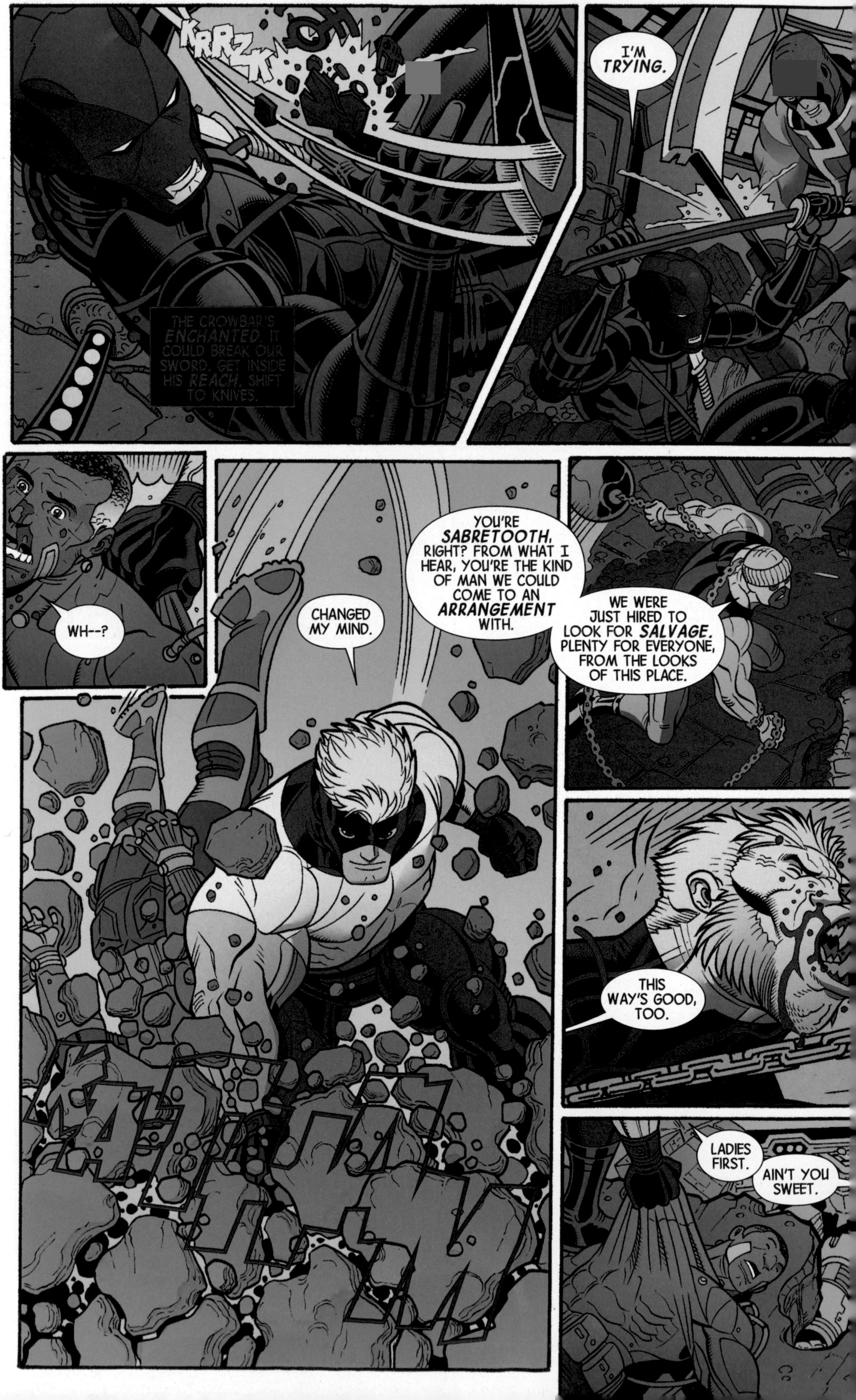
KRRZK
THE CROWBAR'S ENCHANTED. IT COULD BREAK OUR SWORD. GET INSIDE HIS REACH. SHIFT TO KNIVES.
I'M TRYING.
WH--?
CHANGED MY MIND.
YOU'RE SABRETOOTH, RIGHT? FROM WHAT I HEAR, YOU'RE THE KIND OF MAN WE COULD COME TO AN ARRANGEMENT WITH.
WE WERE JUST HIRED TO LOOK FOR SALVAGE. PLENTY FOR EVERYONE, FROM THE LOOKS OF THIS PLACE.
THIS WAY'S GOOD, TOO.
LADIES FIRST.
AIN'T YOU SWEET.

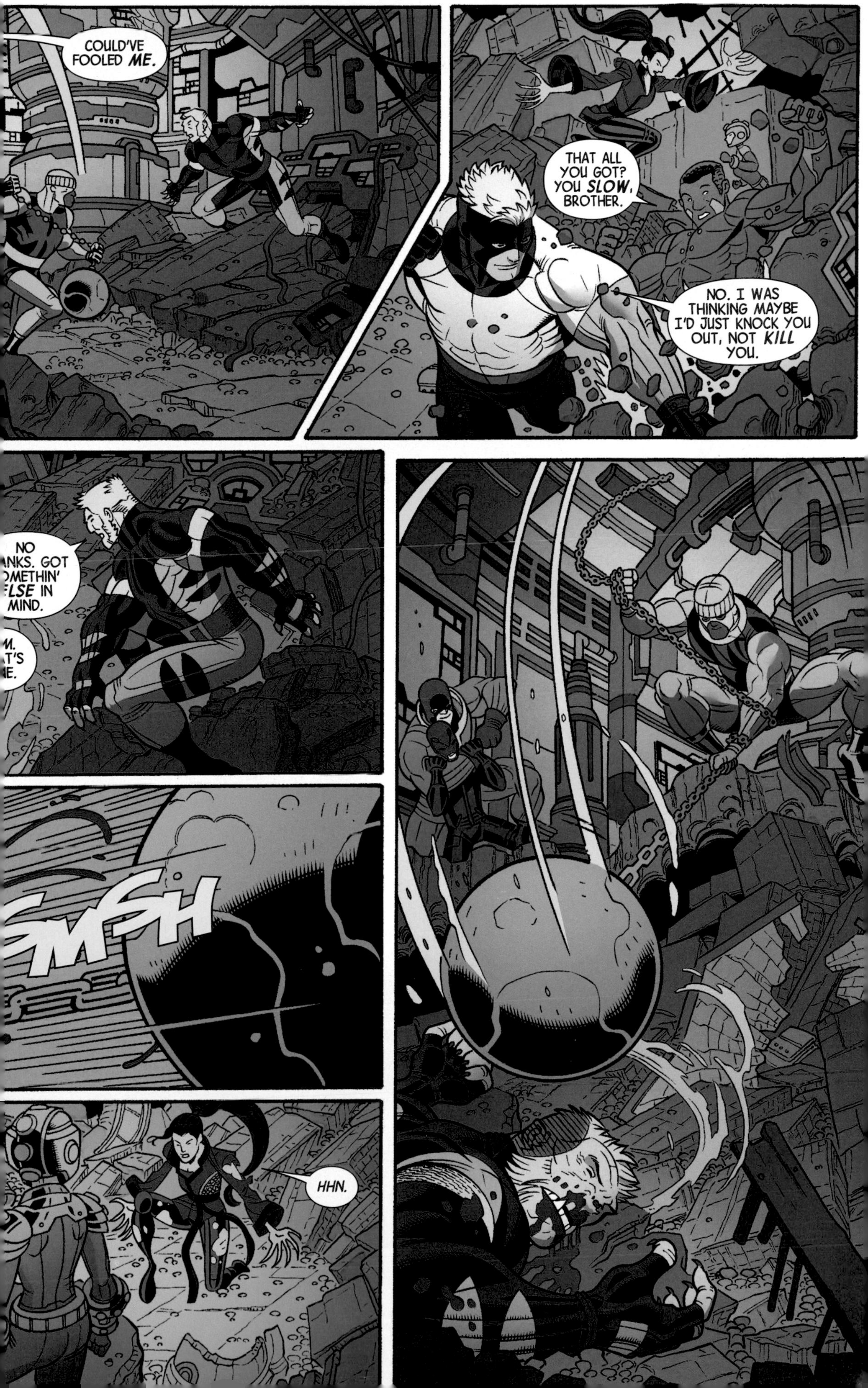
COULD'VE FOOLED ME.
THAT ALL YOU GOT? YOU SLOW, BROTHER.
NO. I WAS THINKING MAYBE I'D JUST KNOCK YOU OUT, NOT KILL YOU.
NO ANKS. GOT OMETHIN' ELSE IN MIND.
SMASH
HHN.

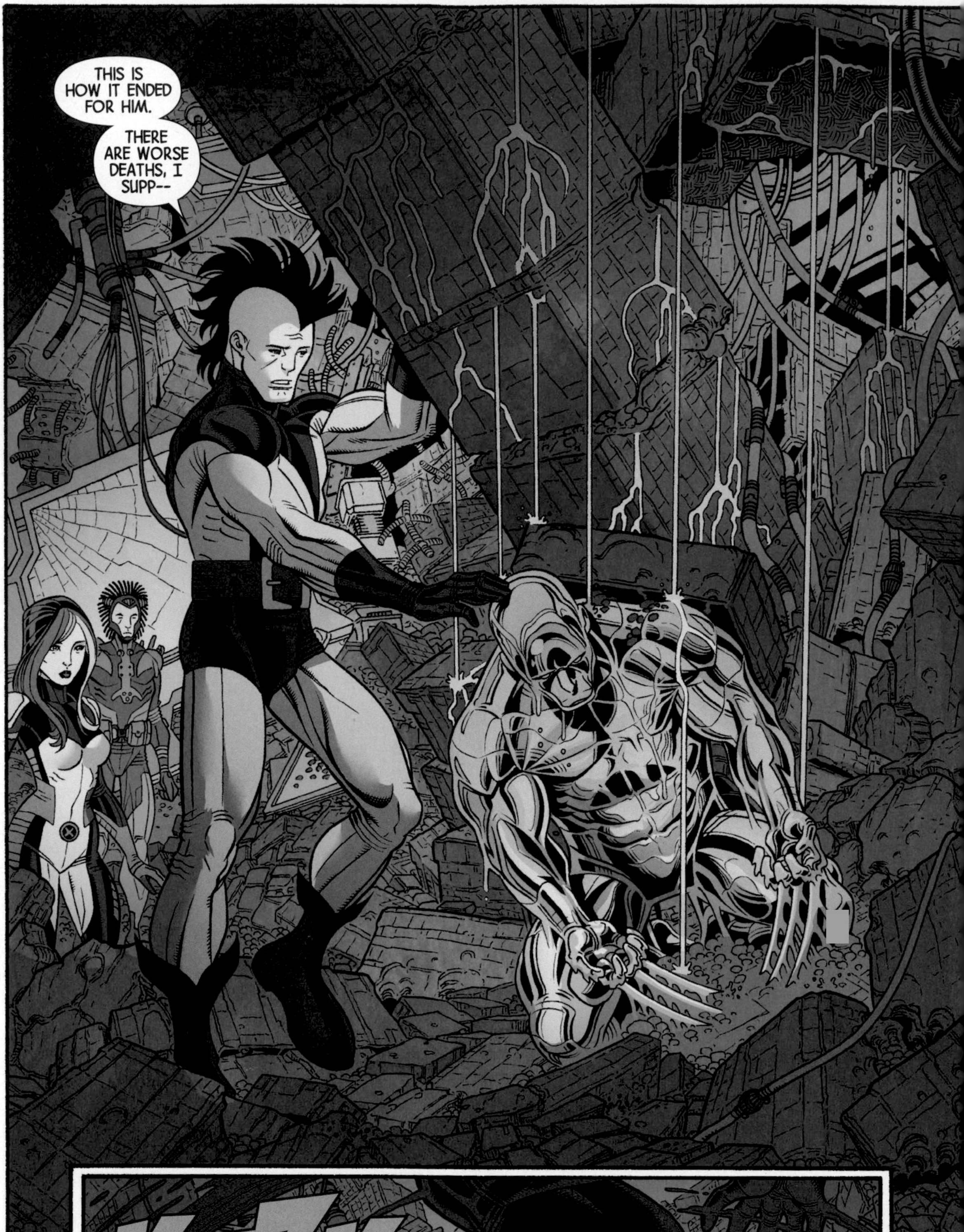
THIS IS HOW IT ENDED FOR HIM.
THERE ARE WORSE DEATHS, I SUPP--

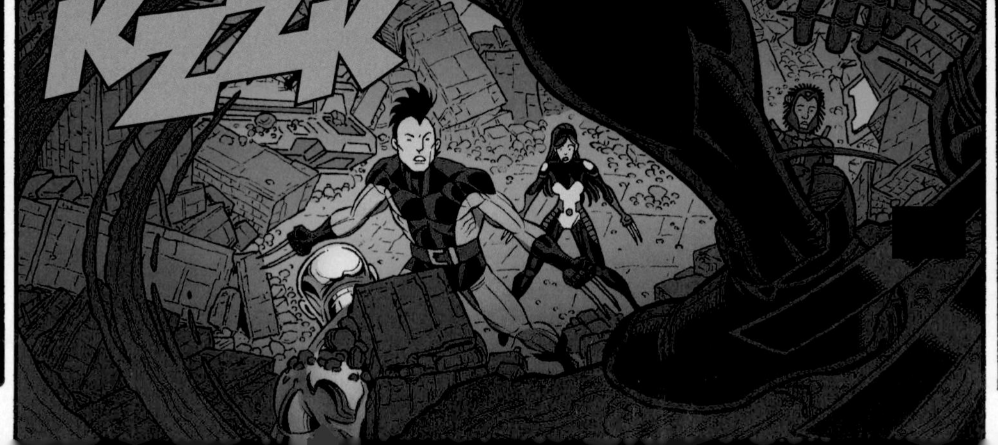
KZZK

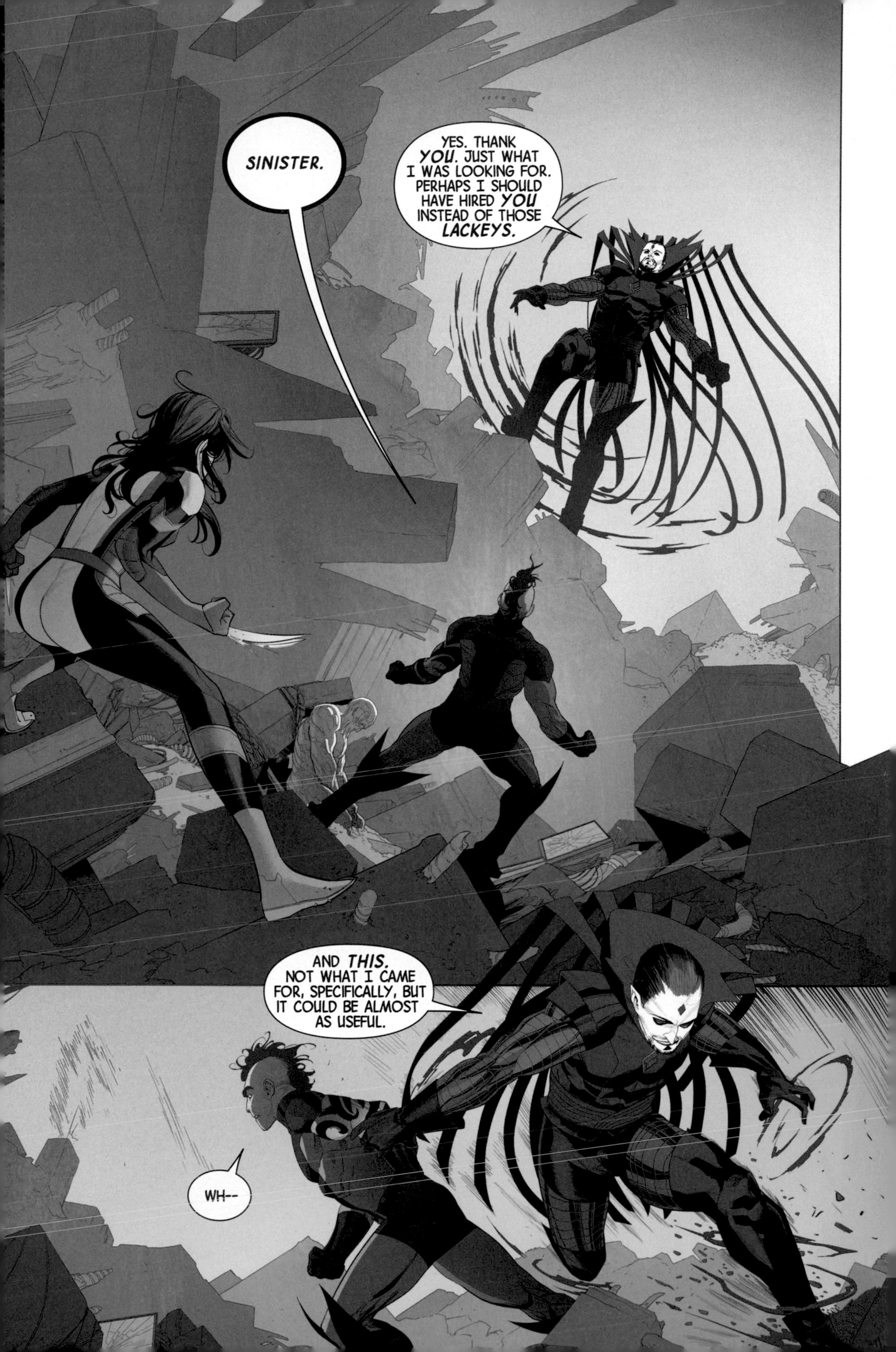
SINISTER.
YES. THANK YOU. JUST WHAT I WAS LOOKING FOR. PERHAPS I SHOULD HAVE HIRED YOU INSTEAD OF THOSE LACKEYS.
AND THIS. NOT WHAT I CAME FOR, SPECIFICALLY, BUT IT COULD BE ALMOST AS USEFUL.
WH--

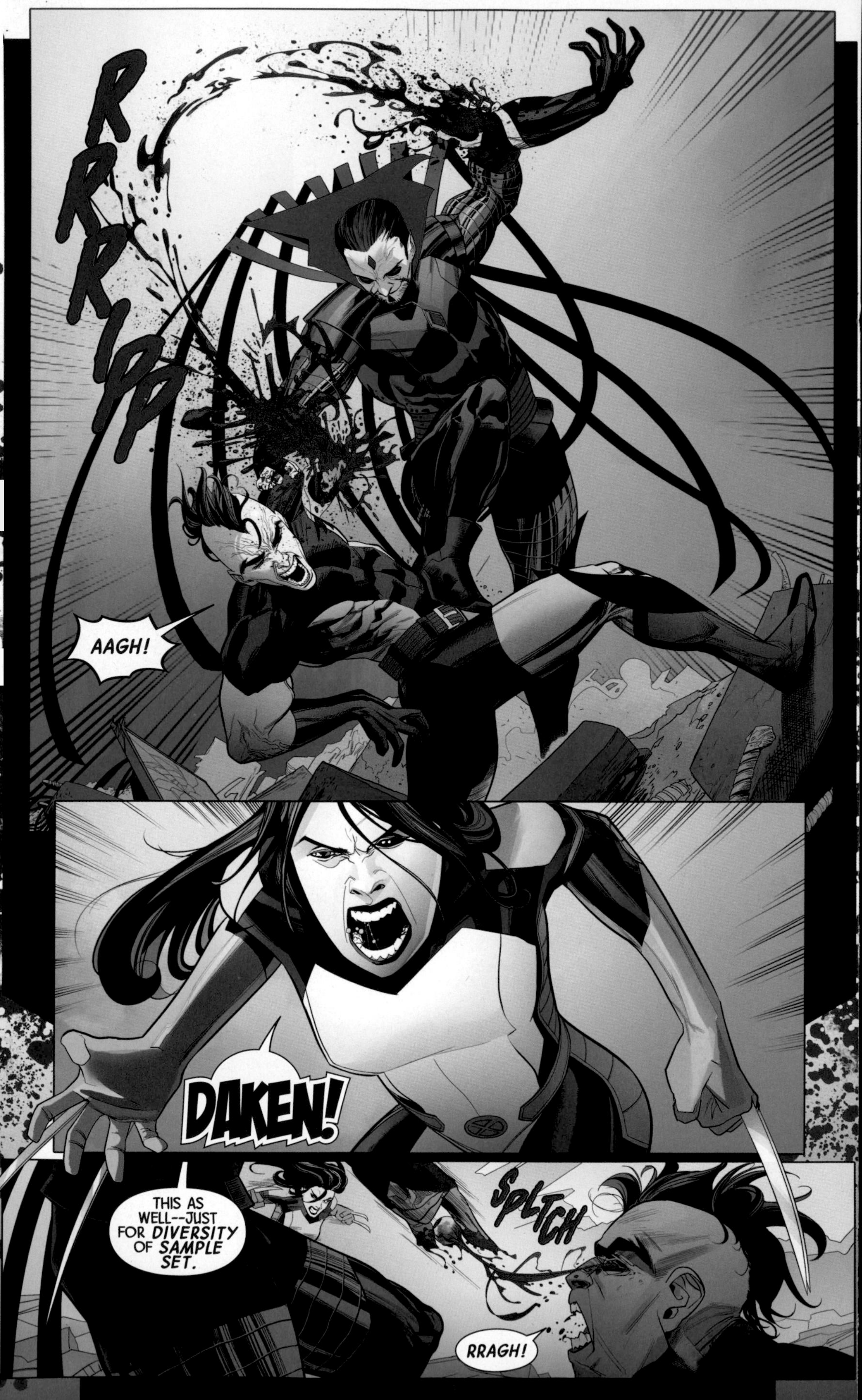
RRRIPP
AAGH!
DAKEN!
THIS AS WELL--JUST FOR DIVERSITY OF SAMPLE SET.
SPLTCH
RRAGH!

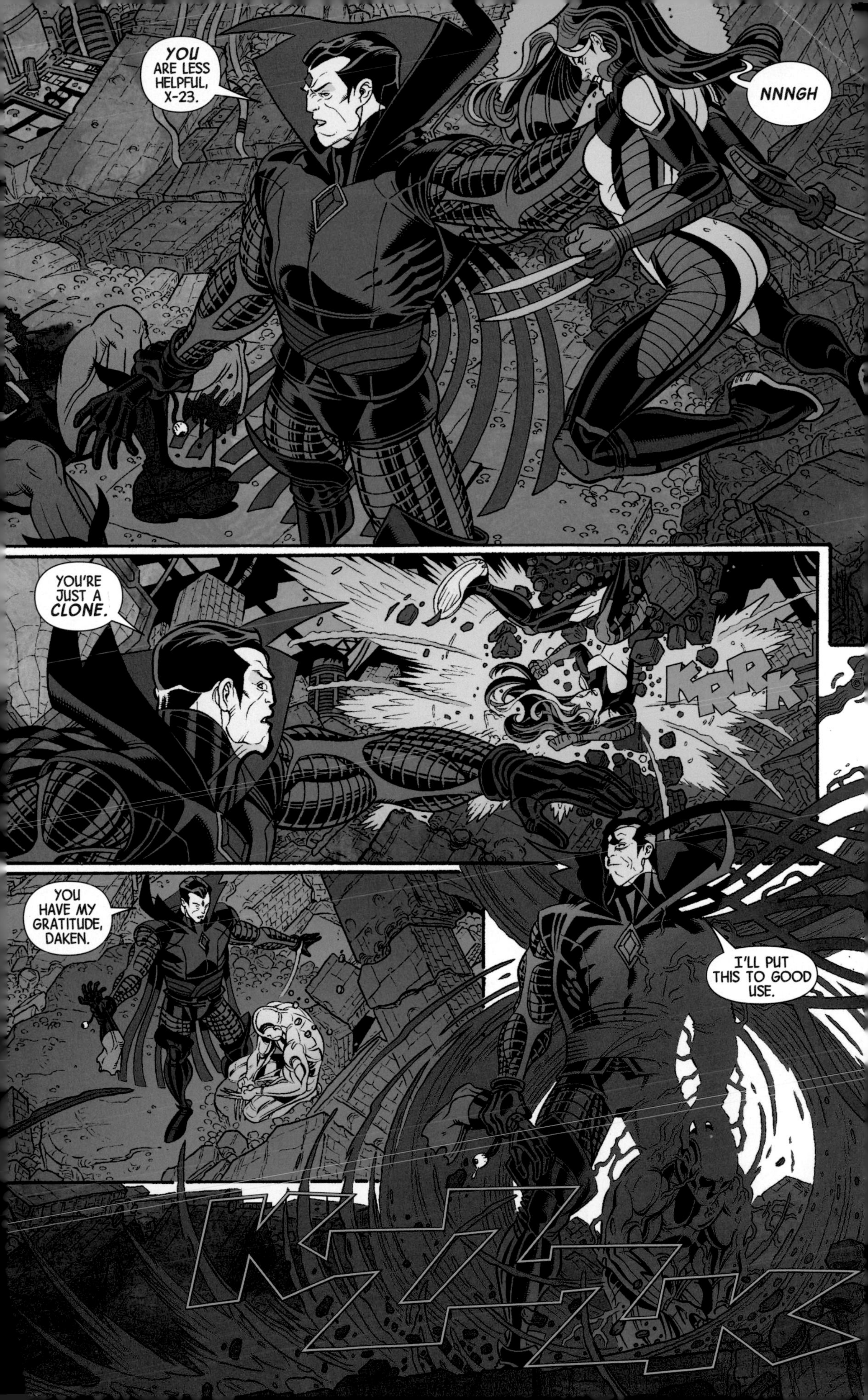

YOU ARE LESS HELPFUL, X-23.
NNNGH
YOU'RE JUST A CLONE.
KRRK
YOU HAVE MY GRATITUDE, DAKEN.
I'LL PUT THIS TO GOOD USE.
KZZK

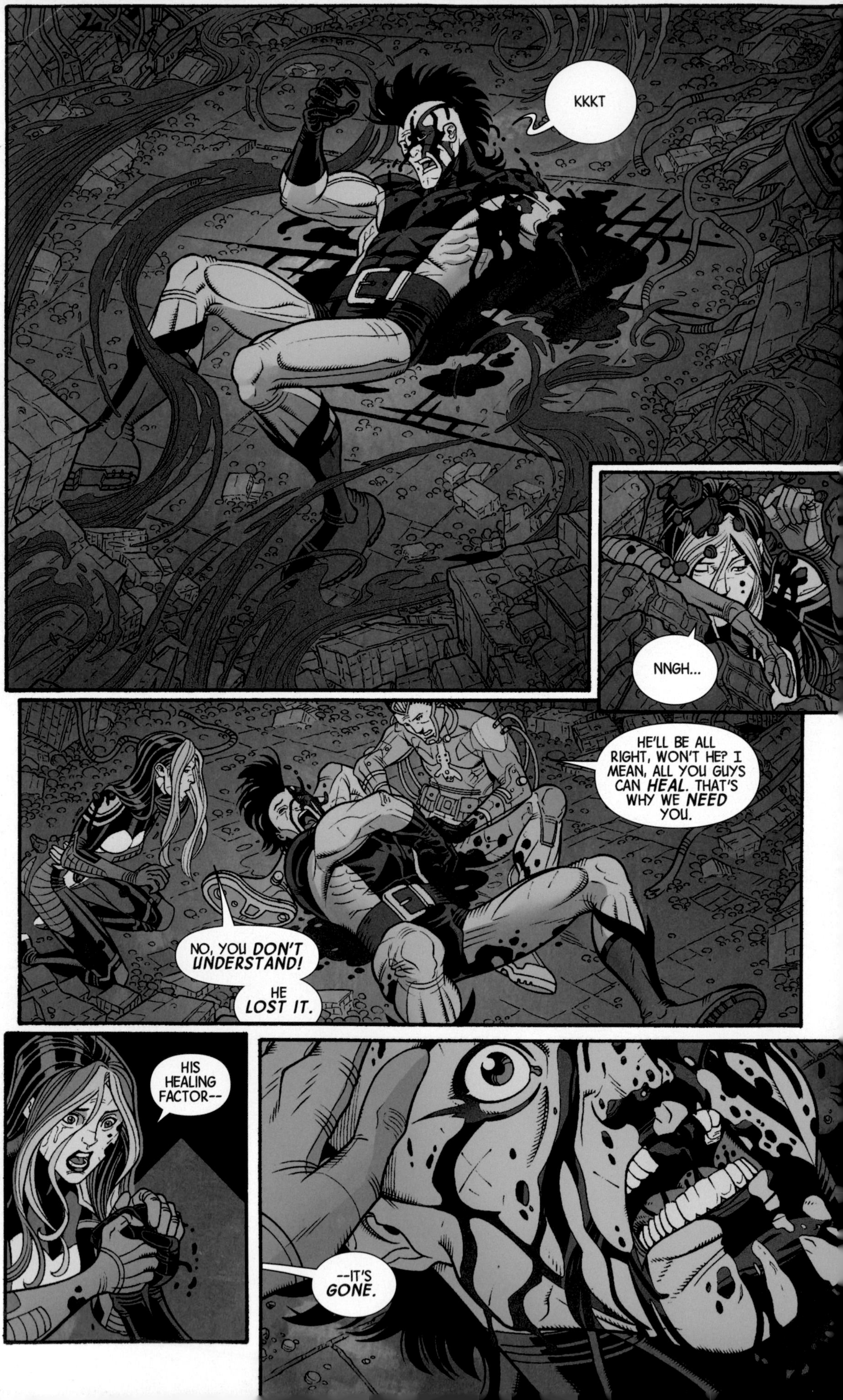
KKKT
NNGH...
HE'LL BE ALL RIGHT, WON'T HE? I MEAN, ALL YOU GUYS CAN HEAL. THAT'S WHY WE NEED YOU.
NO, YOU DON'T UNDERSTAND!
HE LOST IT.
HIS HEALING FACTOR--
--IT'S GONE.

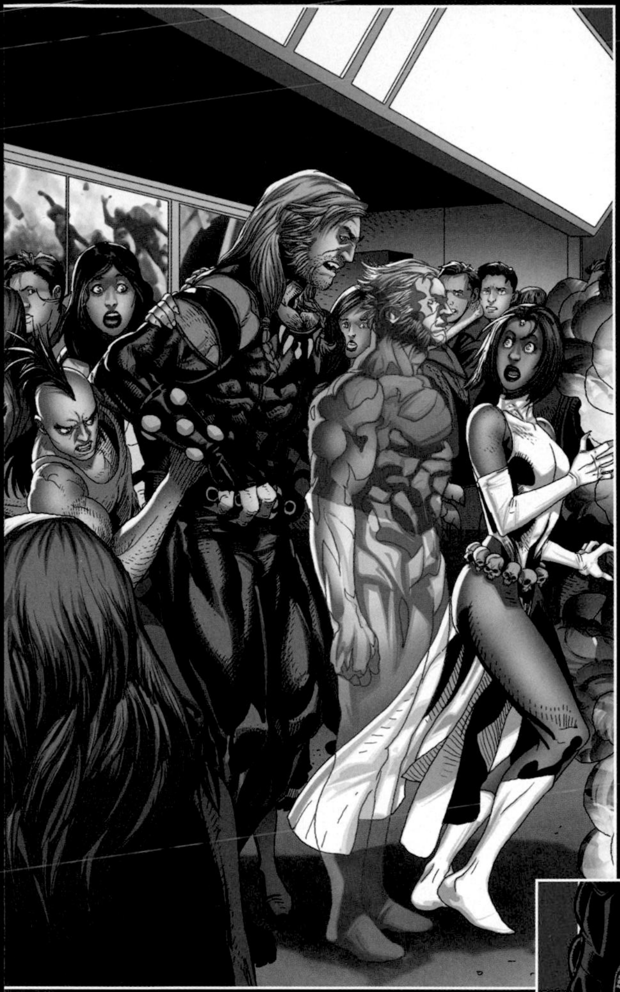

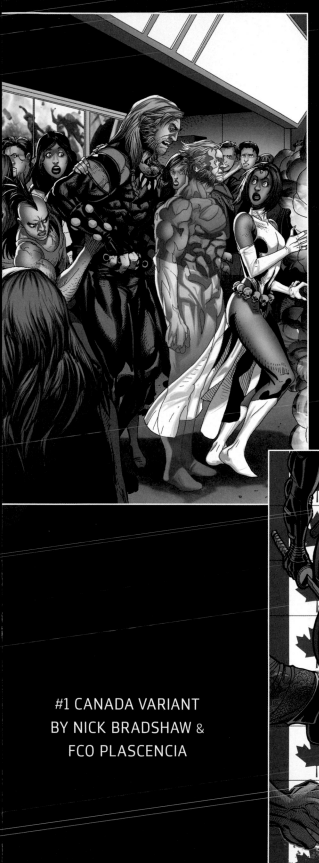

#1 WELCOME HOME VARIANT
BY SALVADOR LARROCA &
ISRAEL SILVA

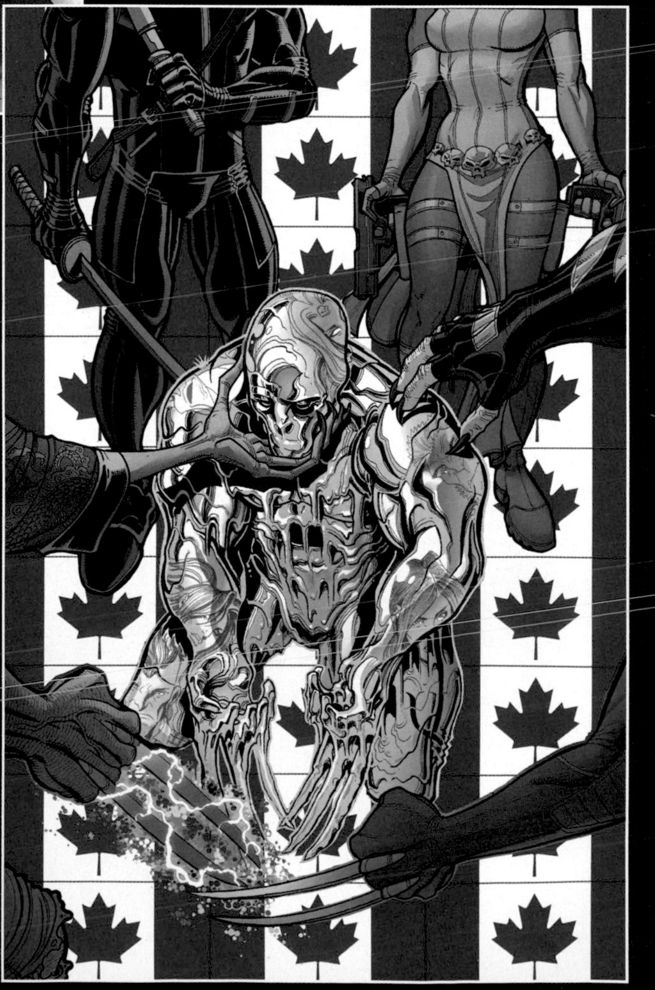

#1 CANADA VARIANT
BY NICK BRADSHAW &
FCO PLASCENCIA

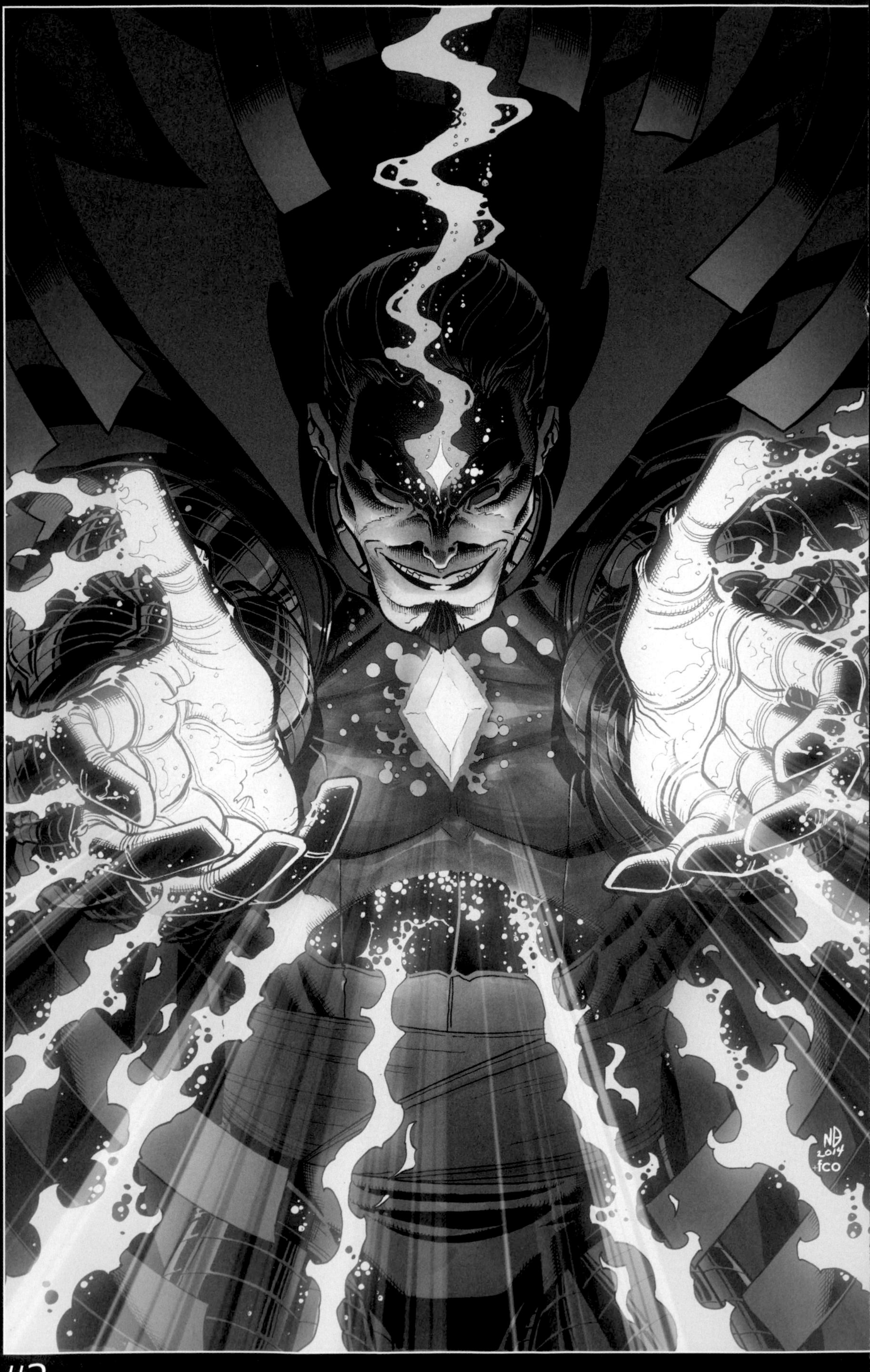

#2

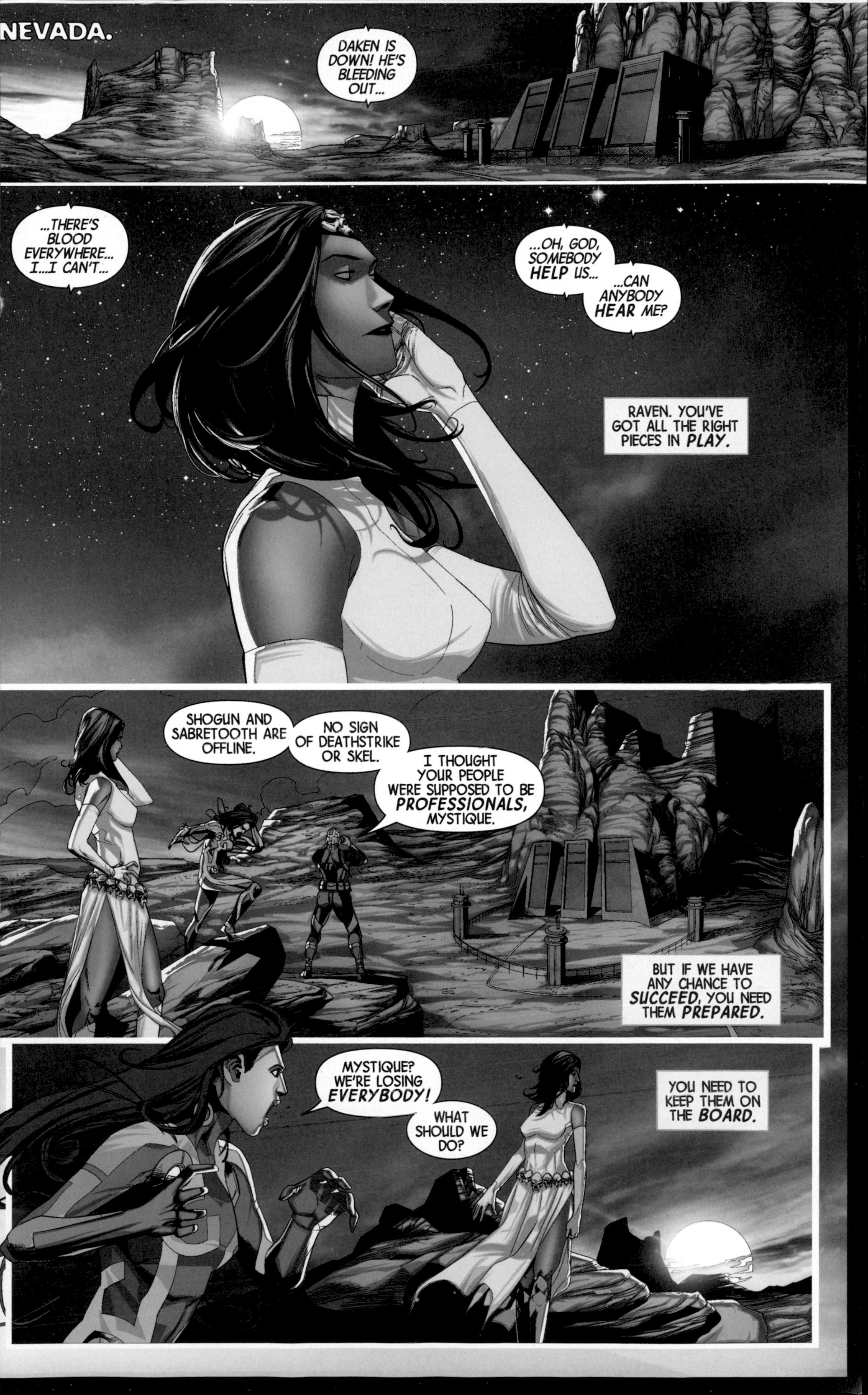
NEVADA.
DAKEN IS DOWN! HE'S BLEEDING OUT...
...THERE'S BLOOD EVERYWHERE... I...I CAN'T...
...OH, GOD, SOMEBODY HELP US...
...CAN ANYBODY HEAR ME?
RAVEN. YOU'VE GOT ALL THE RIGHT PIECES IN PLAY.
SHOGUN AND SABRETOOTH ARE OFFLINE.
NO SIGN OF DEATHSTRIKE OR SKEL.
I THOUGHT YOUR PEOPLE WERE SUPPOSED TO BE PROFESSIONALS, MYSTIQUE.
BUT IF WE HAVE ANY CHANCE TO SUCCEED, YOU NEED THEM PREPARED.
MYSTIQUE? WE'RE LOSING EVERYBODY!
WHAT SHOULD WE DO?
YOU NEED TO KEEP THEM ON THE BOARD.

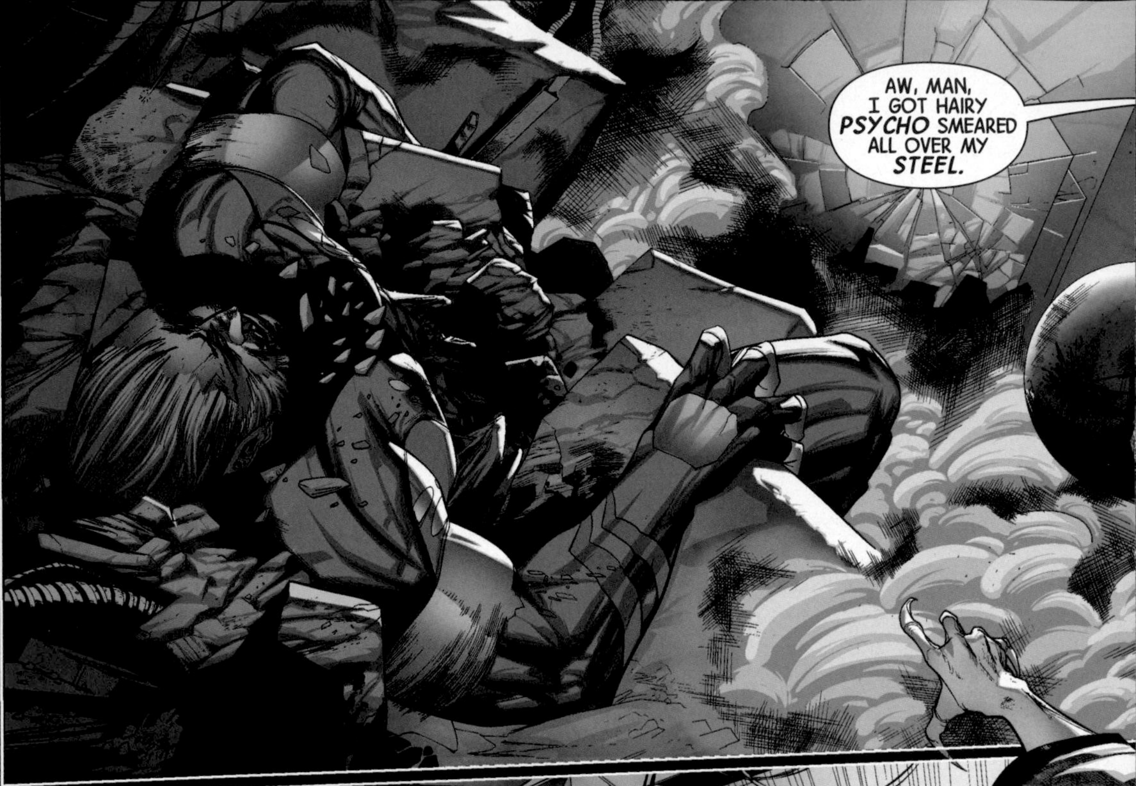
AW, MAN, I GOT HAIRY PSYCHO SMEARED ALL OVER MY STEEL.

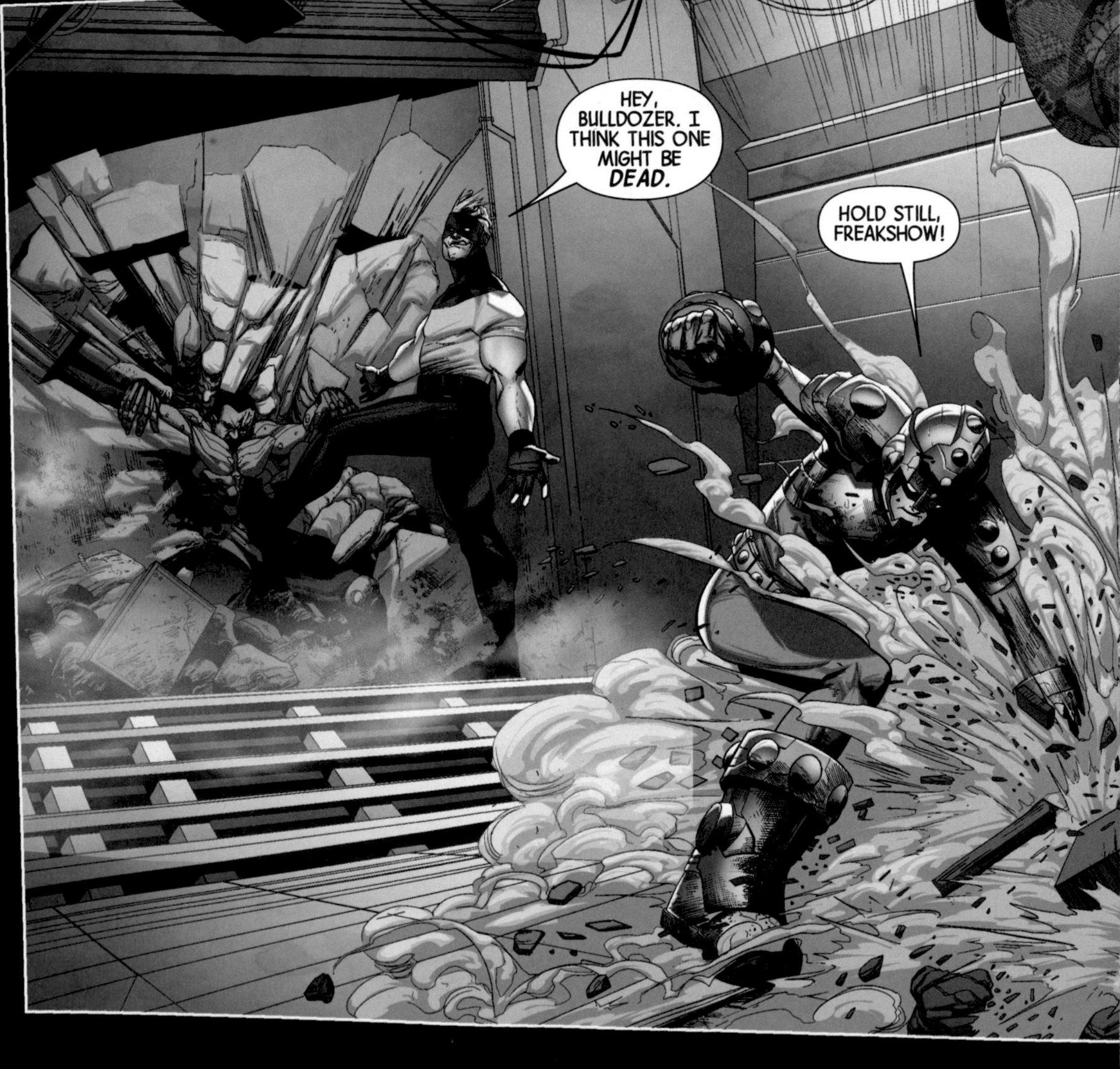
HEY, BULLDOZER. I THINK THIS ONE MIGHT BE DEAD.
HOLD STILL, FREAKSHOW!

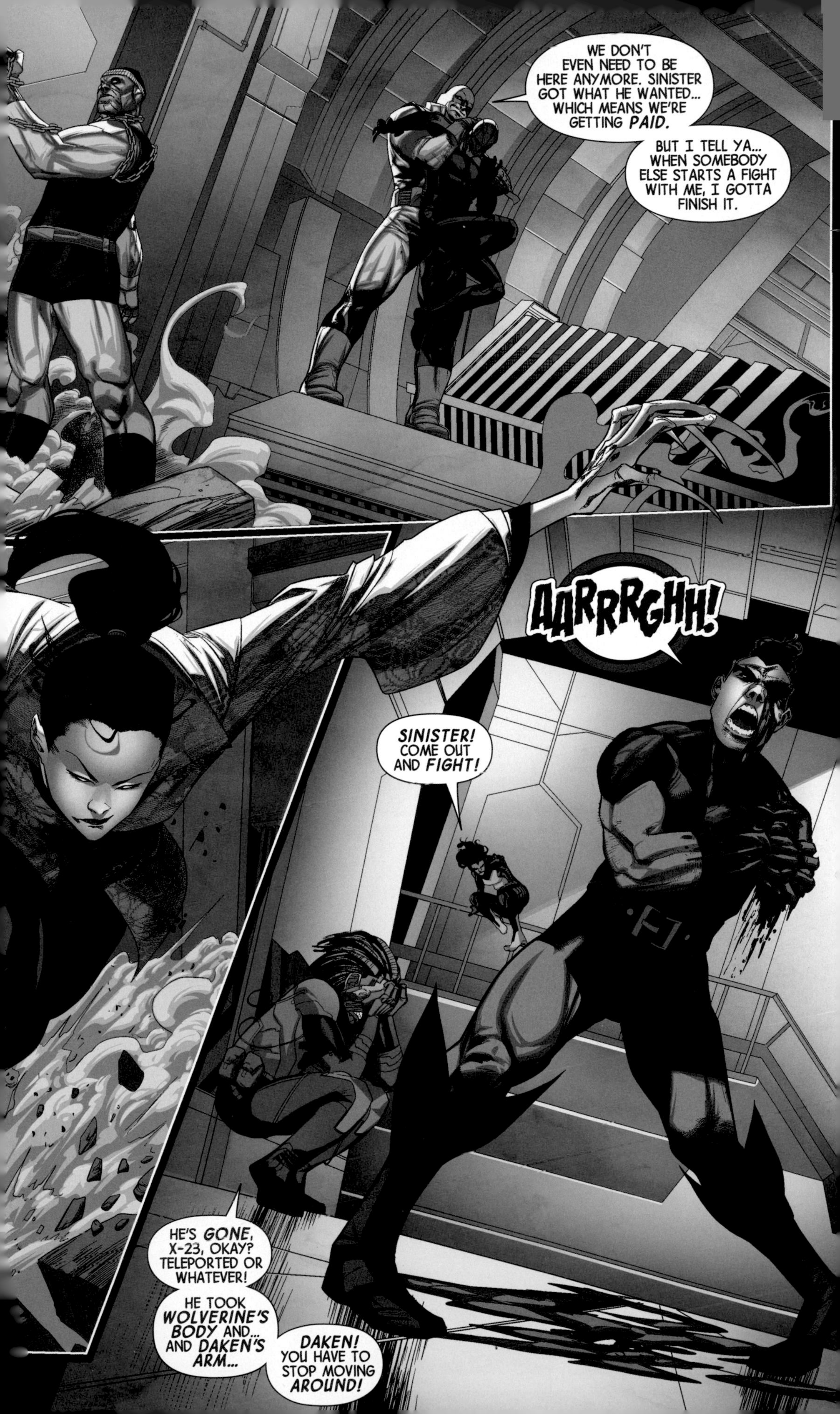
WE DON'T EVEN NEED TO BE HERE ANYMORE. SINISTER GOT WHAT HE WANTED... WHICH MEANS WE'RE GETTING PAID.
BUT I TELL YA... WHEN SOMEBODY ELSE STARTS A FIGHT WITH ME, I GOTTA FINISH IT.
AARRRGHH!
SINISTER! COME OUT AND FIGHT!
HE'S GONE, X-23, OKAY? TELEPORTED OR WHATEVER!
HE TOOK WOLVERINE'S BODY AND... AND DAKEN'S ARM...
DAKEN! YOU HAVE TO STOP MOVING AROUND!

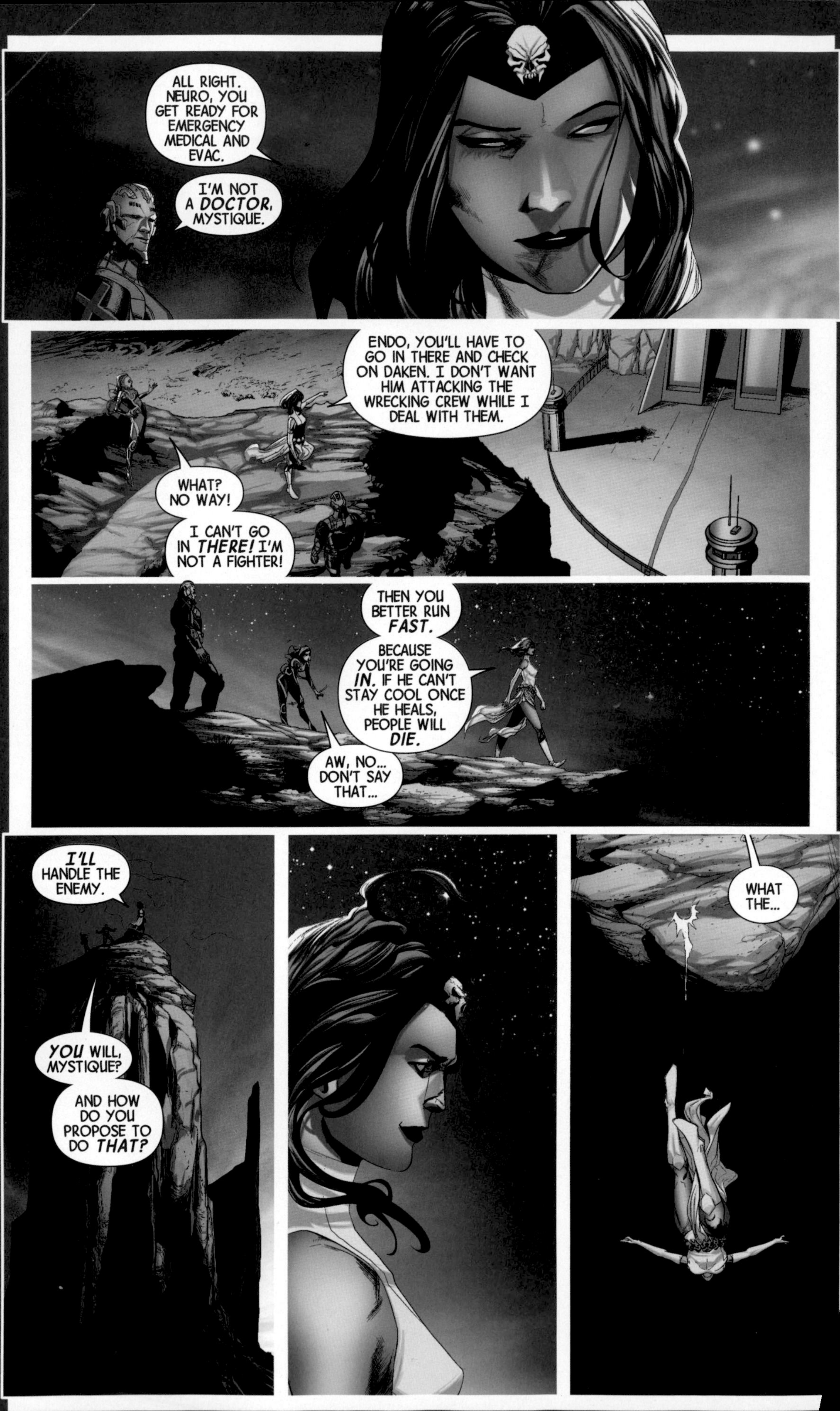
ALL RIGHT. NEURO, YOU GET READY FOR EMERGENCY MEDICAL AND EVAC.
I'M NOT A *DOCTOR*, MYSTIQUE.
ENDO, YOU'LL HAVE TO GO IN THERE AND CHECK ON DAKEN. I DON'T WANT HIM ATTACKING THE WRECKING CREW WHILE I DEAL WITH THEM.
WHAT? NO WAY!
I CAN'T GO IN *THERE!* I'M NOT A FIGHTER!
THEN YOU BETTER RUN *FAST.*
BECAUSE YOU'RE GOING *IN.* IF HE CAN'T STAY COOL ONCE HE HEALS, PEOPLE WILL *DIE.*
AW, NO... DON'T SAY THAT...
I'LL HANDLE THE ENEMY.
YOU WILL, MYSTIQUE?
AND HOW DO YOU PROPOSE TO DO *THAT?*
WHAT THE...

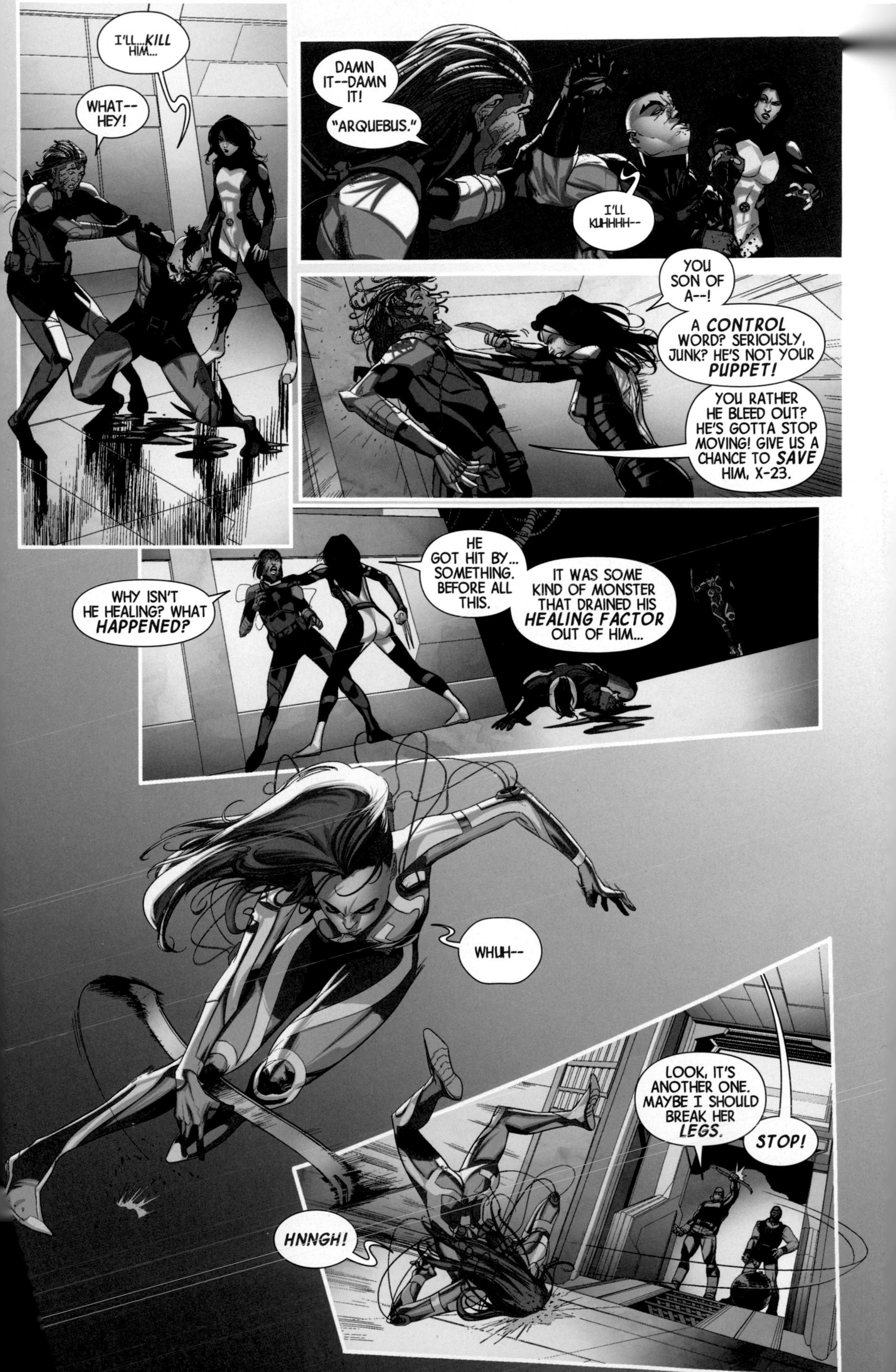
I'LL...KILL HIM...
WHAT-- HEY!
DAMN IT--DAMN IT!
"ARQUEBUS."
I'LL KUHHHH--
YOU SON OF A--!
A CONTROL WORD? SERIOUSLY, JUNK? HE'S NOT YOUR PUPPET!
YOU RATHER HE BLEED OUT? HE'S GOTTA STOP MOVING! GIVE US A CHANCE TO SAVE HIM, X-23.
WHY ISN'T HE HEALING? WHAT HAPPENED?
HE GOT HIT BY... SOMETHING. BEFORE ALL THIS.
IT WAS SOME KIND OF MONSTER THAT DRAINED HIS HEALING FACTOR OUT OF HIM...
WHUH--
LOOK, IT'S ANOTHER ONE. MAYBE I SHOULD BREAK HER LEGS.
STOP!
HNNGH!

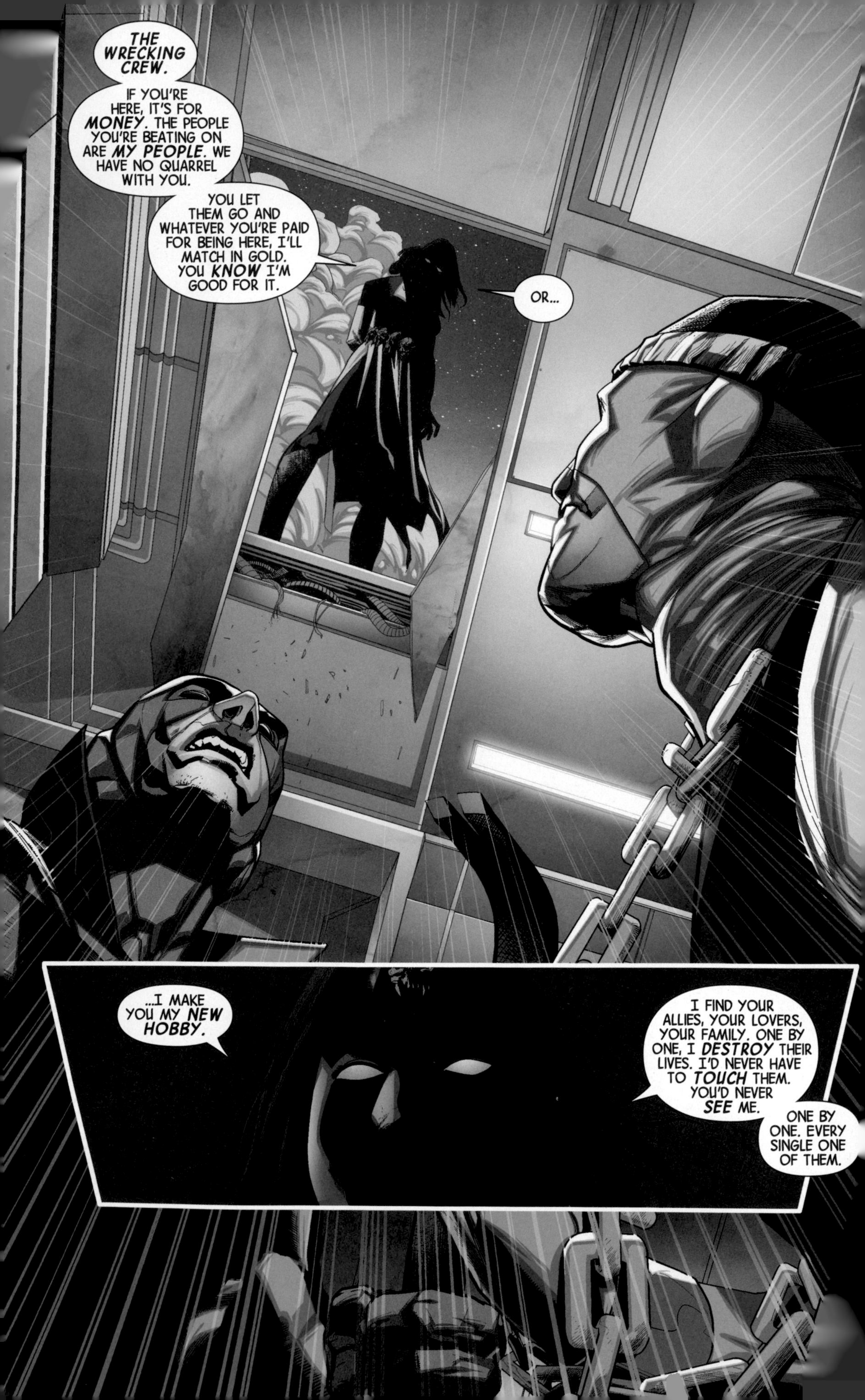
THE WRECKING CREW.
IF YOU'RE HERE, IT'S FOR MONEY. THE PEOPLE YOU'RE BEATING ON ARE MY PEOPLE. WE HAVE NO QUARREL WITH YOU.
YOU LET THEM GO AND WHATEVER YOU'RE PAID FOR BEING HERE, I'LL MATCH IN GOLD. YOU KNOW I'M GOOD FOR IT.
OR...
...I MAKE YOU MY NEW HOBBY.
I FIND YOUR ALLIES, YOUR LOVERS, YOUR FAMILY. ONE BY ONE, I DESTROY THEIR LIVES. I'D NEVER HAVE TO TOUCH THEM. YOU'D NEVER SEE ME.
ONE BY ONE. EVERY SINGLE ONE OF THEM.

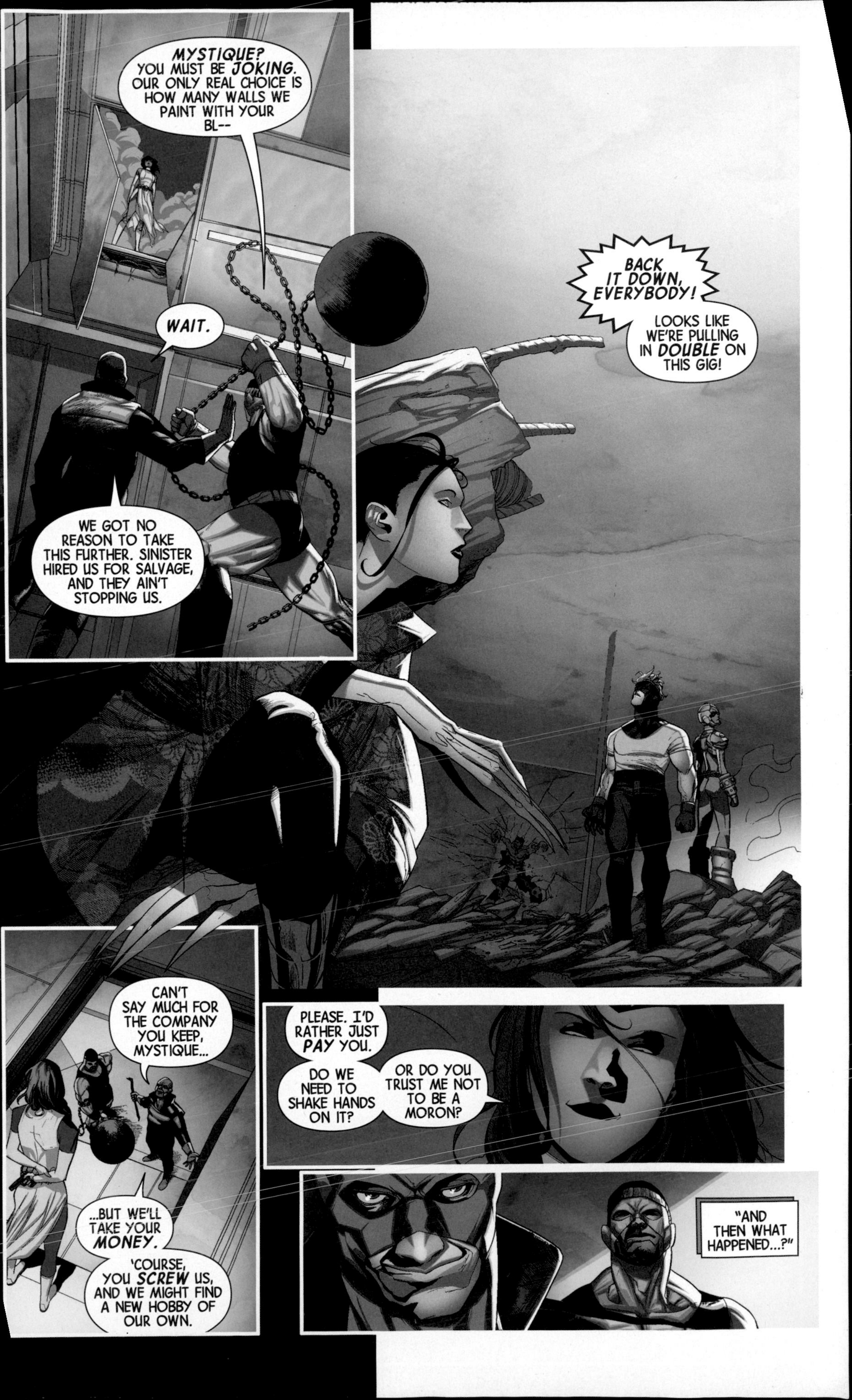

MYSTIQUE? YOU MUST BE JOKING. OUR ONLY REAL CHOICE IS HOW MANY WALLS WE PAINT WITH YOUR BL--
WAIT.
WE GOT NO REASON TO TAKE THIS FURTHER. SINISTER HIRED US FOR SALVAGE, AND THEY AIN'T STOPPING US.
BACK IT DOWN, EVERYBODY!
LOOKS LIKE WE'RE PULLING IN DOUBLE ON THIS GIG!
CAN'T SAY MUCH FOR THE COMPANY YOU KEEP, MYSTIQUE...
...BUT WE'LL TAKE YOUR MONEY.
'COURSE, YOU SCREW US, AND WE MIGHT FIND A NEW HOBBY OF OUR OWN.
PLEASE. I'D RATHER JUST PAY YOU.
DO WE NEED TO SHAKE HANDS ON IT?
OR DO YOU TRUST ME NOT TO BE A MORON?
"AND THEN WHAT HAPPENED...?"

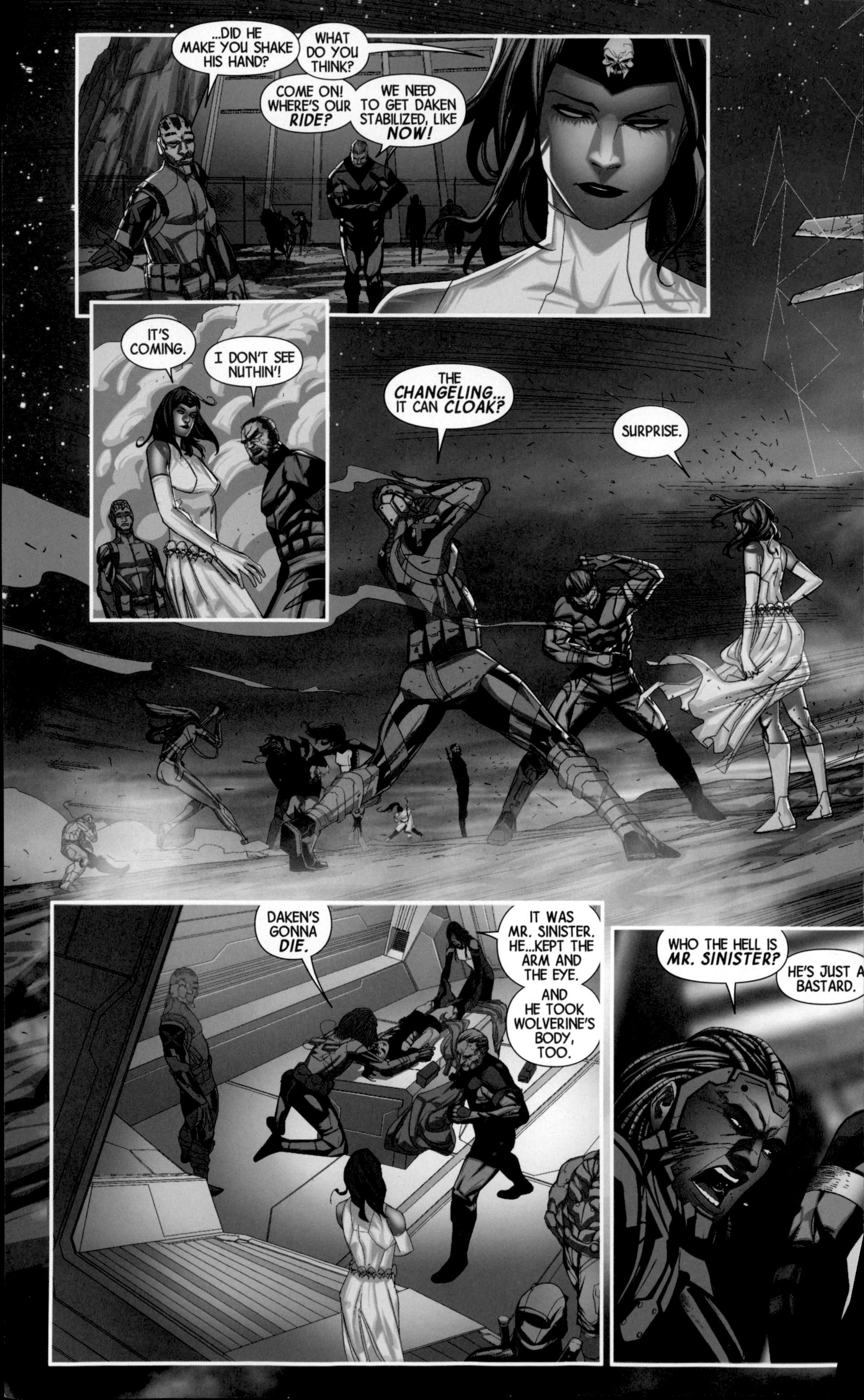

...DID HE MAKE YOU SHAKE HIS HAND?
WHAT DO YOU THINK?
COME ON! WHERE'S OUR RIDE?
WE NEED TO GET DAKEN STABILIZED, LIKE NOW!
IT'S COMING.
I DON'T SEE NUTHIN'!
THE CHANGELING... IT CAN CLOAK?
SURPRISE.
DAKEN'S GONNA DIE.
IT WAS MR. SINISTER. HE...KEPT THE ARM AND THE EYE.
AND HE TOOK WOLVERINE'S BODY, TOO.
WHO THE HELL IS MR. SINISTER?
HE'S JUST A BASTARD.

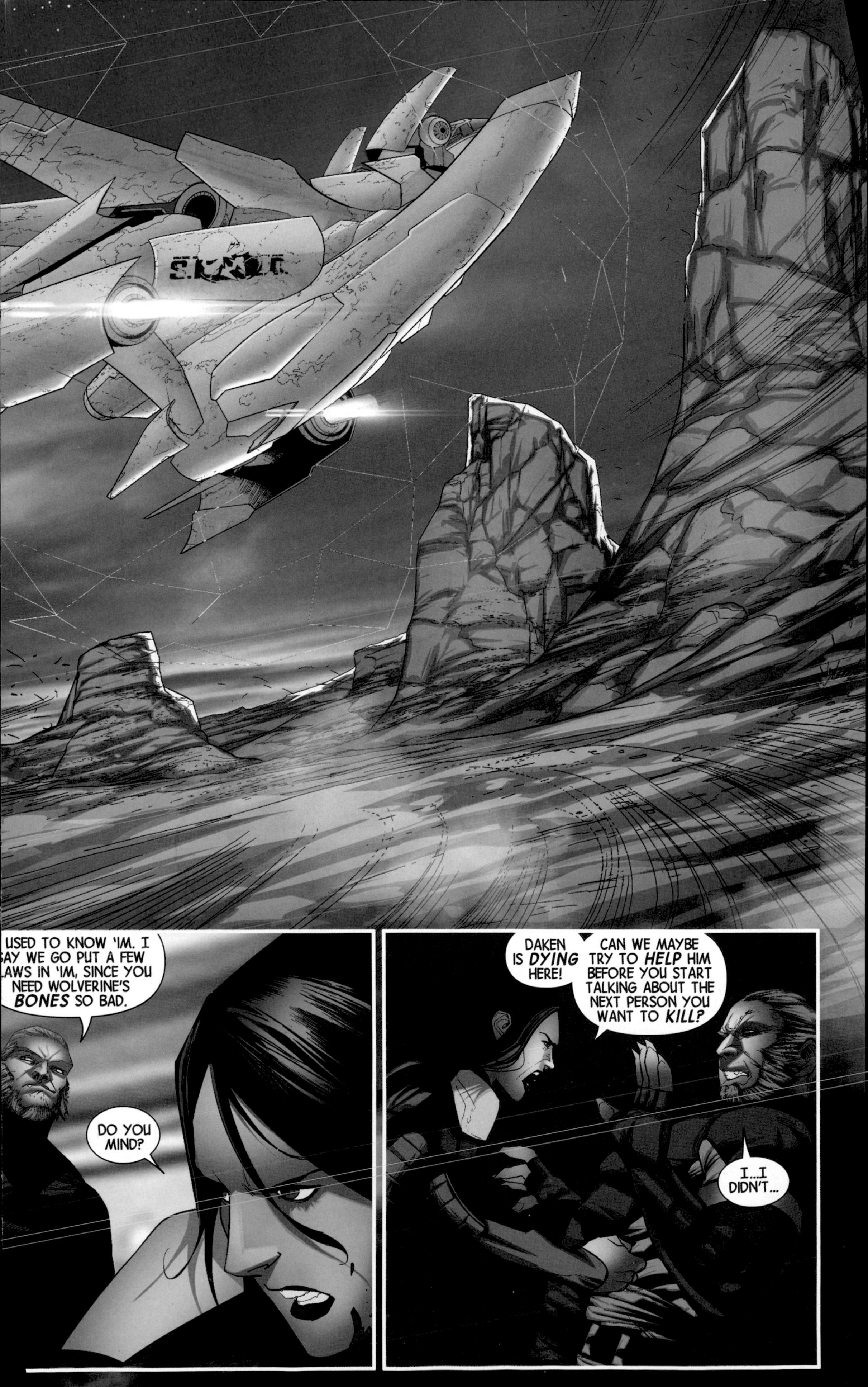
USED TO KNOW 'IM. I AY WE GO PUT A FEW LAWS IN 'IM, SINCE YOU NEED WOLVERINE'S BONES SO BAD.
DO YOU MIND?
DAKEN IS DYING HERE!
CAN WE MAYBE TRY TO HELP HIM BEFORE YOU START TALKING ABOUT THE NEXT PERSON YOU WANT TO KILL?
I...I DIDN'T...

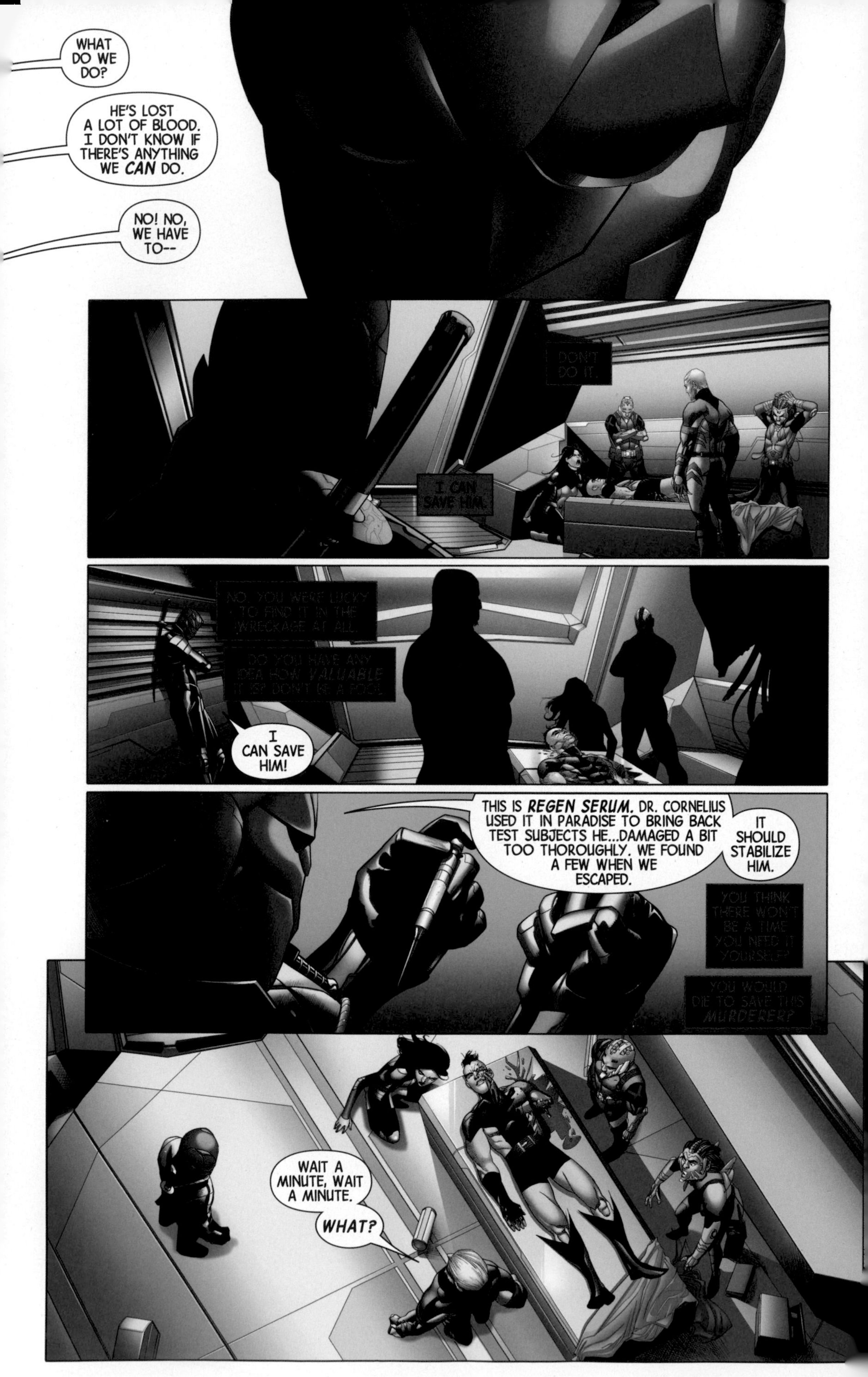
WHAT DO WE DO?
HE'S LOST A LOT OF BLOOD. I DON'T KNOW IF THERE'S ANYTHING WE CAN DO.
NO! NO, WE HAVE TO--
DON'T DO IT.
I CAN SAVE HIM.
NO. YOU WERE LUCKY TO FIND IT IN THE WRECKAGE AT ALL.
DO YOU HAVE ANY IDEA HOW VALUABLE IT IS? DON'T BE A FOOL.
I CAN SAVE HIM!
THIS IS REGEN SERUM. DR. CORNELIUS USED IT IN PARADISE TO BRING BACK TEST SUBJECTS HE...DAMAGED A BIT TOO THOROUGHLY. WE FOUND A FEW WHEN WE ESCAPED.
IT SHOULD STABILIZE HIM.
YOU THINK THERE WON'T BE A TIME YOU NEED IT YOURSELF?
YOU WOULD DIE TO SAVE THIS MURDERER?
WAIT A MINUTE, WAIT A MINUTE.
WHAT?

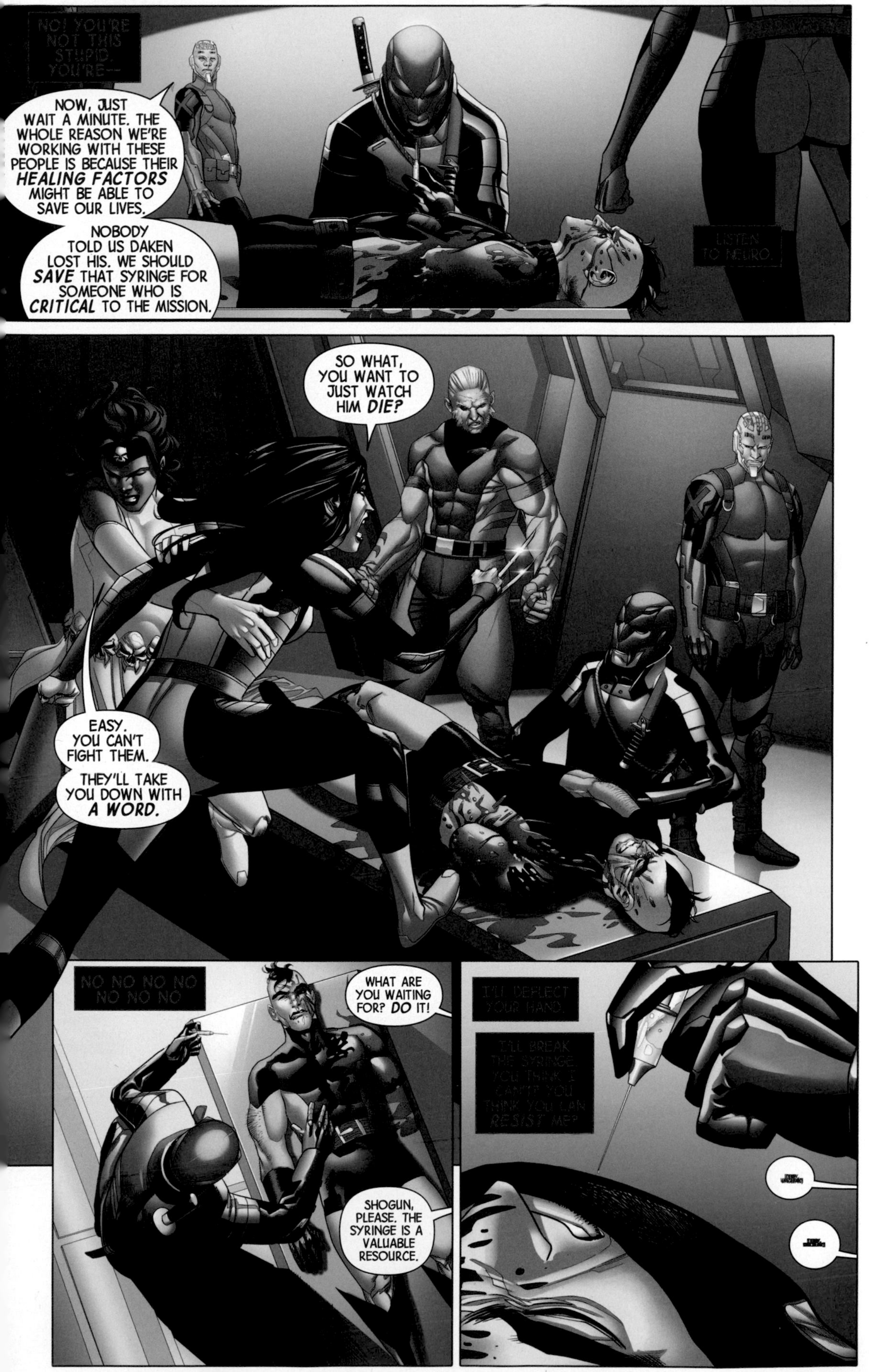
NO! YOU'RE NOT THIS STUPID. YOU'RE--
NOW, JUST WAIT A MINUTE. THE WHOLE REASON WE'RE WORKING WITH THESE PEOPLE IS BECAUSE THEIR HEALING FACTORS MIGHT BE ABLE TO SAVE OUR LIVES.
NOBODY TOLD US DAKEN LOST HIS. WE SHOULD SAVE THAT SYRINGE FOR SOMEONE WHO IS CRITICAL TO THE MISSION.
LISTEN TO NEURO.
SO WHAT, YOU WANT TO JUST WATCH HIM DIE?
EASY. YOU CAN'T FIGHT THEM.
THEY'LL TAKE YOU DOWN WITH A WORD.
NO NO NO NO NO NO NO
WHAT ARE YOU WAITING FOR? DO IT!
SHOGUN, PLEASE. THE SYRINGE IS A VALUABLE RESOURCE.
I'LL DEFLECT YOUR HAND.
I'LL BREAK THE SYRINGE. YOU THINK I CAN'T? YOU THINK YOU CAN RESIST ME?

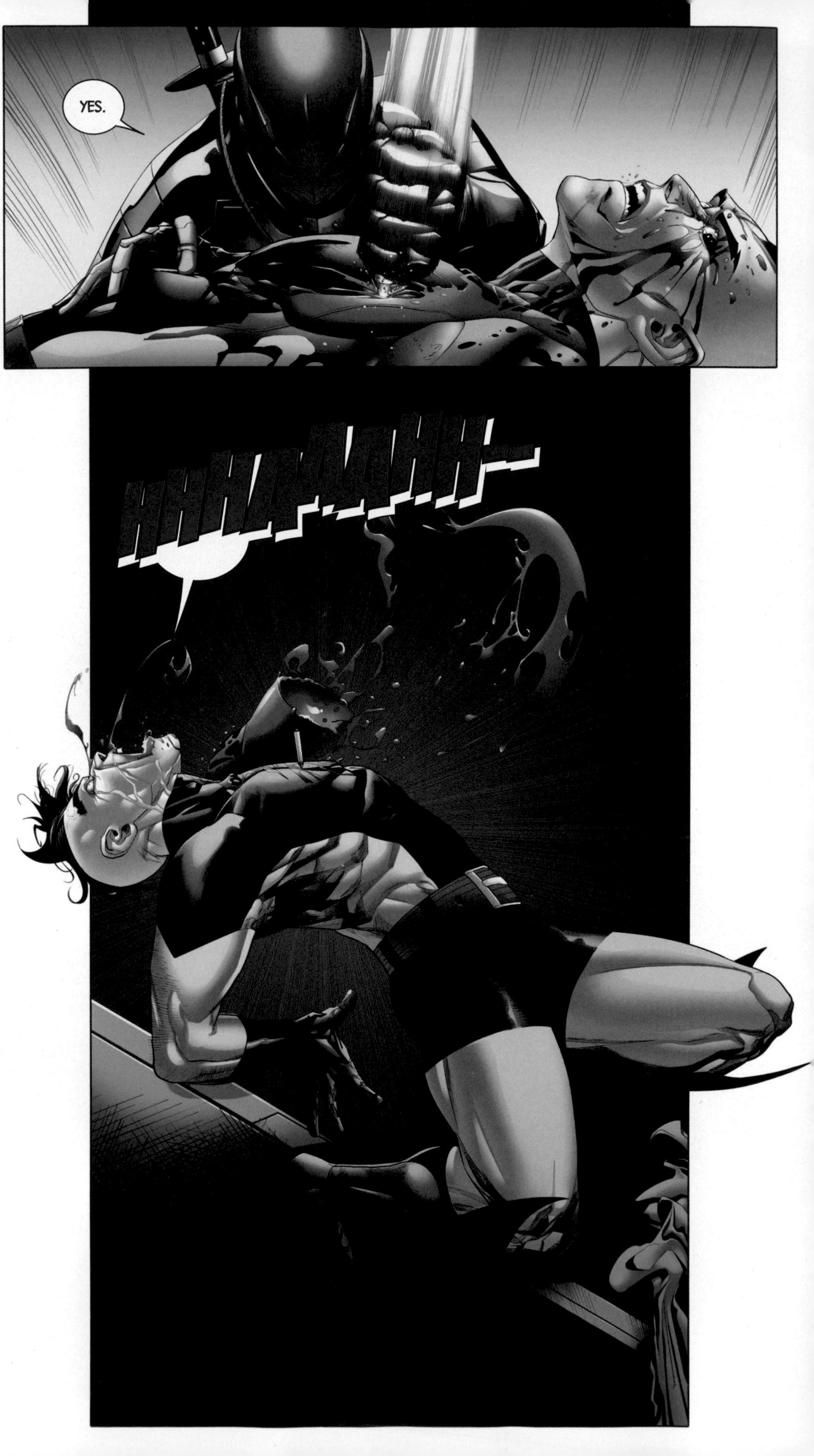
YES.
HHHAAAAHH—

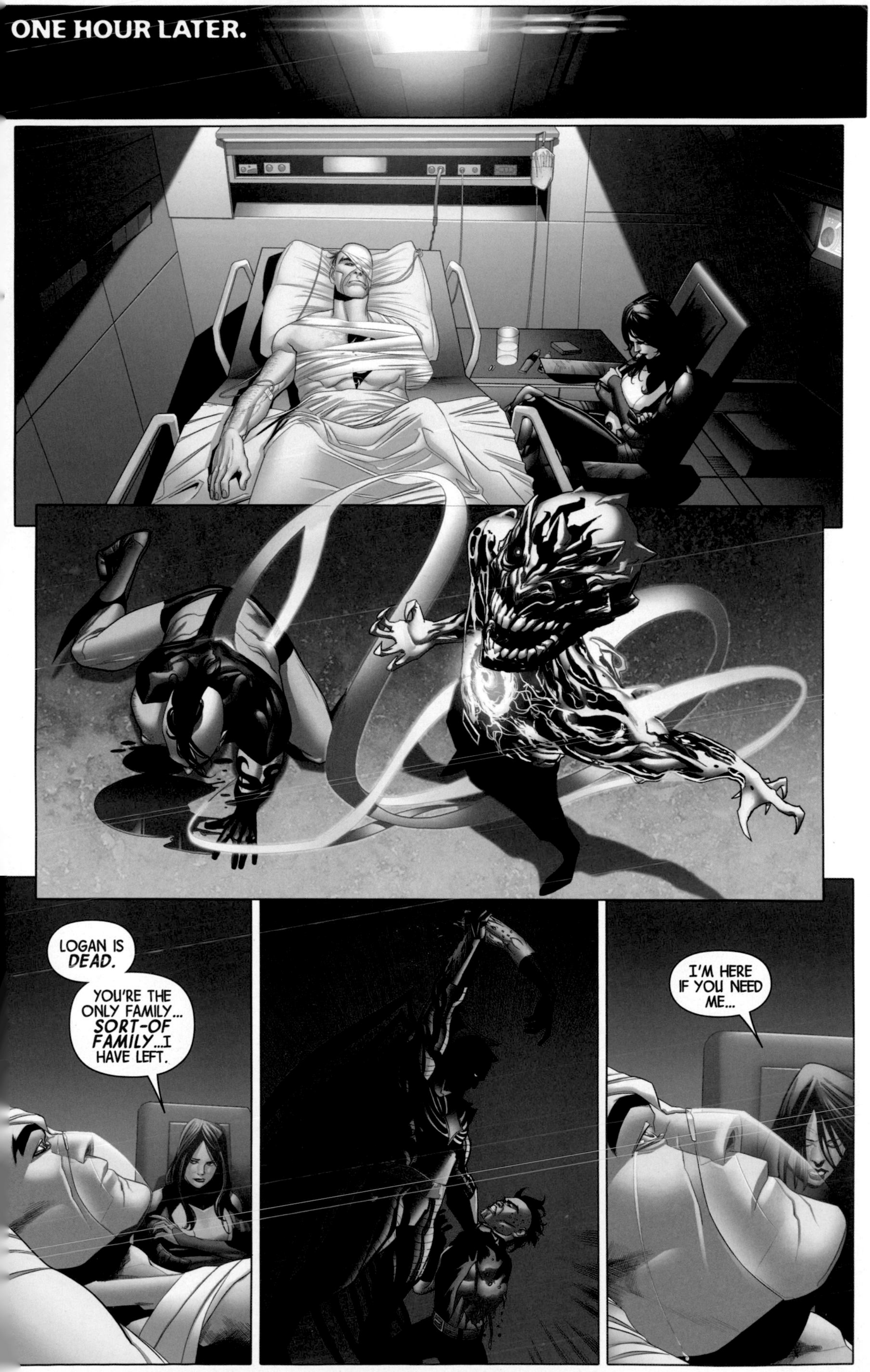
ONE HOUR LATER.
LOGAN IS DEAD.
YOU'RE THE ONLY FAMILY... SORT-OF FAMILY...I HAVE LEFT.
I'M HERE IF YOU NEED ME...

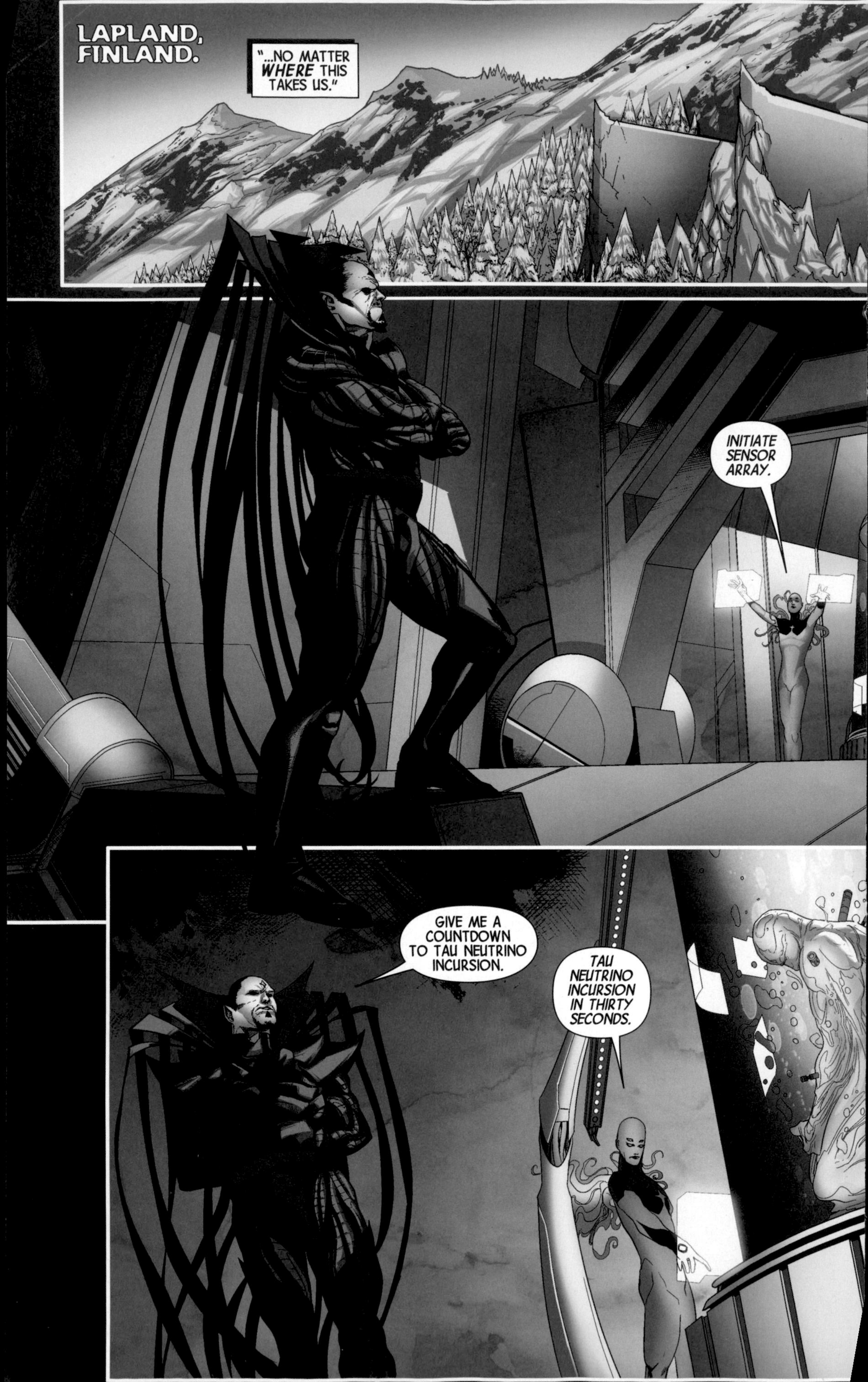
LAPLAND, FINLAND.
"...NO MATTER WHERE THIS TAKES US."
INITIATE SENSOR ARRAY.
GIVE ME A COUNTDOWN TO TAU NEUTRINO INCURSION.
TAU NEUTRINO INCURSION IN THIRTY SECONDS.

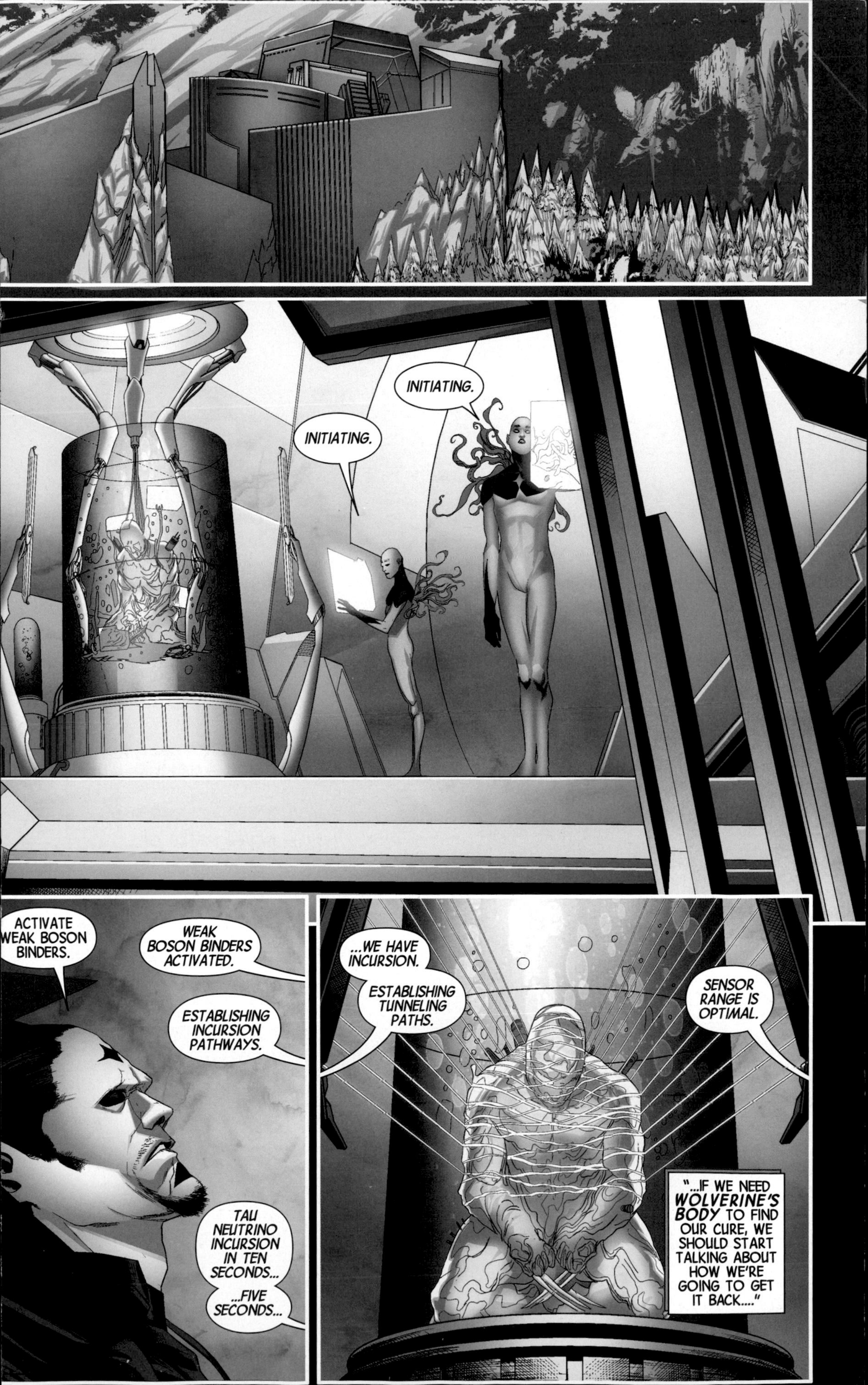
INITIATING.
INITIATING.
ACTIVATE WEAK BOSON BINDERS.
WEAK BOSON BINDERS ACTIVATED.
ESTABLISHING INCURSION PATHWAYS.
TAU NEUTRINO INCURSION IN TEN SECONDS...
...FIVE SECONDS...
...WE HAVE INCURSION.
ESTABLISHING TUNNELING PATHS.
SENSOR RANGE IS OPTIMAL.
"...IF WE NEED WOLVERINE'S BODY TO FIND OUR CURE, WE SHOULD START TALKING ABOUT HOW WE'RE GOING TO GET IT BACK...."

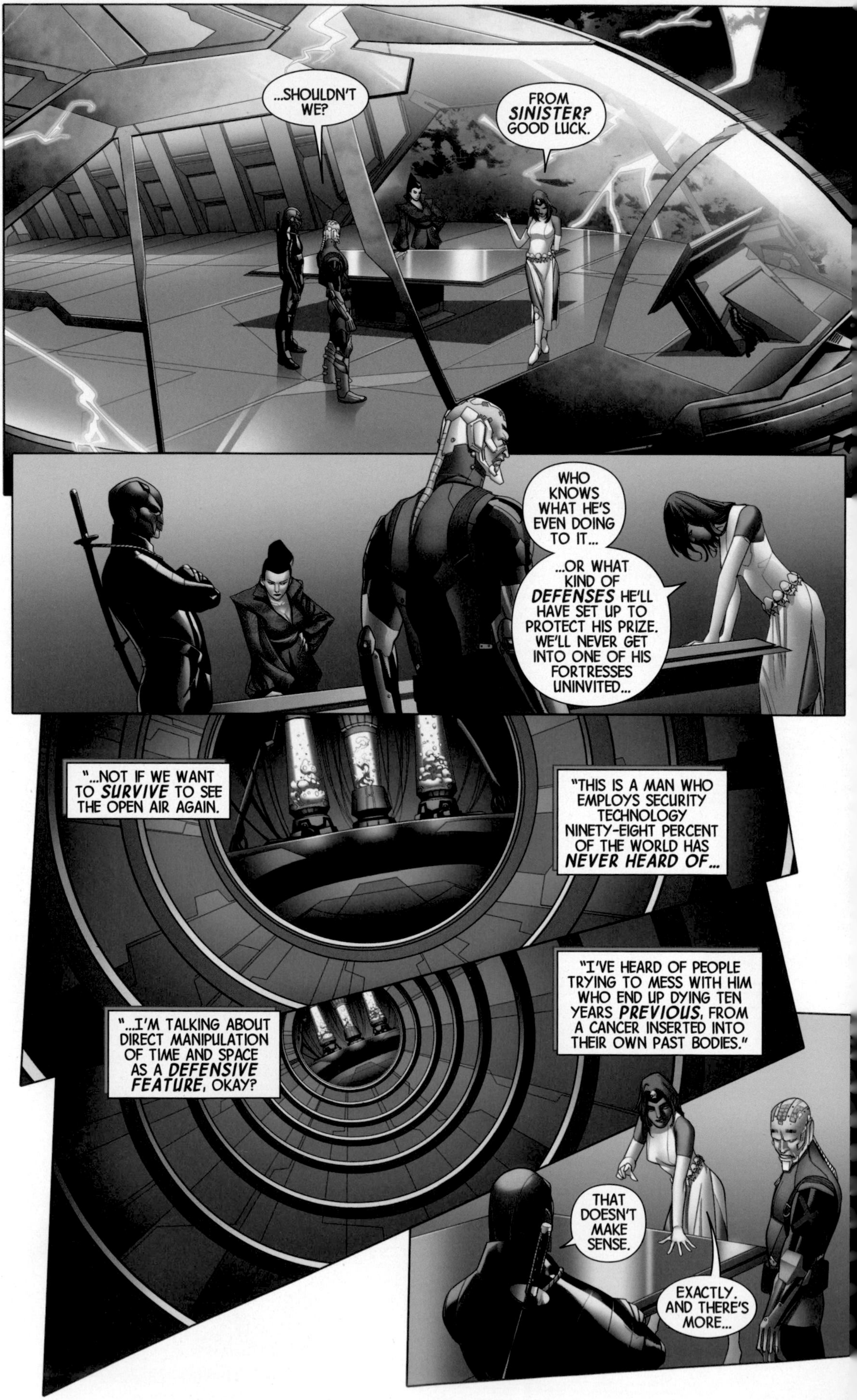
...SHOULDN'T WE?
FROM SINISTER? GOOD LUCK.
WHO KNOWS WHAT HE'S EVEN DOING TO IT...
...OR WHAT KIND OF DEFENSES HE'LL HAVE SET UP TO PROTECT HIS PRIZE. WE'LL NEVER GET INTO ONE OF HIS FORTRESSES UNINVITED...
"...NOT IF WE WANT TO SURVIVE TO SEE THE OPEN AIR AGAIN.
"THIS IS A MAN WHO EMPLOYS SECURITY TECHNOLOGY NINETY-EIGHT PERCENT OF THE WORLD HAS NEVER HEARD OF...
"...I'M TALKING ABOUT DIRECT MANIPULATION OF TIME AND SPACE AS A DEFENSIVE FEATURE, OKAY?
"I'VE HEARD OF PEOPLE TRYING TO MESS WITH HIM WHO END UP DYING TEN YEARS PREVIOUS, FROM A CANCER INSERTED INTO THEIR OWN PAST BODIES."
THAT DOESN'T MAKE SENSE.
EXACTLY. AND THERE'S MORE...

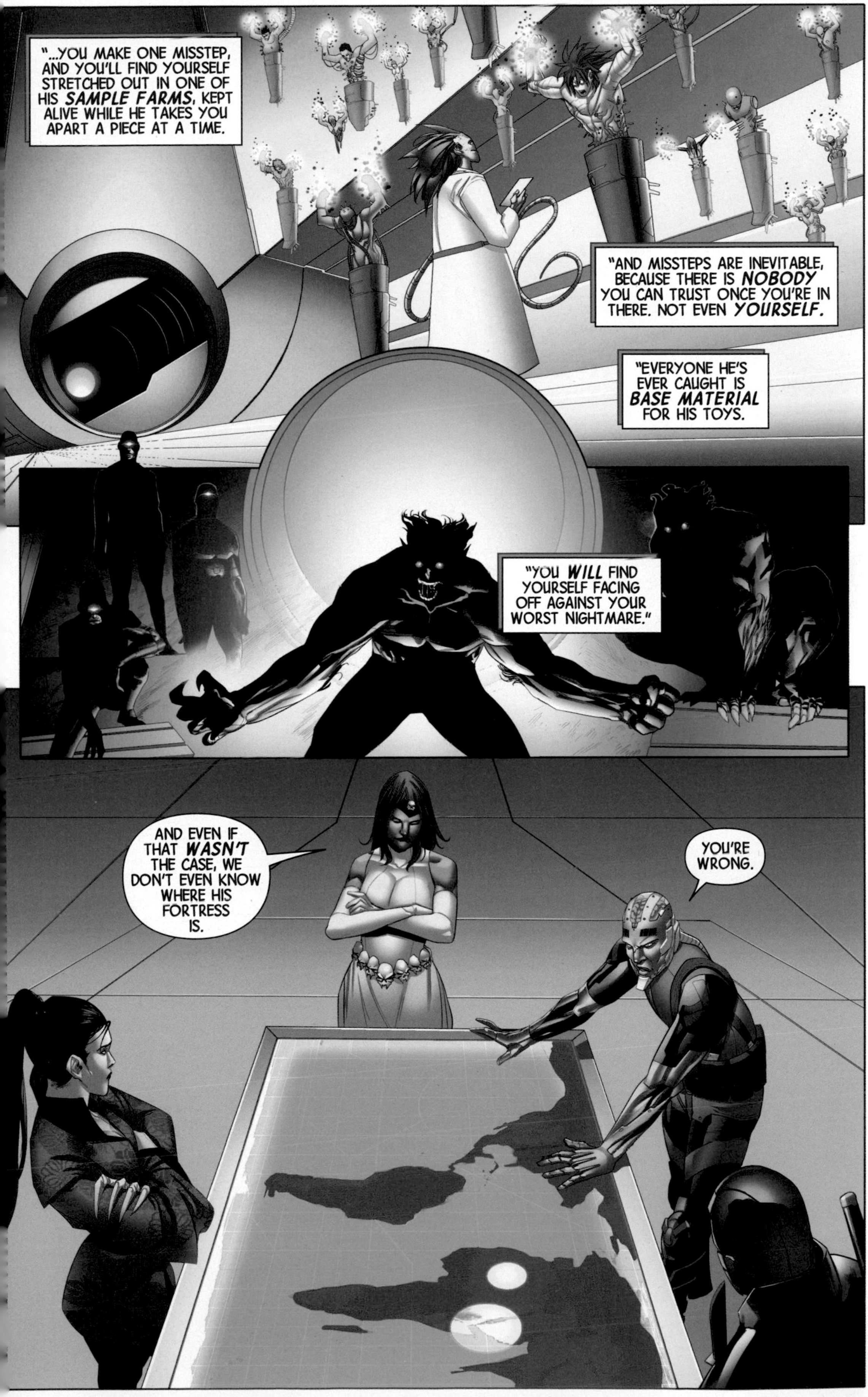
"...YOU MAKE ONE MISSTEP, AND YOU'LL FIND YOURSELF STRETCHED OUT IN ONE OF HIS SAMPLE FARMS, KEPT ALIVE WHILE HE TAKES YOU APART A PIECE AT A TIME.
"AND MISSTEPS ARE INEVITABLE, BECAUSE THERE IS NOBODY YOU CAN TRUST ONCE YOU'RE IN THERE. NOT EVEN YOURSELF.
"EVERYONE HE'S EVER CAUGHT IS BASE MATERIAL FOR HIS TOYS.
"YOU WILL FIND YOURSELF FACING OFF AGAINST YOUR WORST NIGHTMARE."
AND EVEN IF THAT WASN'T THE CASE, WE DON'T EVEN KNOW WHERE HIS FORTRESS IS.
YOU'RE WRONG.

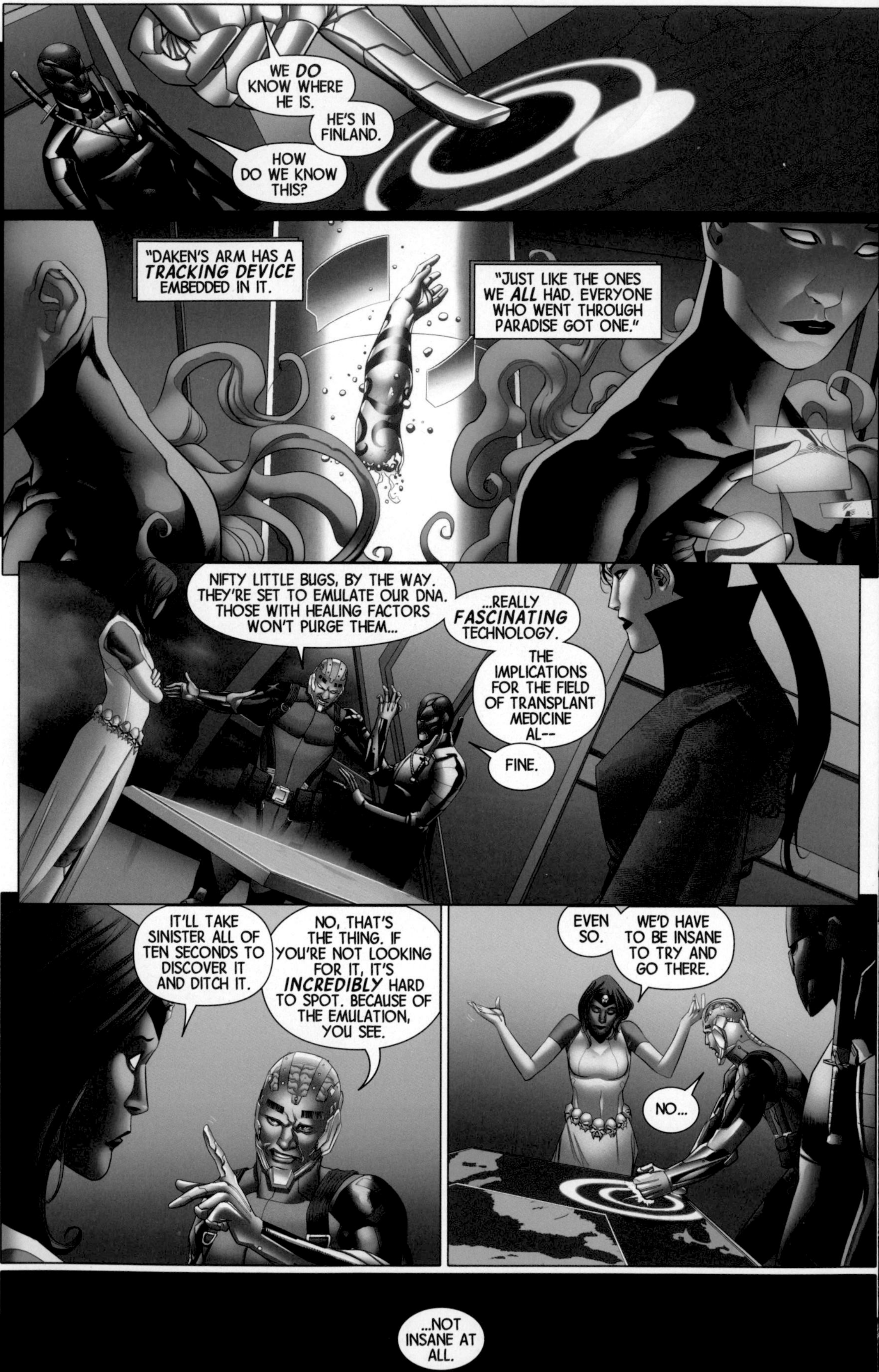
WE DO KNOW WHERE HE IS.
HE'S IN FINLAND.
HOW DO WE KNOW THIS?
"DAKEN'S ARM HAS A TRACKING DEVICE EMBEDDED IN IT.
"JUST LIKE THE ONES WE ALL HAD. EVERYONE WHO WENT THROUGH PARADISE GOT ONE."
NIFTY LITTLE BUGS, BY THE WAY. THEY'RE SET TO EMULATE OUR DNA. THOSE WITH HEALING FACTORS WON'T PURGE THEM...
...REALLY FASCINATING TECHNOLOGY.
THE IMPLICATIONS FOR THE FIELD OF TRANSPLANT MEDICINE AL--
FINE.
IT'LL TAKE SINISTER ALL OF TEN SECONDS TO DISCOVER IT AND DITCH IT.
NO, THAT'S THE THING. IF YOU'RE NOT LOOKING FOR IT, IT'S INCREDIBLY HARD TO SPOT. BECAUSE OF THE EMULATION, YOU SEE.
EVEN SO.
WE'D HAVE TO BE INSANE TO TRY AND GO THERE.
NO...
...NOT INSANE AT ALL.

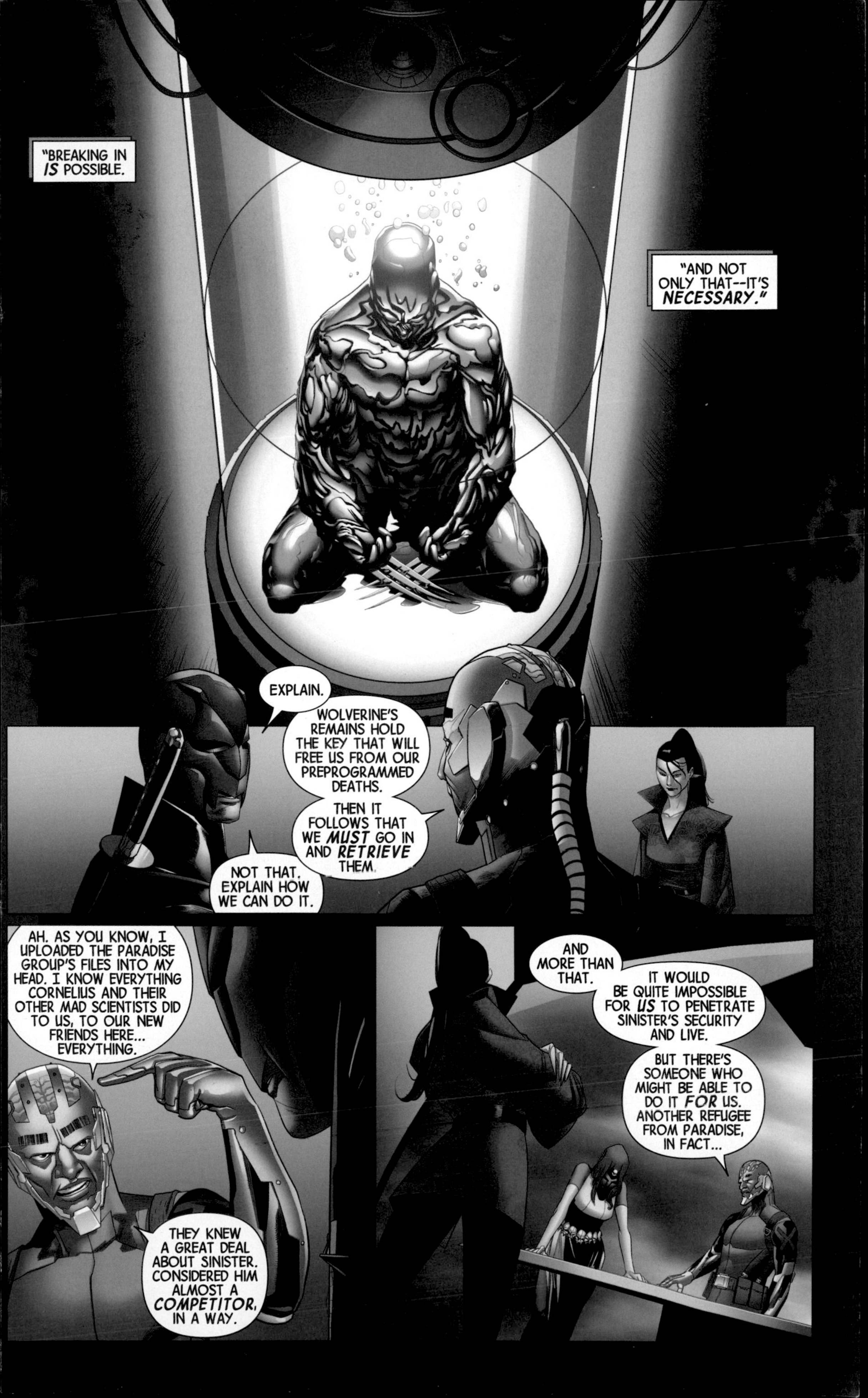
"BREAKING IN IS POSSIBLE.
"AND NOT ONLY THAT--IT'S NECESSARY."
EXPLAIN.
WOLVERINE'S REMAINS HOLD THE KEY THAT WILL FREE US FROM OUR PREPROGRAMMED DEATHS.
THEN IT FOLLOWS THAT WE MUST GO IN AND RETRIEVE THEM.
NOT THAT. EXPLAIN HOW WE CAN DO IT.
AH. AS YOU KNOW, I UPLOADED THE PARADISE GROUP'S FILES INTO MY HEAD. I KNOW EVERYTHING CORNELIUS AND THEIR OTHER MAD SCIENTISTS DID TO US, TO OUR NEW FRIENDS HERE... EVERYTHING.
THEY KNEW A GREAT DEAL ABOUT SINISTER. CONSIDERED HIM ALMOST A COMPETITOR, IN A WAY.
AND MORE THAN THAT.
IT WOULD BE QUITE IMPOSSIBLE FOR US TO PENETRATE SINISTER'S SECURITY AND LIVE.
BUT THERE'S SOMEONE WHO MIGHT BE ABLE TO DO IT FOR US. ANOTHER REFUGEE FROM PARADISE, IN FACT...

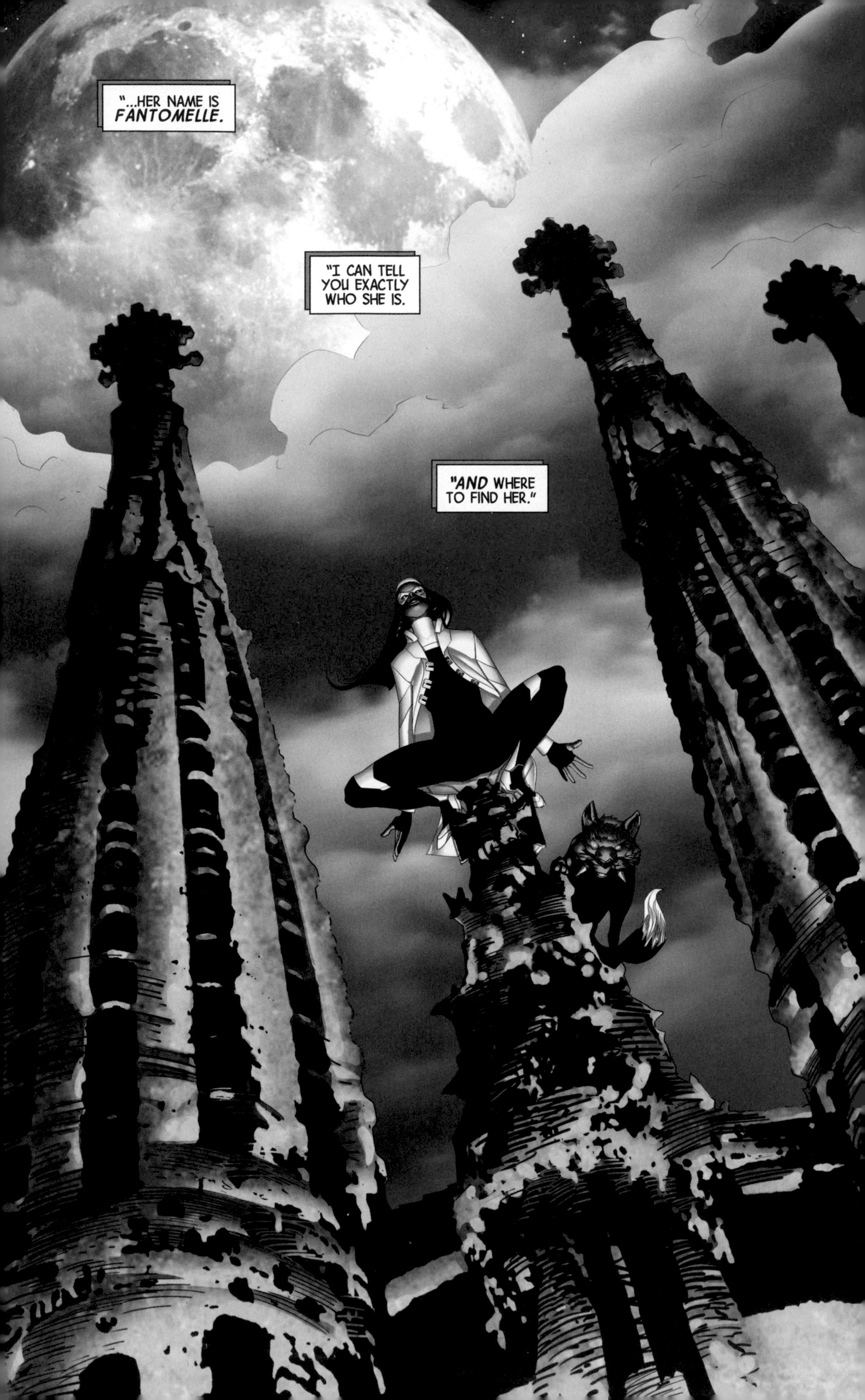
"...HER NAME IS *FANTOMELLE.*
"I CAN TELL YOU EXACTLY WHO SHE IS.
"*AND* WHERE TO FIND HER."

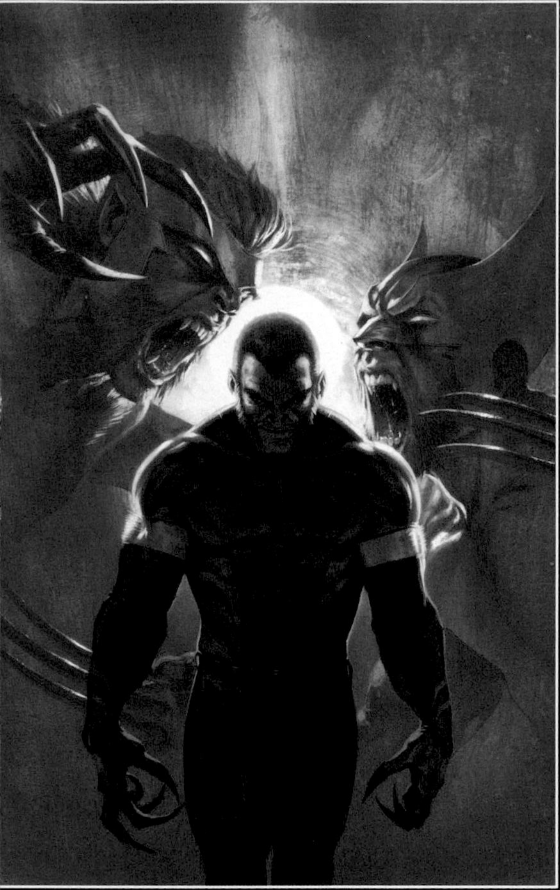

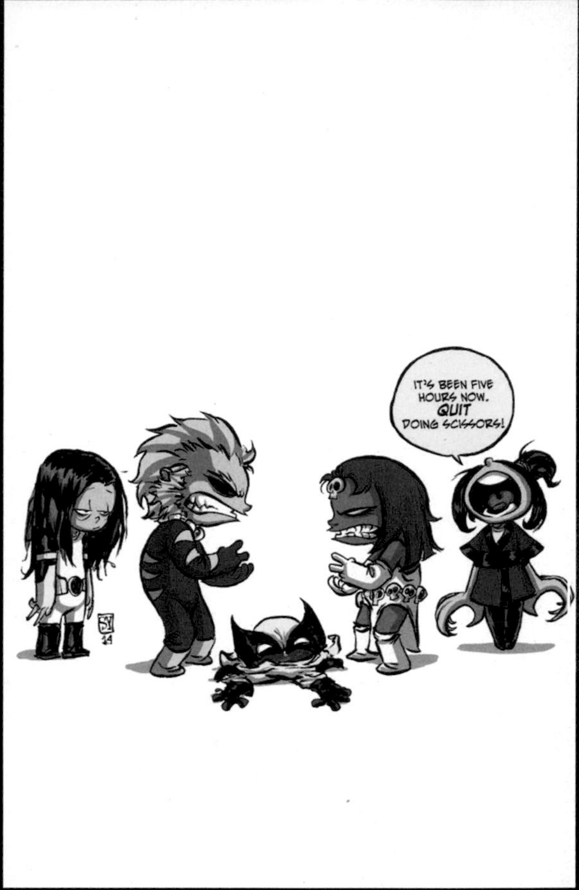
IT'S BEEN FIVE HOURS NOW. QUIT DOING SCISSORS!

#1 VARIANT
BY
GABRIELE
DELL'OTTO

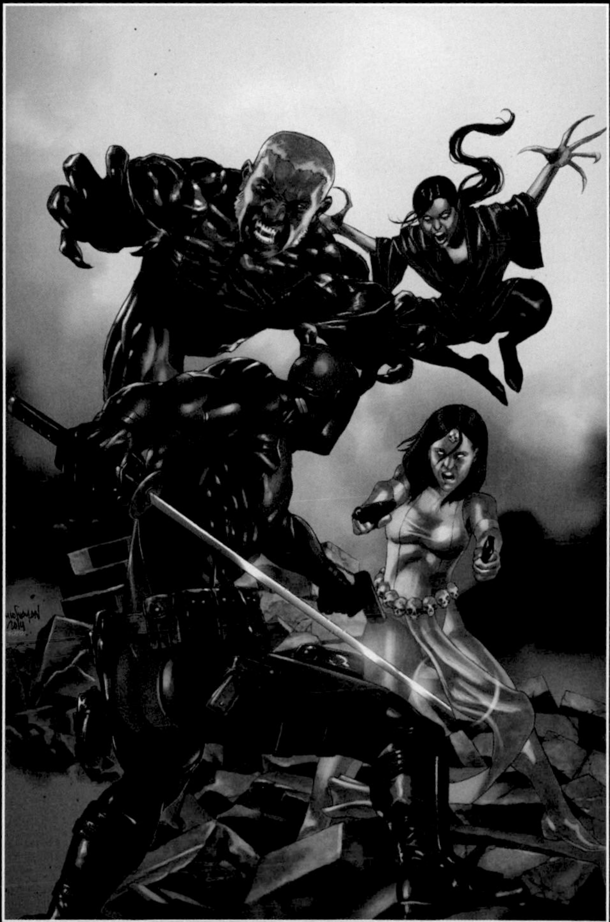

#1 VARIANT
BY
SKOTTIE YOUNG

#1 HASTINGS VARIANT BY MICO SUAYAN & CHRIS SOTOMAYOR

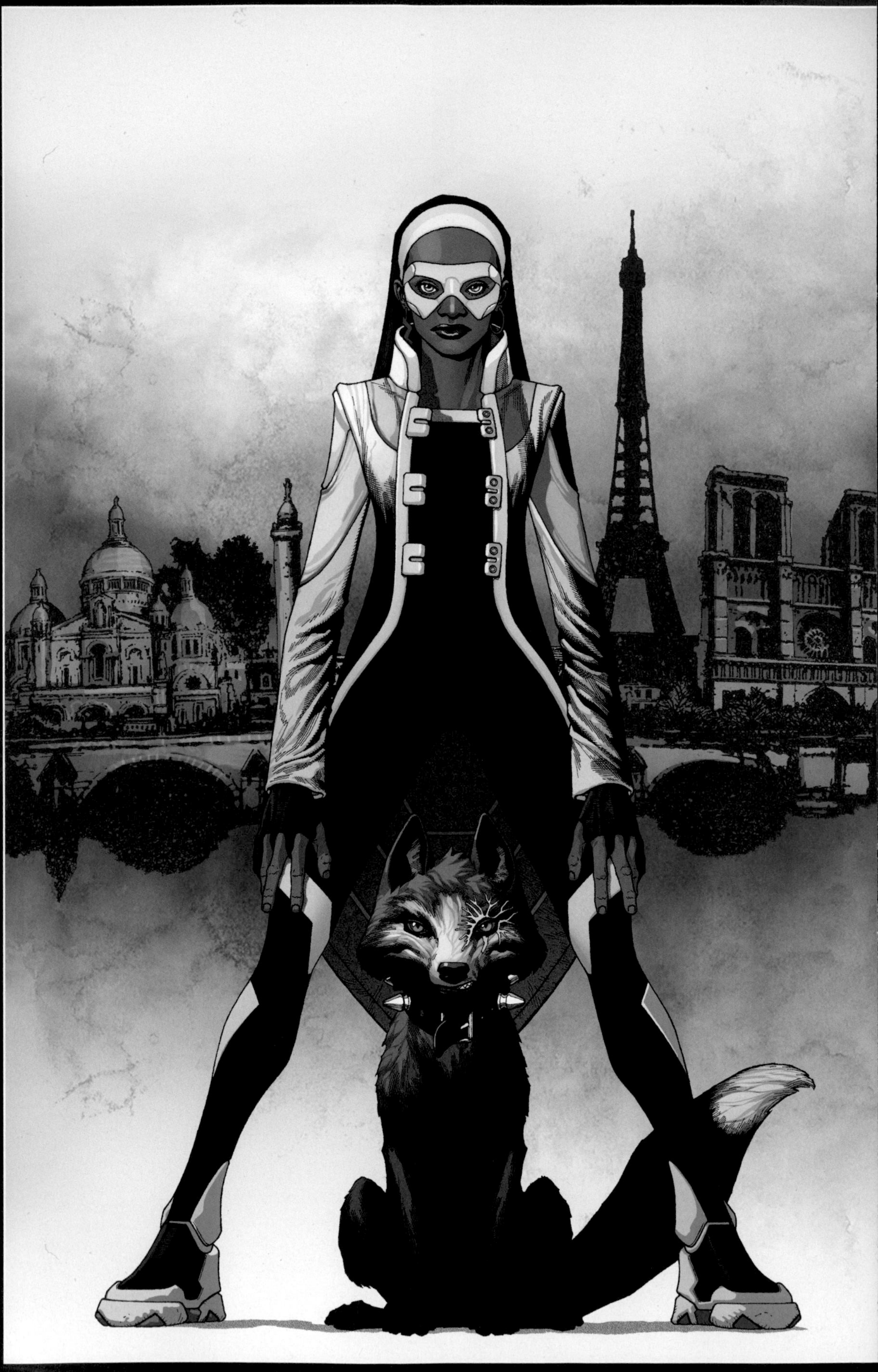

#3

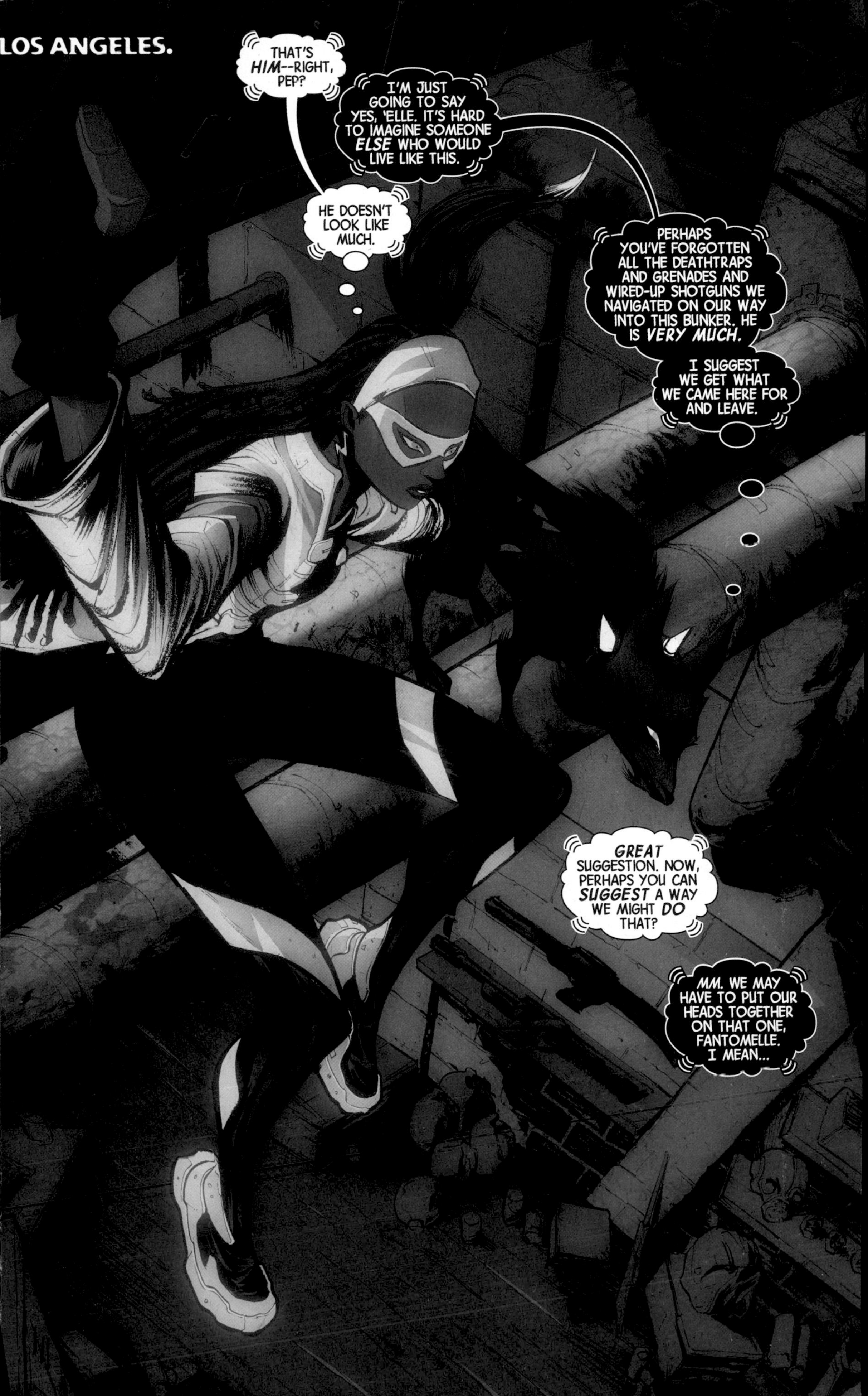
LOS ANGELES.
THAT'S HIM--RIGHT, PEP?
I'M JUST GOING TO SAY YES, 'ELLE. IT'S HARD TO IMAGINE SOMEONE ELSE WHO WOULD LIVE LIKE THIS.
HE DOESN'T LOOK LIKE MUCH.
PERHAPS YOU'VE FORGOTTEN ALL THE DEATHTRAPS AND GRENADES AND WIRED-UP SHOTGUNS WE NAVIGATED ON OUR WAY INTO THIS BUNKER. HE IS VERY MUCH.
I SUGGEST WE GET WHAT WE CAME HERE FOR AND LEAVE.
GREAT SUGGESTION. NOW, PERHAPS YOU CAN SUGGEST A WAY WE MIGHT DO THAT?
MM. WE MAY HAVE TO PUT OUR HEADS TOGETHER ON THAT ONE, FANTOMELLE. I MEAN...

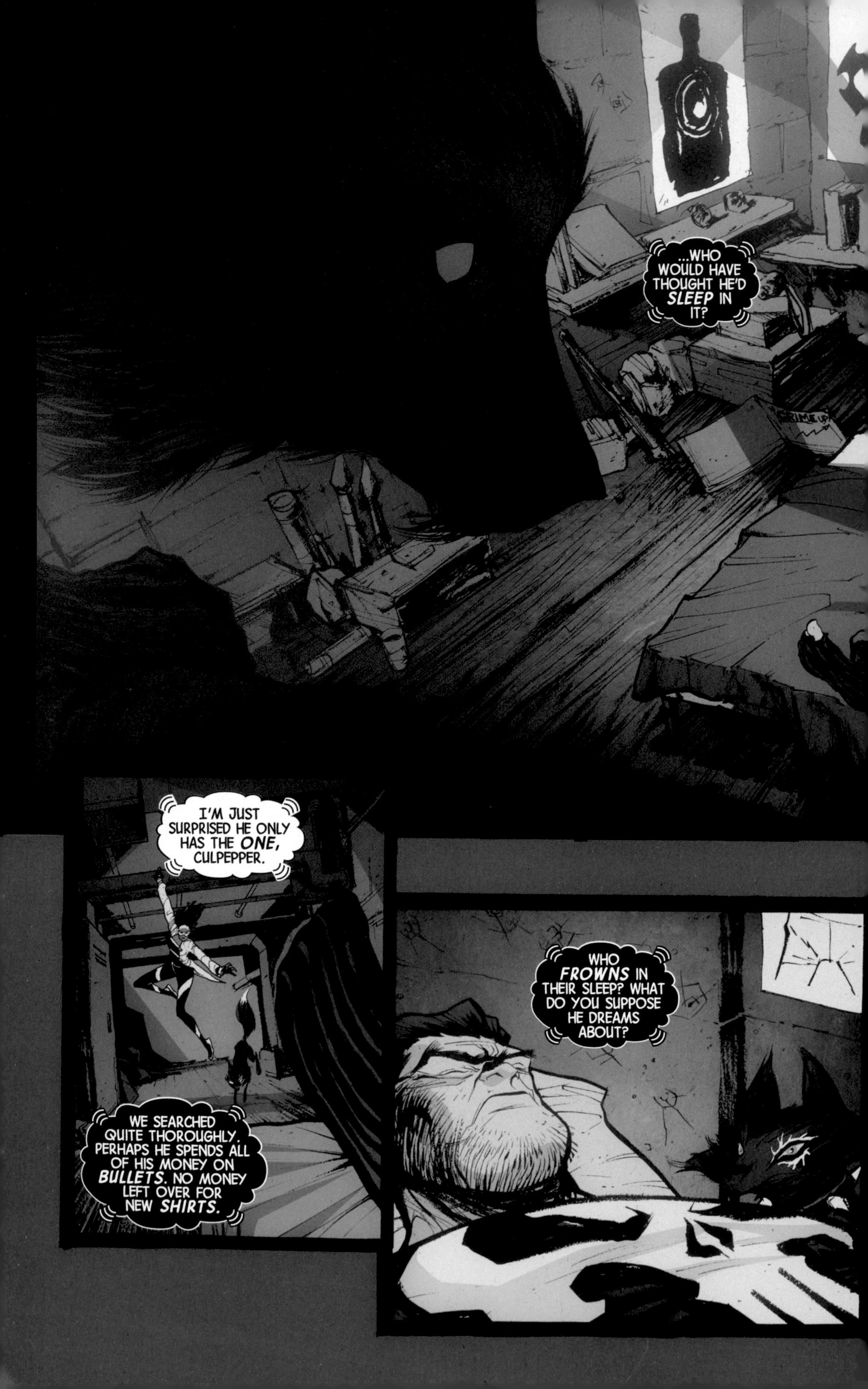
...WHO WOULD HAVE THOUGHT HE'D SLEEP IN IT?
I'M JUST SURPRISED HE ONLY HAS THE ONE, CULPEPPER.
WE SEARCHED QUITE THOROUGHLY. PERHAPS HE SPENDS ALL OF HIS MONEY ON BULLETS. NO MONEY LEFT OVER FOR NEW SHIRTS.
WHO FROWNS IN THEIR SLEEP? WHAT DO YOU SUPPOSE HE DREAMS ABOUT?

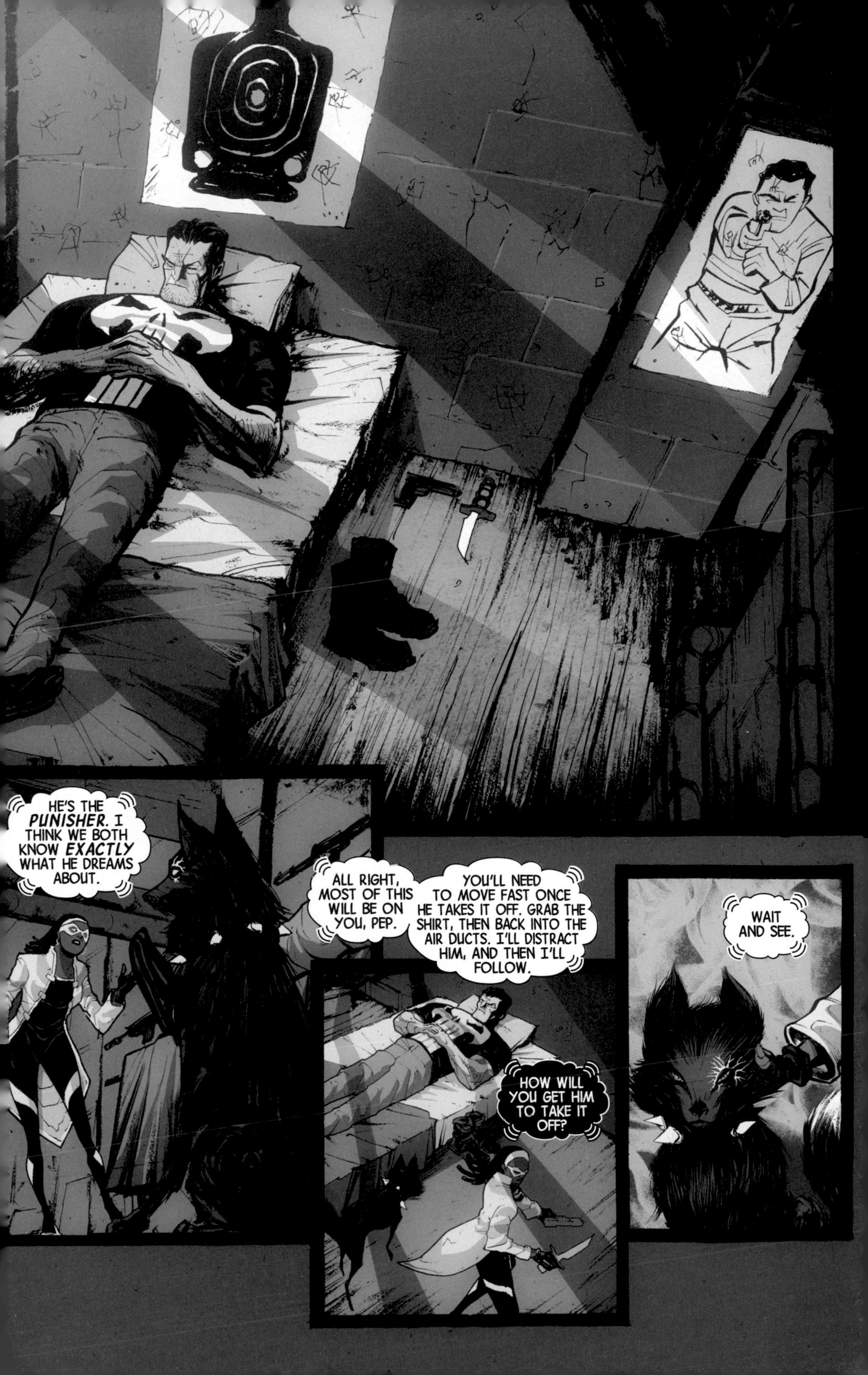
HE'S THE PUNISHER. I THINK WE BOTH KNOW EXACTLY WHAT HE DREAMS ABOUT.
ALL RIGHT, MOST OF THIS WILL BE ON YOU, PEP.
YOU'LL NEED TO MOVE FAST ONCE HE TAKES IT OFF. GRAB THE SHIRT, THEN BACK INTO THE AIR DUCTS. I'LL DISTRACT HIM, AND THEN I'LL FOLLOW.
HOW WILL YOU GET HIM TO TAKE IT OFF?
WAIT AND SEE.

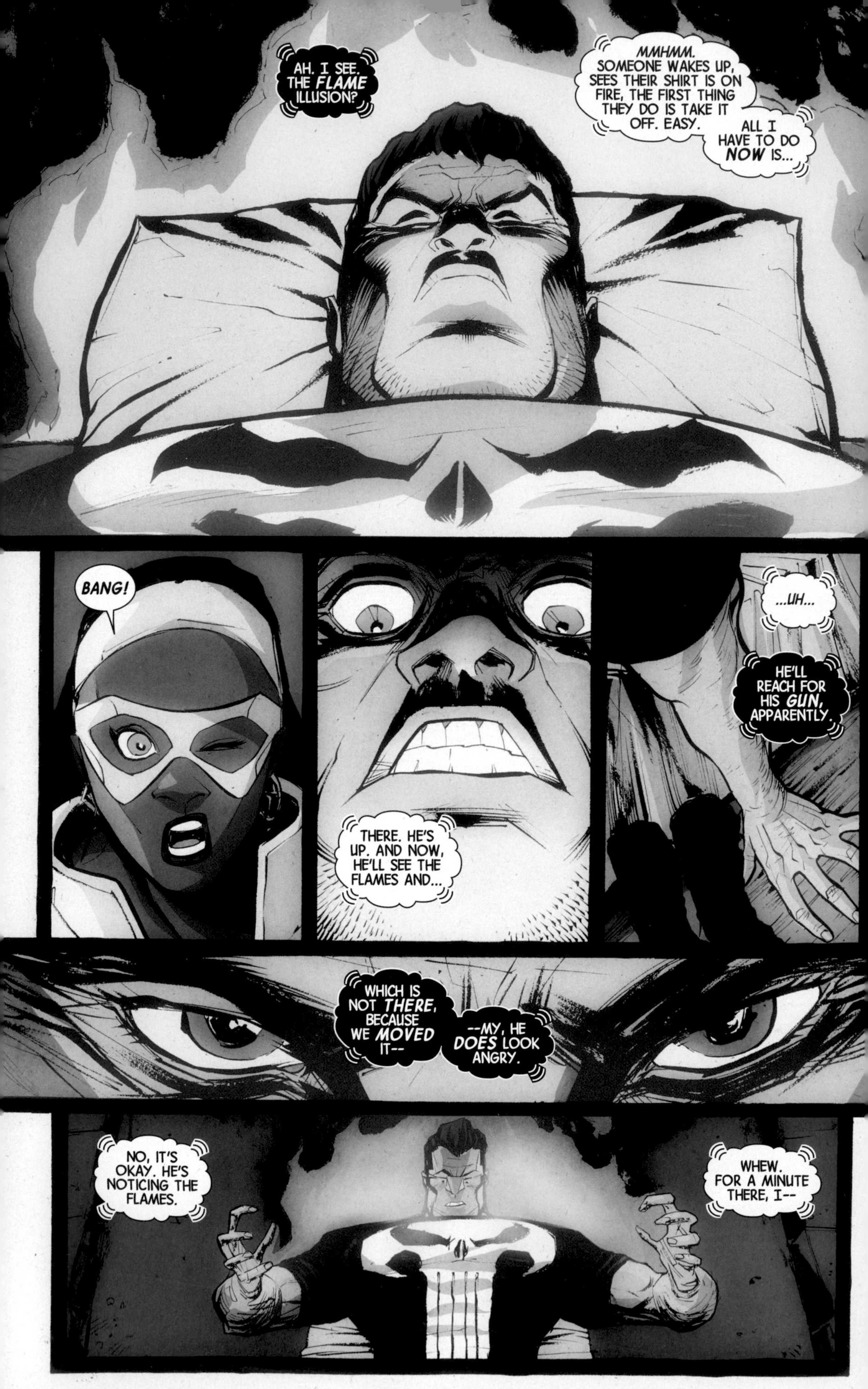
AH. I SEE. THE FLAME ILLUSION?
MMHMM. SOMEONE WAKES UP, SEES THEIR SHIRT IS ON FIRE, THE FIRST THING THEY DO IS TAKE IT OFF. EASY.
ALL I HAVE TO DO NOW IS...
BANG!
THERE. HE'S UP. AND NOW, HE'LL SEE THE FLAMES AND...
...UH...
HE'LL REACH FOR HIS GUN, APPARENTLY.
WHICH IS NOT THERE, BECAUSE WE MOVED IT--
--MY, HE DOES LOOK ANGRY.
NO, IT'S OKAY. HE'S NOTICING THE FLAMES.
WHEW. FOR A MINUTE THERE, I--

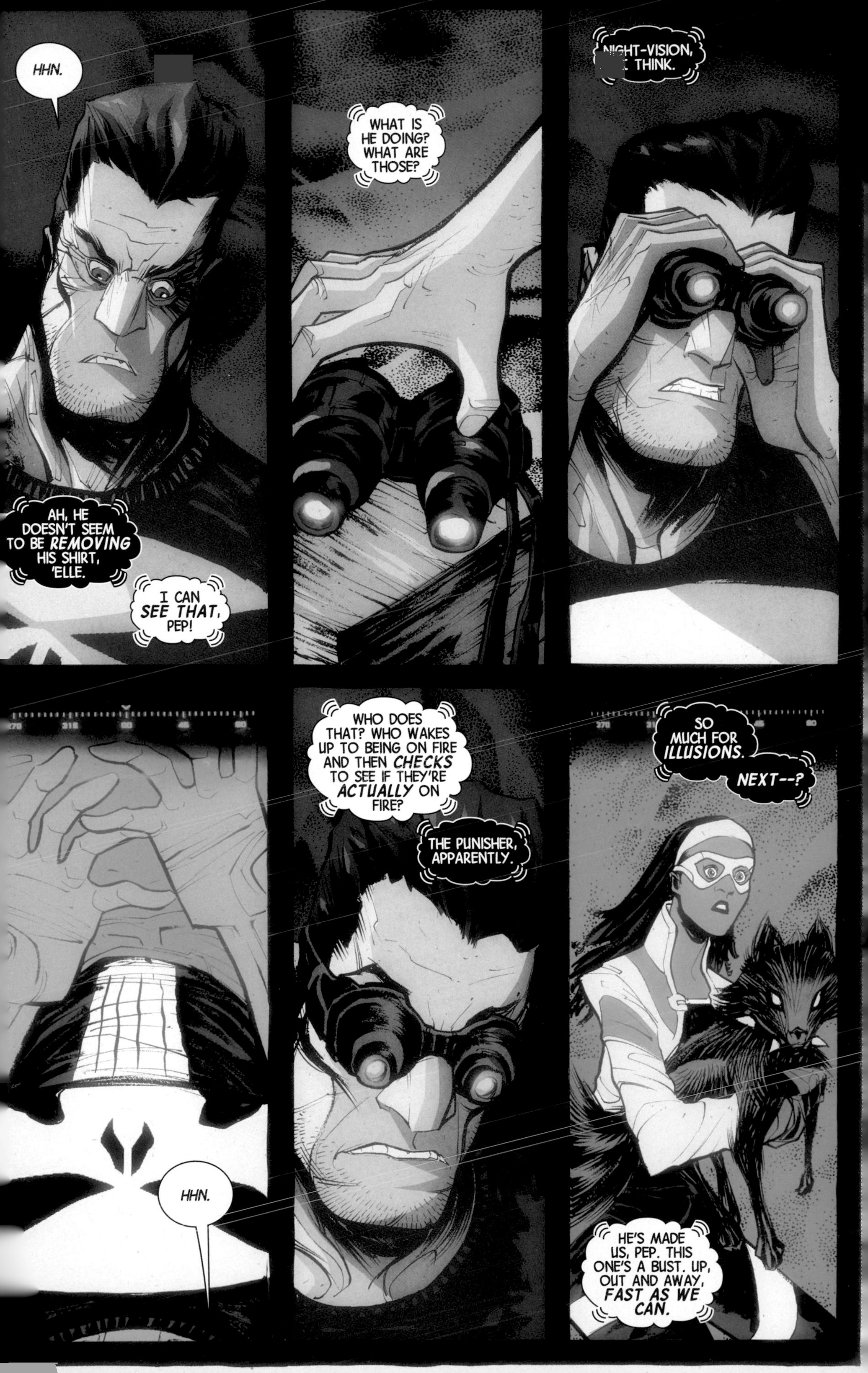
HHN.
WHAT IS HE DOING? WHAT ARE THOSE?
N[redacted]HT-VISION,
[redacted] THINK.
AH, HE DOESN'T SEEM TO BE *REMOVING* HIS SHIRT, 'ELLE.
I CAN *SEE THAT*, PEP!
270 315 00 45 90
WHO DOES THAT? WHO WAKES UP TO BEING ON FIRE AND THEN *CHECKS* TO SEE IF THEY'RE *ACTUALLY* ON FIRE?
THE PUNISHER, APPARENTLY.
SO MUCH FOR *ILLUSIONS*.
NEXT--?
HHN.
HE'S MADE US, PEP. THIS ONE'S A BUST. UP, OUT AND AWAY, *FAST AS WE CAN.*

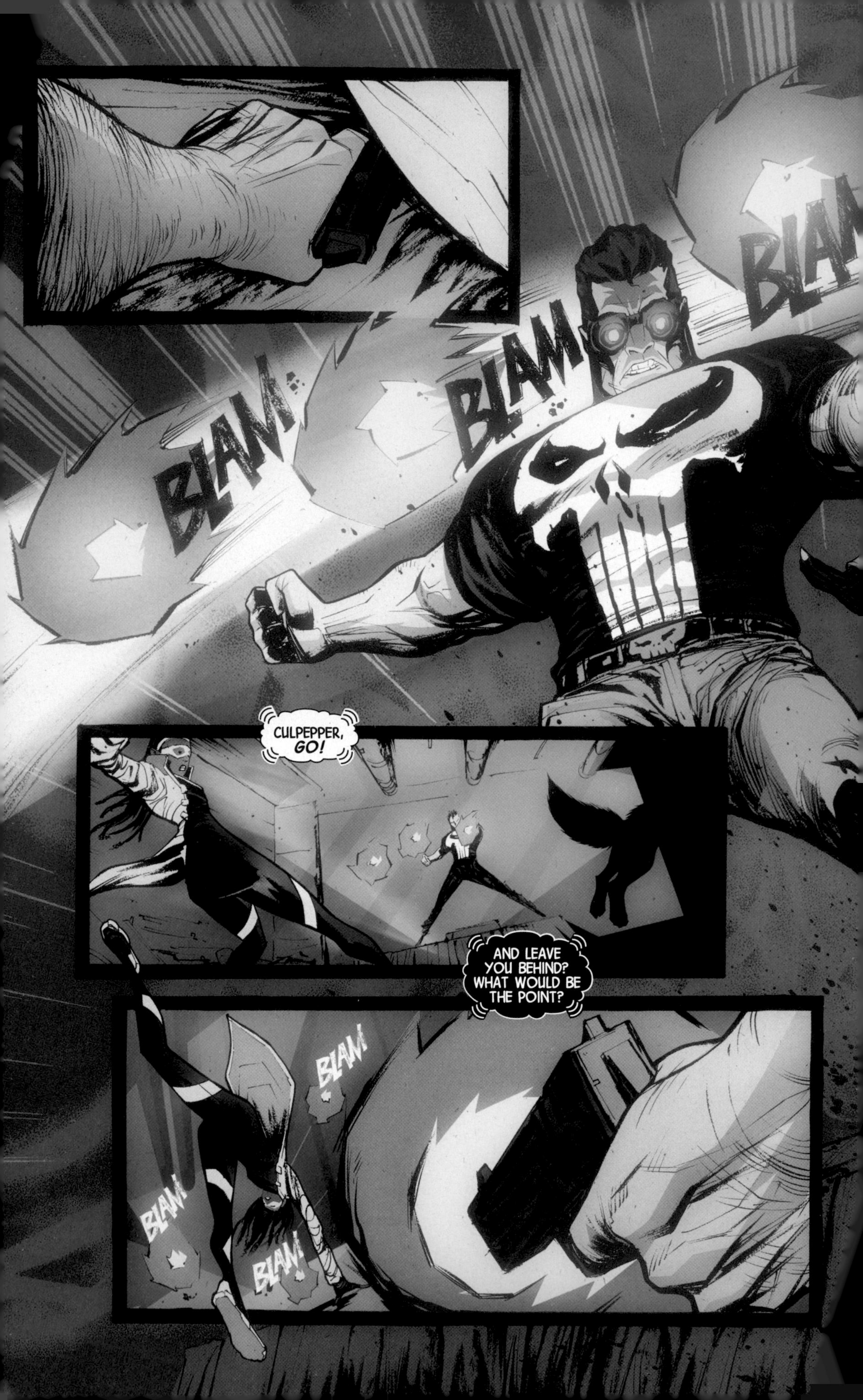
BLAM
BLAM
BLAM
BLAM
CULPEPPER, GO!
AND LEAVE YOU BEHIND? WHAT WOULD BE THE POINT?
BLAM
BLAM
BLAM

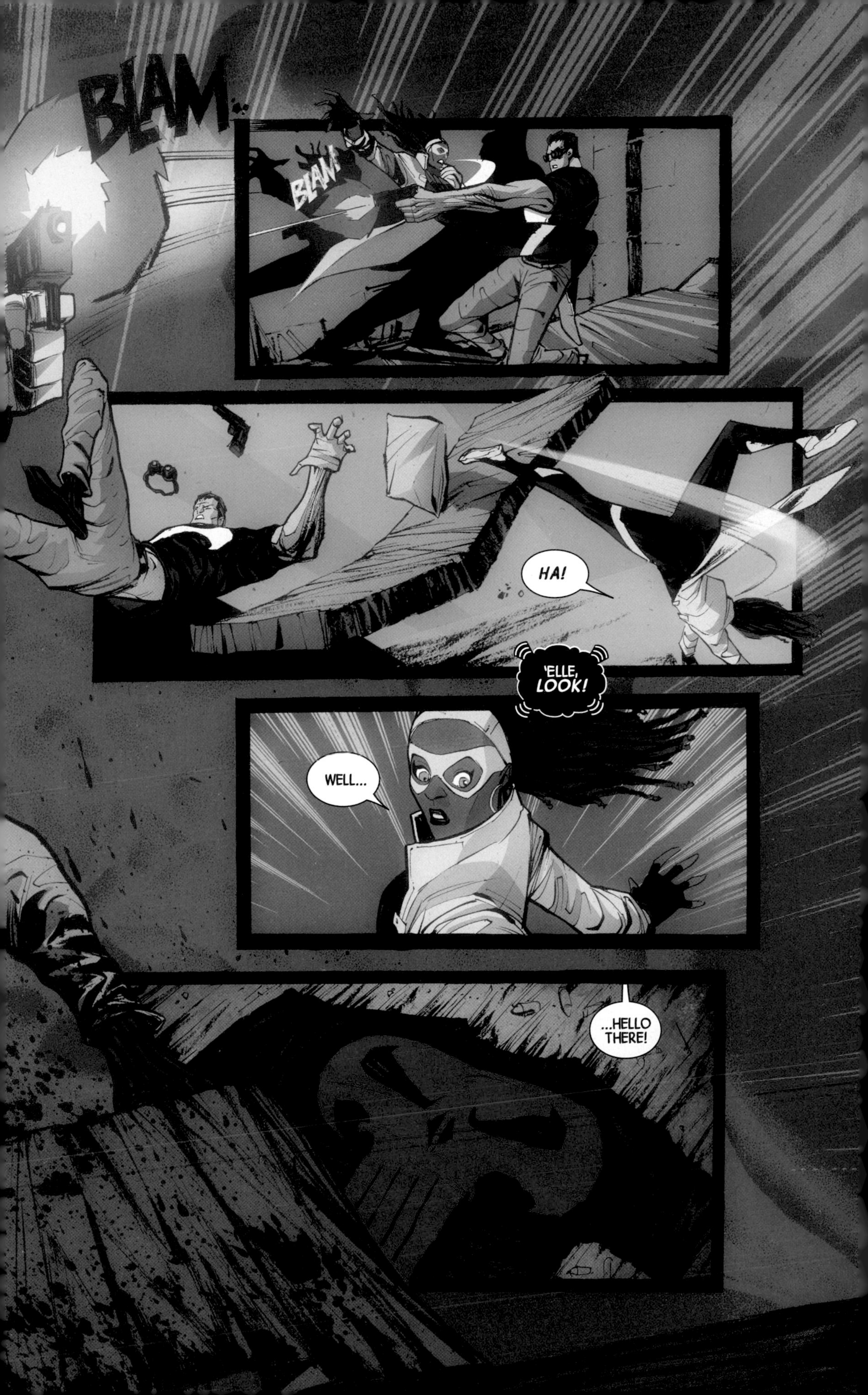
BLAM
BLAM!
HA!
'ELLE, LOOK!
WELL...
...HELLO THERE!

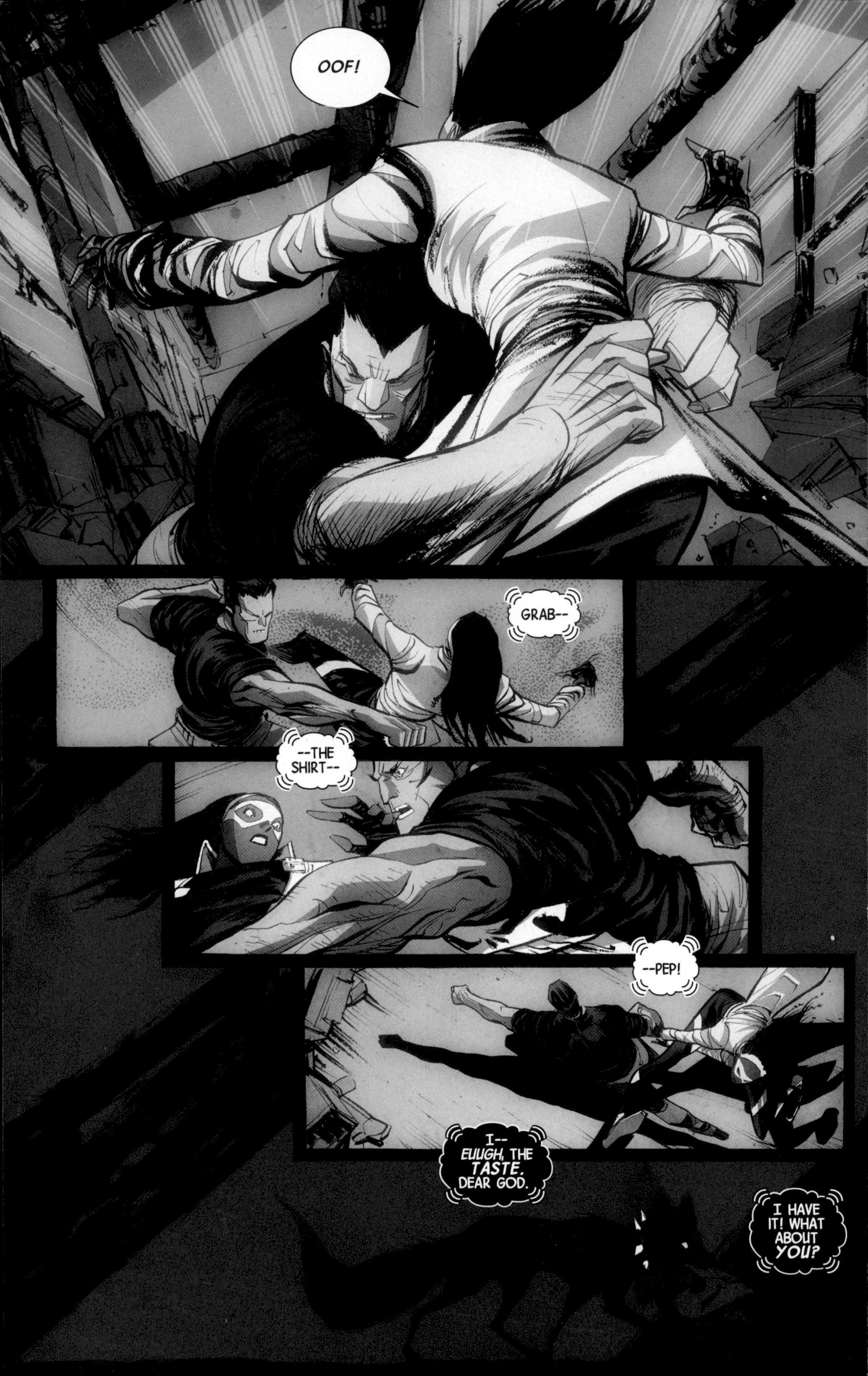
OOF!
GRAB--
--THE SHIRT--
--PEP!
I-- EUUGH, THE TASTE. DEAR GOD.
I HAVE IT! WHAT ABOUT YOU?

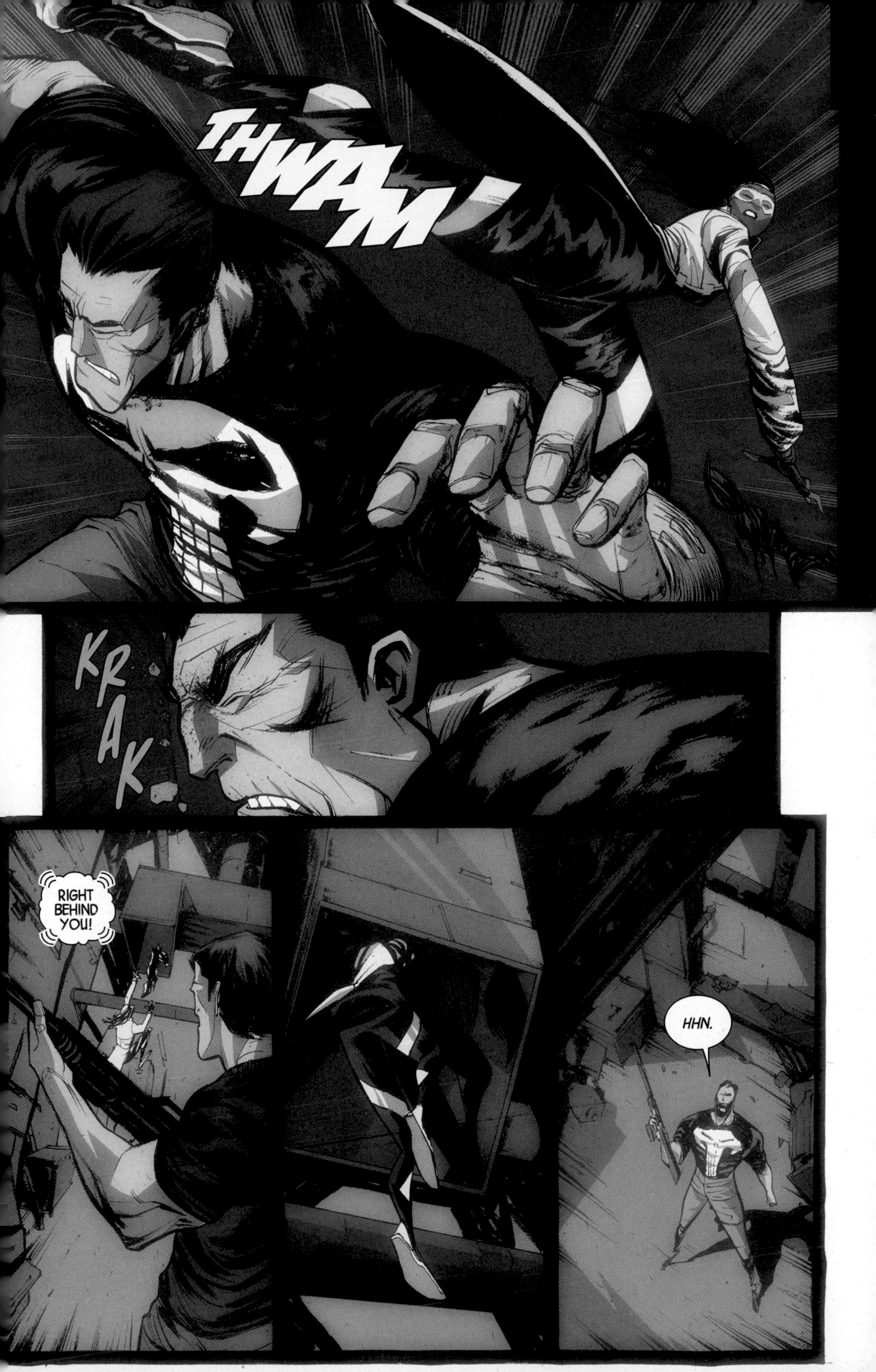
THWAM
KRAK
RIGHT BEHIND YOU!
HHN.

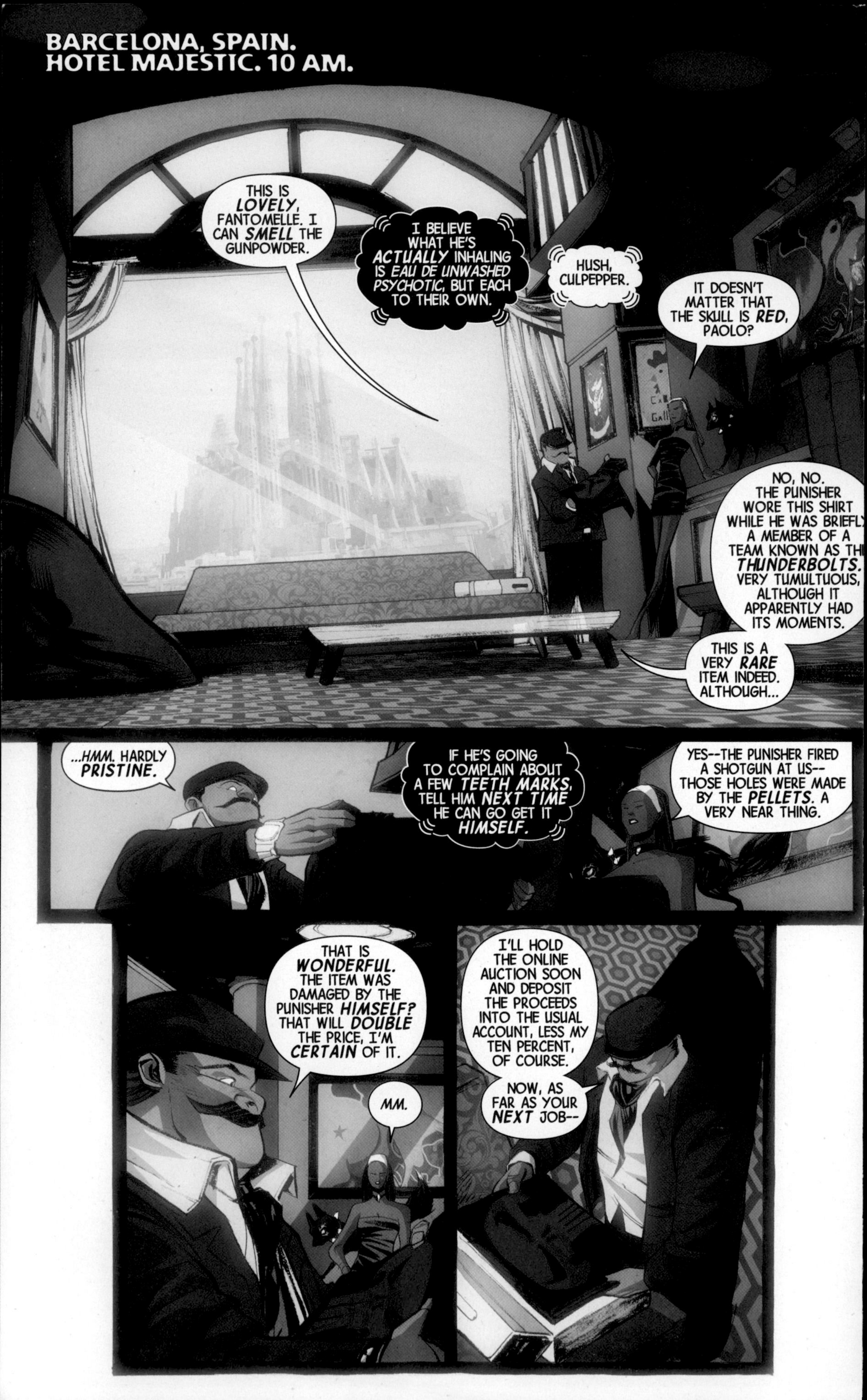
BARCELONA, SPAIN.
HOTEL MAJESTIC. 10 AM.
THIS IS LOVELY, FANTOMELLE. I CAN SMELL THE GUNPOWDER.
I BELIEVE WHAT HE'S ACTUALLY INHALING IS EAU DE UNWASHED PSYCHOTIC, BUT EACH TO THEIR OWN.
HUSH, CULPEPPER.
IT DOESN'T MATTER THAT THE SKULL IS RED, PAOLO?
NO, NO. THE PUNISHER WORE THIS SHIRT WHILE HE WAS BRIEFLY A MEMBER OF A TEAM KNOWN AS THE THUNDERBOLTS. VERY TUMULTUOUS, ALTHOUGH IT APPARENTLY HAD ITS MOMENTS.
THIS IS A VERY RARE ITEM INDEED. ALTHOUGH...
...HMM. HARDLY PRISTINE.
IF HE'S GOING TO COMPLAIN ABOUT A FEW TEETH MARKS, TELL HIM NEXT TIME HE CAN GO GET IT HIMSELF.
YES--THE PUNISHER FIRED A SHOTGUN AT US--THOSE HOLES WERE MADE BY THE PELLETS. A VERY NEAR THING.
THAT IS WONDERFUL. THE ITEM WAS DAMAGED BY THE PUNISHER HIMSELF? THAT WILL DOUBLE THE PRICE, I'M CERTAIN OF IT.
MM.
I'LL HOLD THE ONLINE AUCTION SOON AND DEPOSIT THE PROCEEDS INTO THE USUAL ACCOUNT, LESS MY TEN PERCENT, OF COURSE.
NOW, AS FAR AS YOUR NEXT JOB--

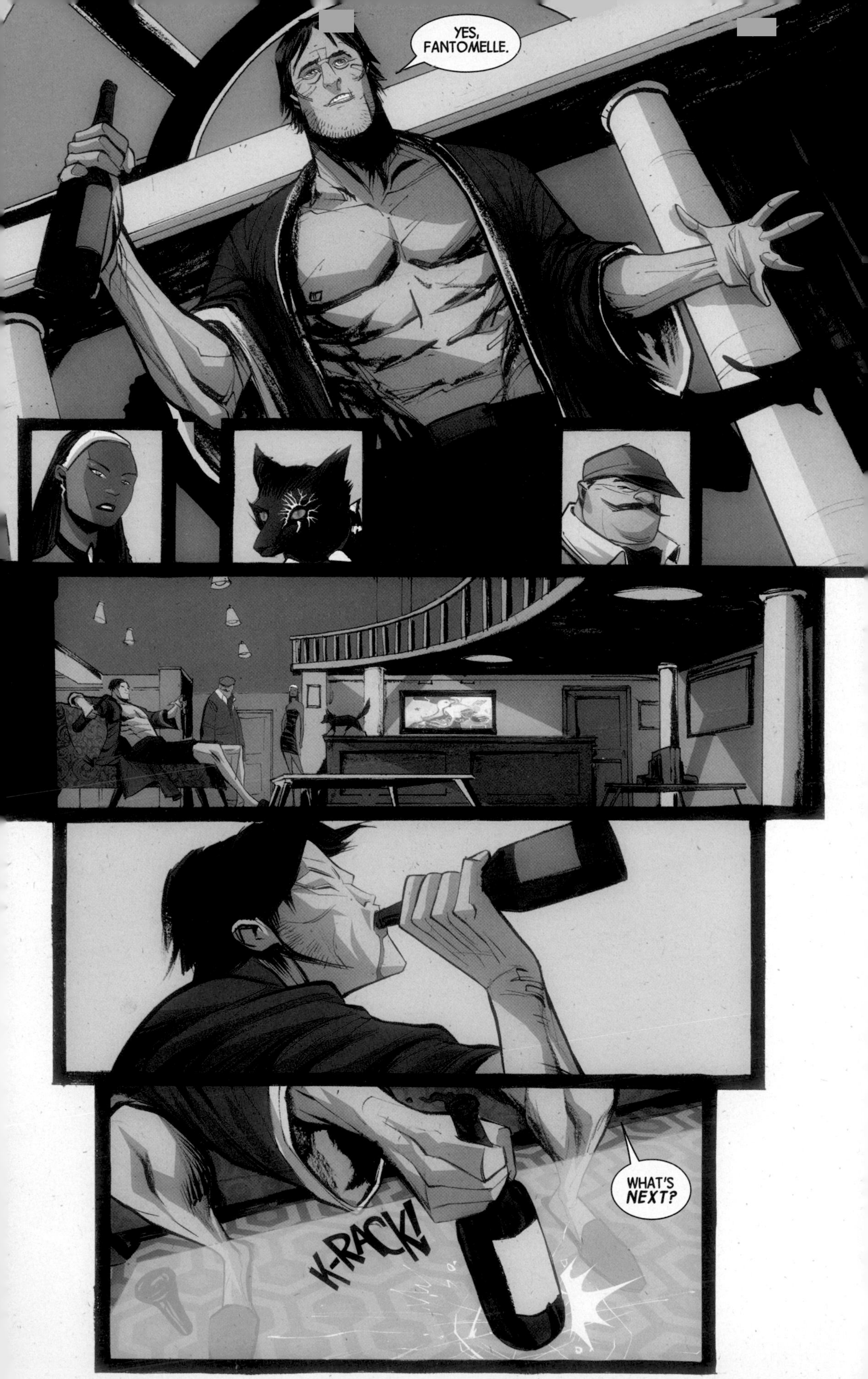
YES, FANTOMELLE.
WHAT'S NEXT?
K-RACK!

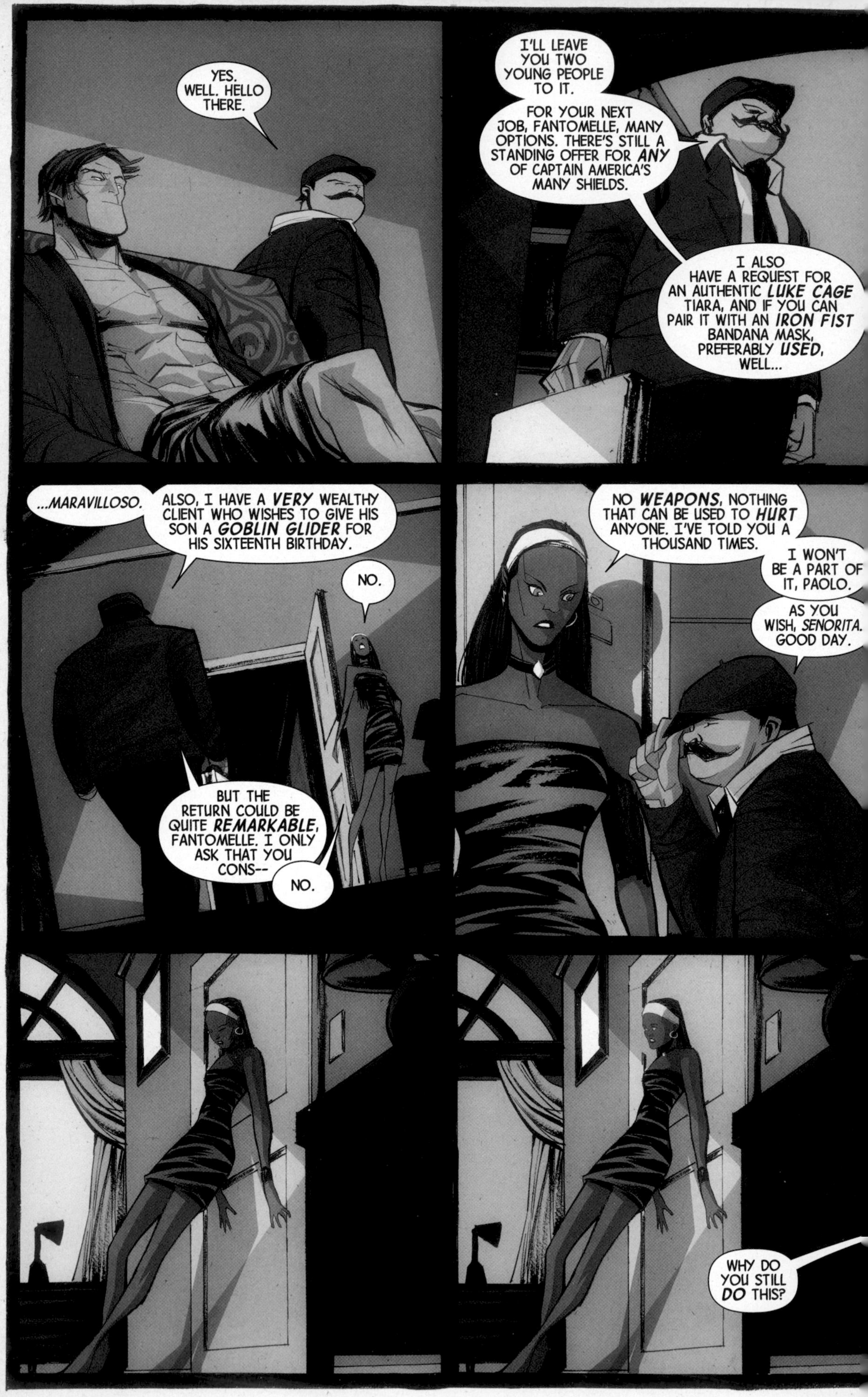
YES. WELL. HELLO THERE.
I'LL LEAVE YOU TWO YOUNG PEOPLE TO IT.
FOR YOUR NEXT JOB, FANTOMELLE, MANY OPTIONS. THERE'S STILL A STANDING OFFER FOR ANY OF CAPTAIN AMERICA'S MANY SHIELDS.
I ALSO HAVE A REQUEST FOR AN AUTHENTIC LUKE CAGE TIARA, AND IF YOU CAN PAIR IT WITH AN IRON FIST BANDANA MASK, PREFERABLY USED, WELL...
...MARAVILLOSO.
ALSO, I HAVE A VERY WEALTHY CLIENT WHO WISHES TO GIVE HIS SON A GOBLIN GLIDER FOR HIS SIXTEENTH BIRTHDAY.
NO.
BUT THE RETURN COULD BE QUITE REMARKABLE, FANTOMELLE. I ONLY ASK THAT YOU CONS--
NO.
NO WEAPONS, NOTHING THAT CAN BE USED TO HURT ANYONE. I'VE TOLD YOU A THOUSAND TIMES.
I WON'T BE A PART OF IT, PAOLO.
AS YOU WISH, SENORITA. GOOD DAY.
WHY DO YOU STILL DO THIS?

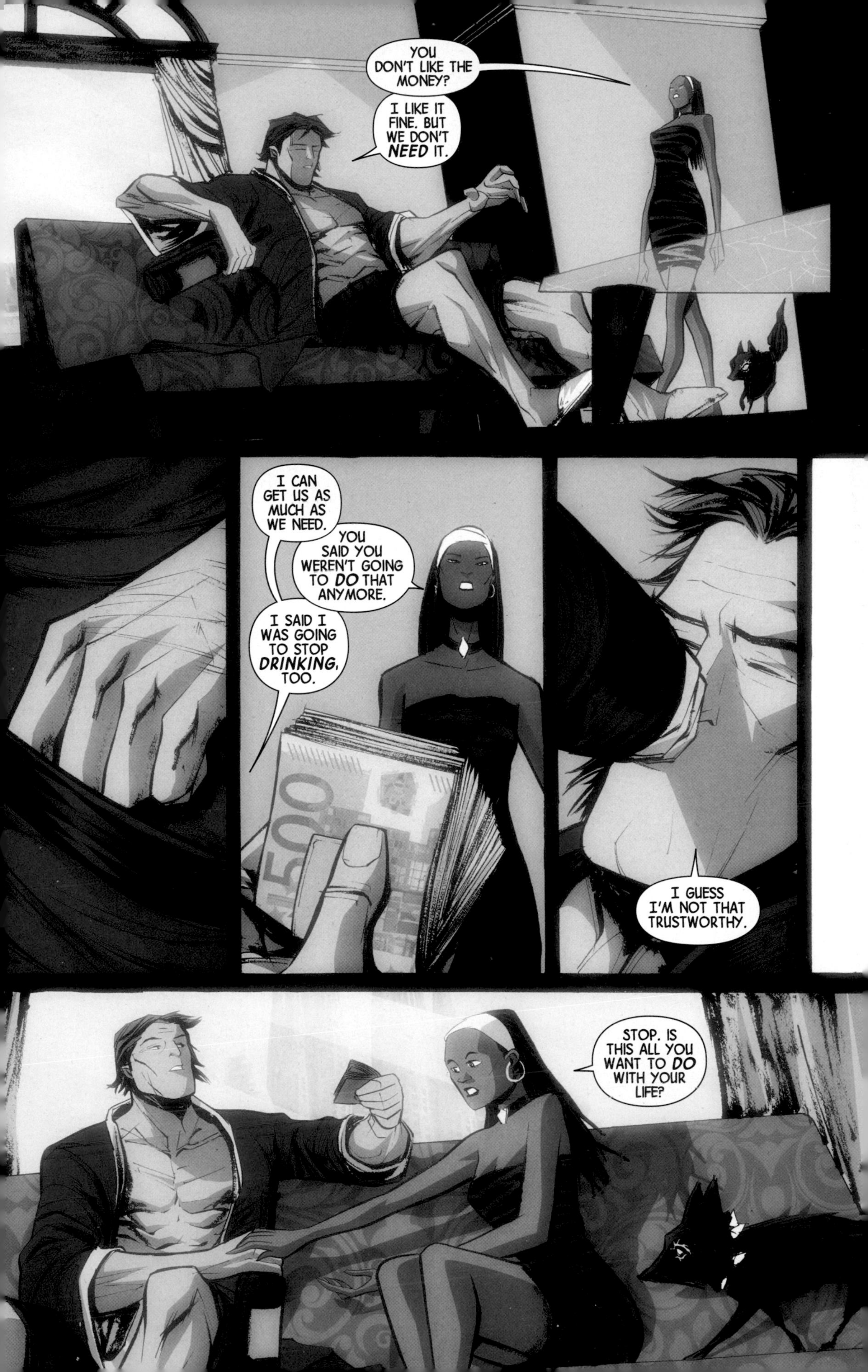
YOU DON'T LIKE THE MONEY?
I LIKE IT FINE. BUT WE DON'T NEED IT.
I CAN GET US AS MUCH AS WE NEED.
YOU SAID YOU WEREN'T GOING TO DO THAT ANYMORE.
I SAID I WAS GOING TO STOP DRINKING, TOO.
500
I GUESS I'M NOT THAT TRUSTWORTHY.
STOP. IS THIS ALL YOU WANT TO DO WITH YOUR LIFE?

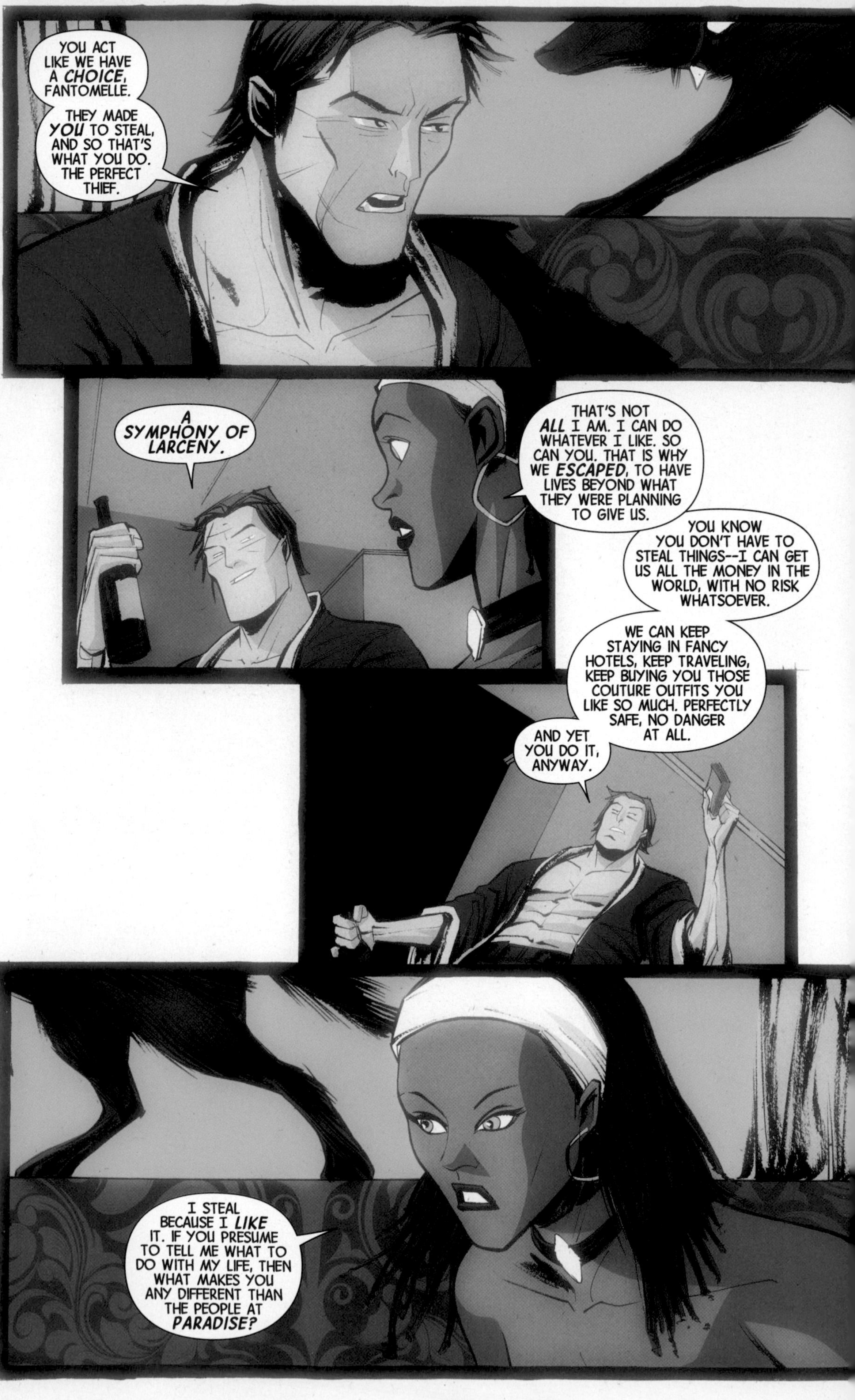
YOU ACT LIKE WE HAVE A CHOICE, FANTOMELLE.
THEY MADE YOU TO STEAL, AND SO THAT'S WHAT YOU DO. THE PERFECT THIEF.
A SYMPHONY OF LARCENY.
THAT'S NOT ALL I AM. I CAN DO WHATEVER I LIKE. SO CAN YOU. THAT IS WHY WE ESCAPED, TO HAVE LIVES BEYOND WHAT THEY WERE PLANNING TO GIVE US.
YOU KNOW YOU DON'T HAVE TO STEAL THINGS--I CAN GET US ALL THE MONEY IN THE WORLD, WITH NO RISK WHATSOEVER.
WE CAN KEEP STAYING IN FANCY HOTELS, KEEP TRAVELING, KEEP BUYING YOU THOSE COUTURE OUTFITS YOU LIKE SO MUCH. PERFECTLY SAFE, NO DANGER AT ALL.
AND YET YOU DO IT, ANYWAY.
I STEAL BECAUSE I LIKE IT. IF YOU PRESUME TO TELL ME WHAT TO DO WITH MY LIFE, THEN WHAT MAKES YOU ANY DIFFERENT THAN THE PEOPLE AT PARADISE?

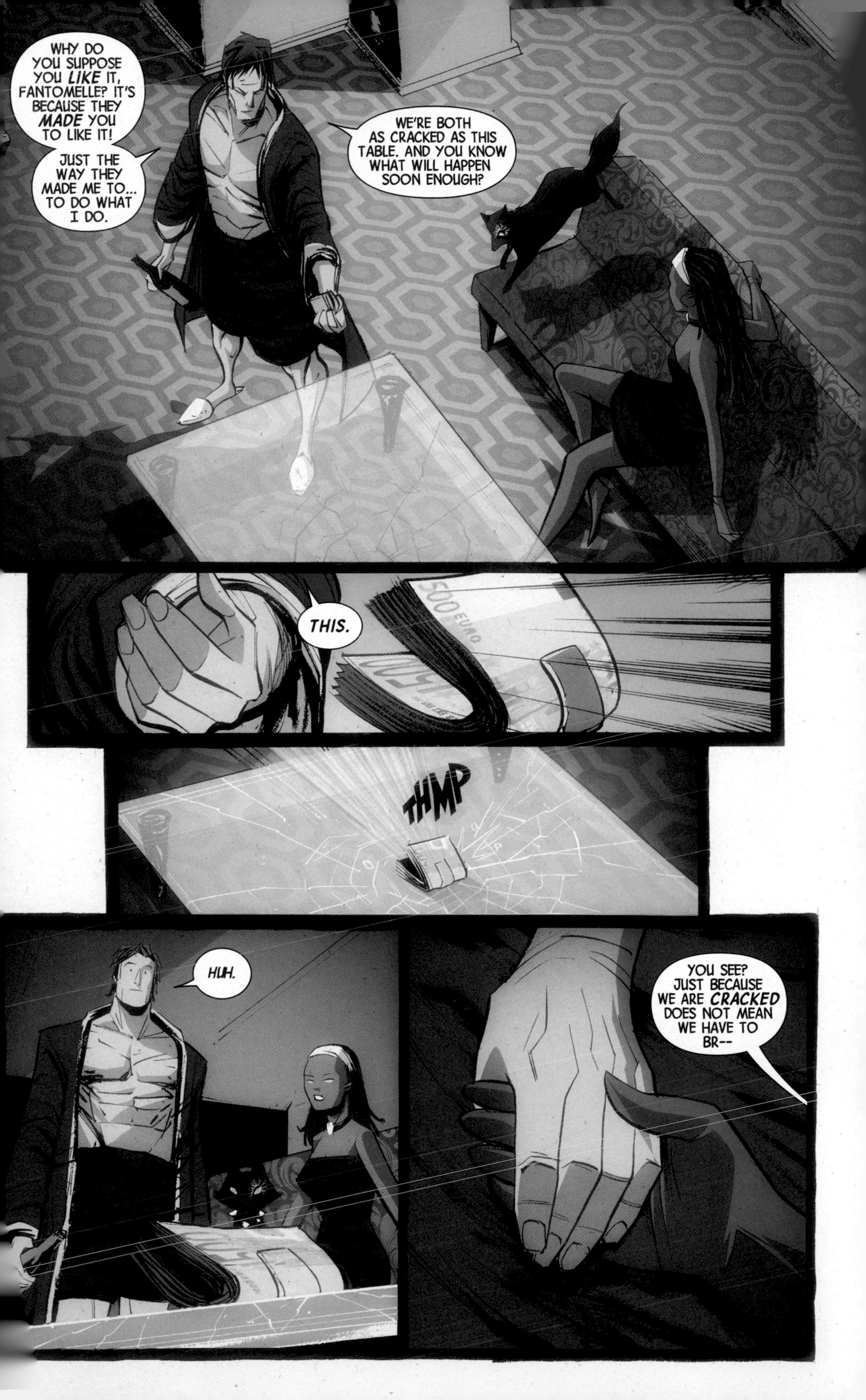
WHY DO YOU SUPPOSE YOU LIKE IT, FANTOMELLE? IT'S BECAUSE THEY MADE YOU TO LIKE IT!
JUST THE WAY THEY MADE ME TO... TO DO WHAT I DO.
WE'RE BOTH AS CRACKED AS THIS TABLE. AND YOU KNOW WHAT WILL HAPPEN SOON ENOUGH?
THIS.
THMP
HUH.
YOU SEE? JUST BECAUSE WE ARE CRACKED DOES NOT MEAN WE HAVE TO BR--

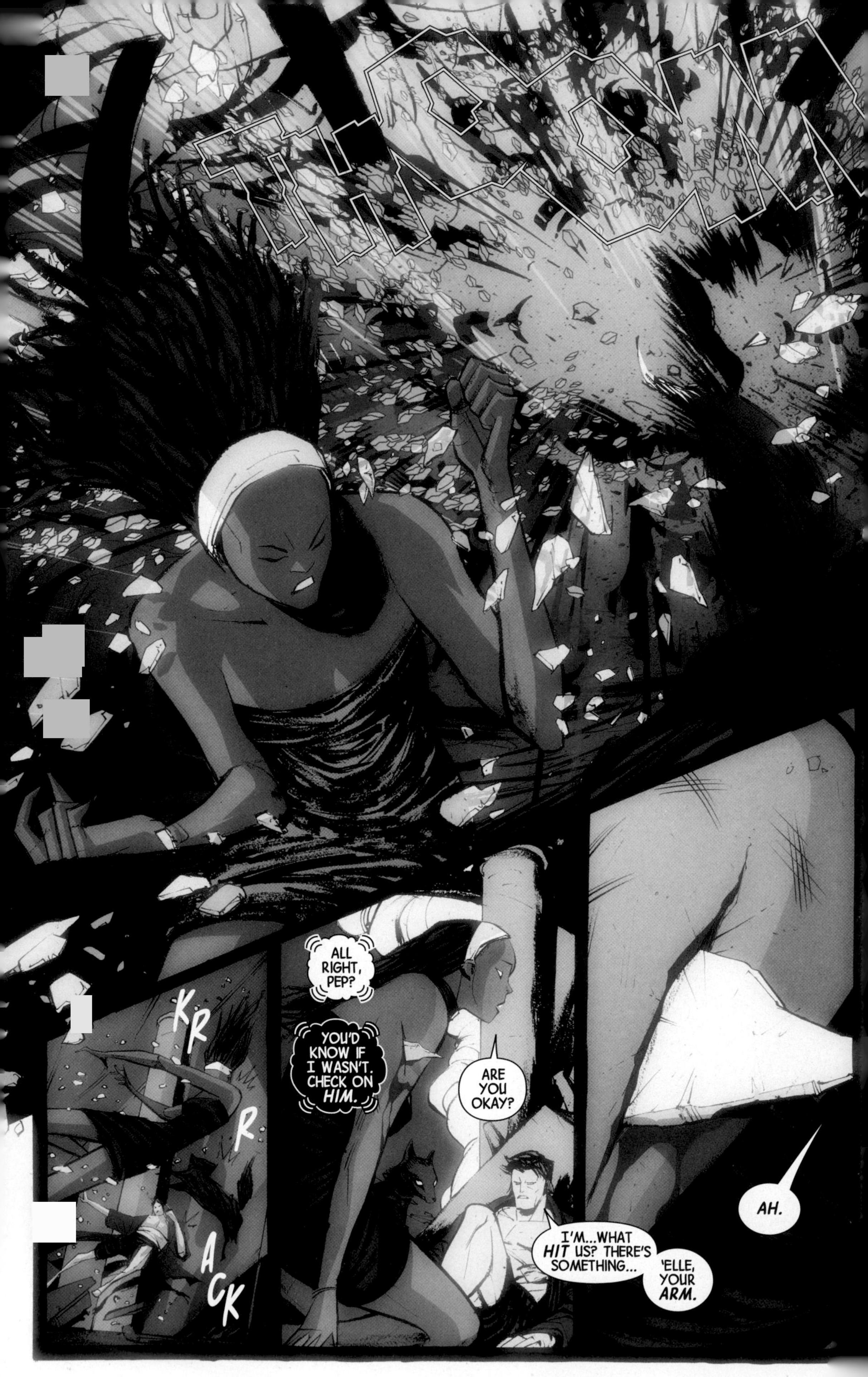
KRRACK
ALL RIGHT, PEP?
YOU'D KNOW IF I WASN'T. CHECK ON HIM.
ARE YOU OKAY?
I'M...WHAT HIT US? THERE'S SOMETHING...
'ELLE, YOUR ARM.
AH.

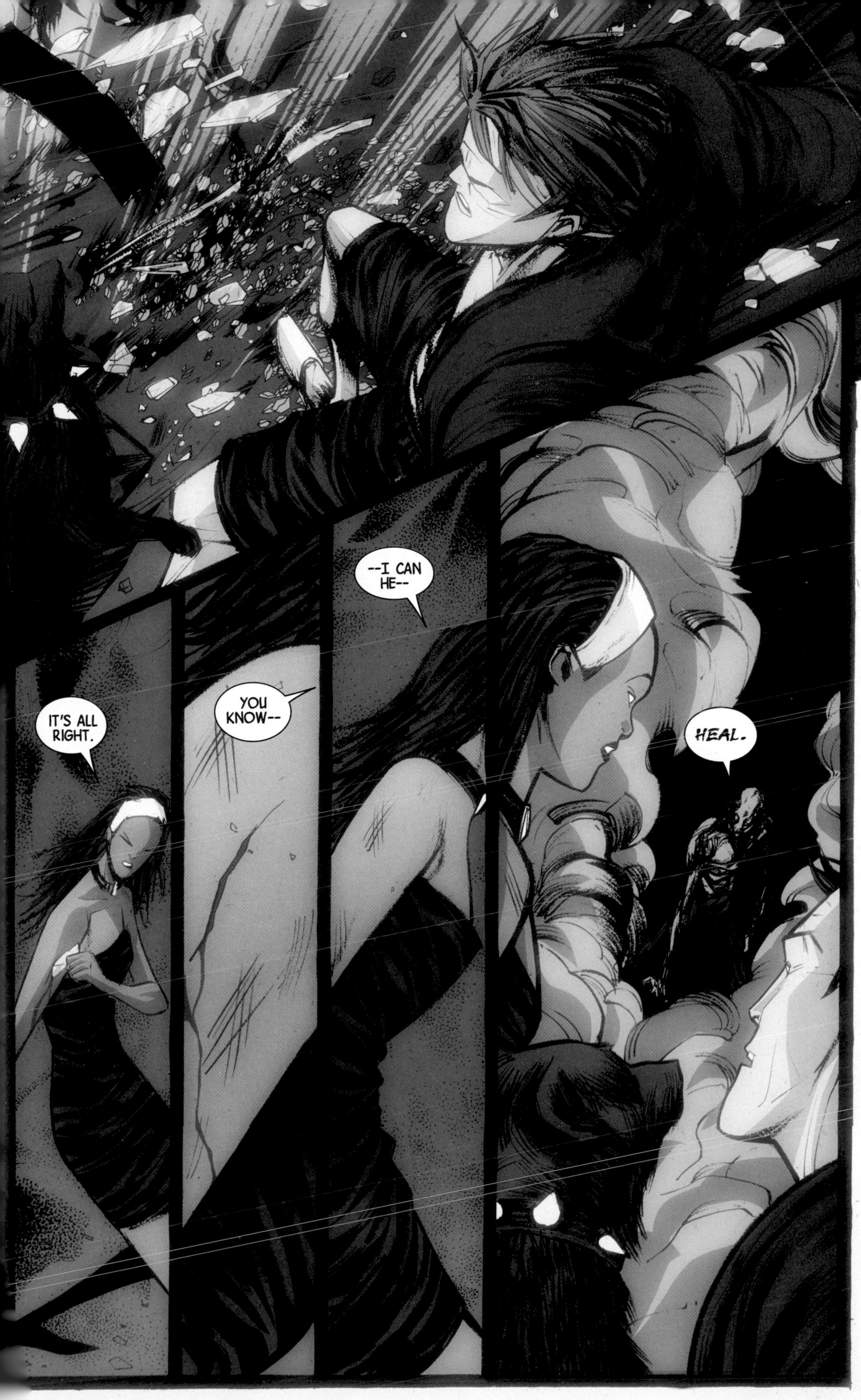
IT'S ALL RIGHT.
YOU KNOW--
--I CAN HE--
HEAL.

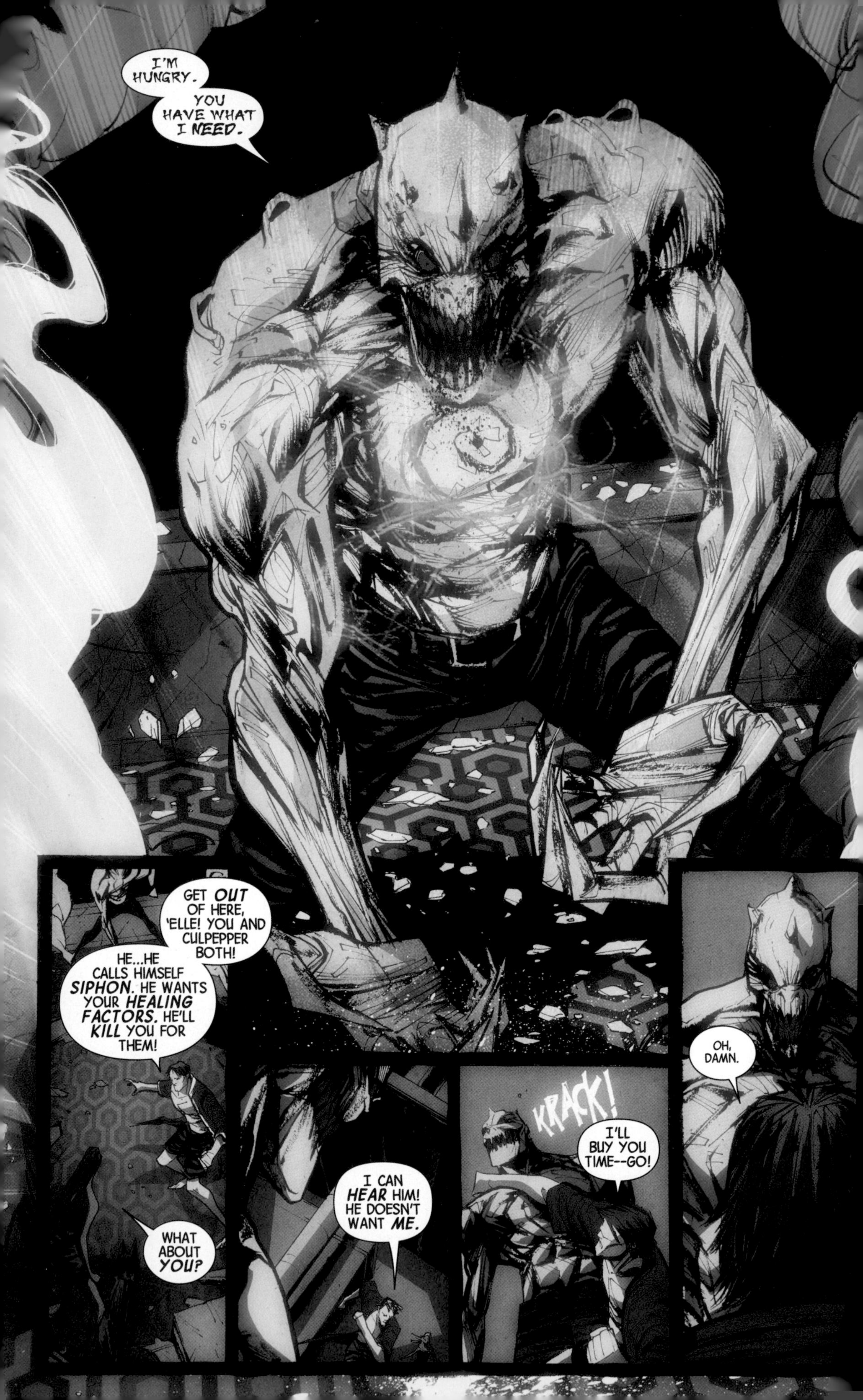
I'M HUNGRY.
YOU HAVE WHAT I NEED.
GET OUT OF HERE, 'ELLE! YOU AND CULPEPPER BOTH!
HE...HE CALLS HIMSELF SIPHON. HE WANTS YOUR HEALING FACTORS. HE'LL KILL YOU FOR THEM!
WHAT ABOUT YOU?
I CAN HEAR HIM! HE DOESN'T WANT ME.
KRACK!
I'LL BUY YOU TIME--GO!
OH, DAMN.

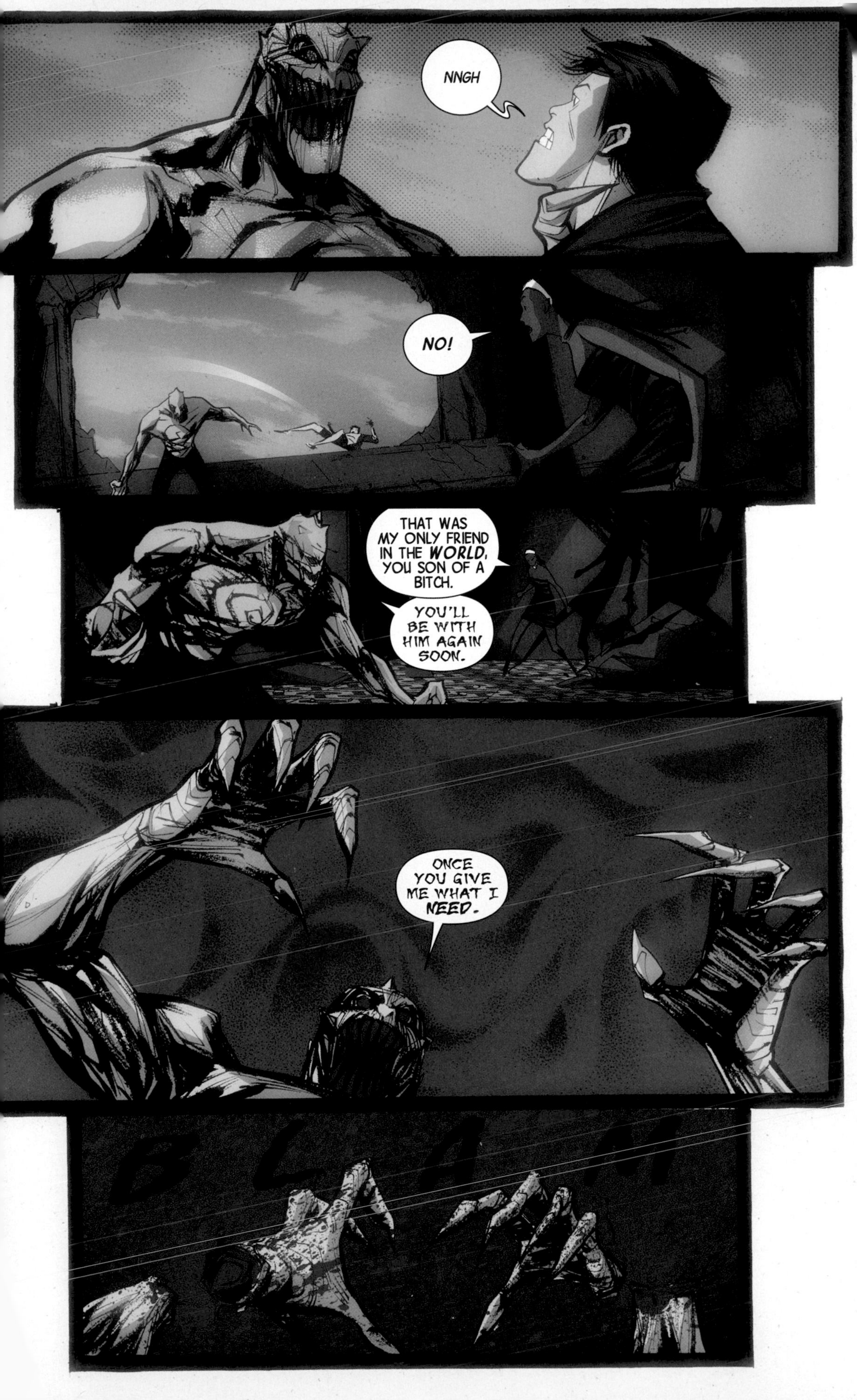
NNGH
NO!
THAT WAS MY ONLY FRIEND IN THE WORLD, YOU SON OF A BITCH.
YOU'LL BE WITH HIM AGAIN SOON.
ONCE YOU GIVE ME WHAT I NEED.
BLAM

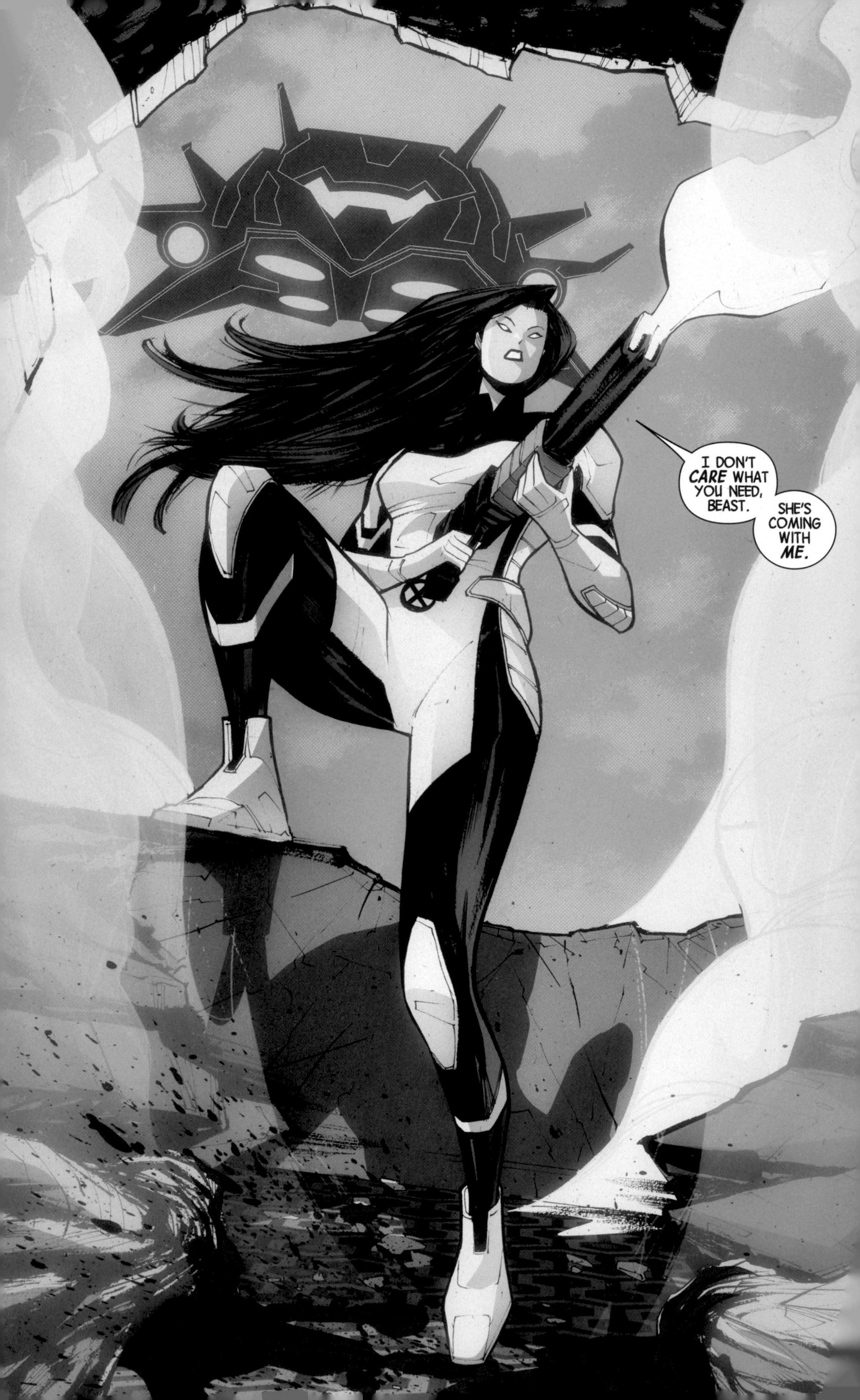
I DON'T CARE WHAT YOU NEED, BEAST.
SHE'S COMING WITH ME.

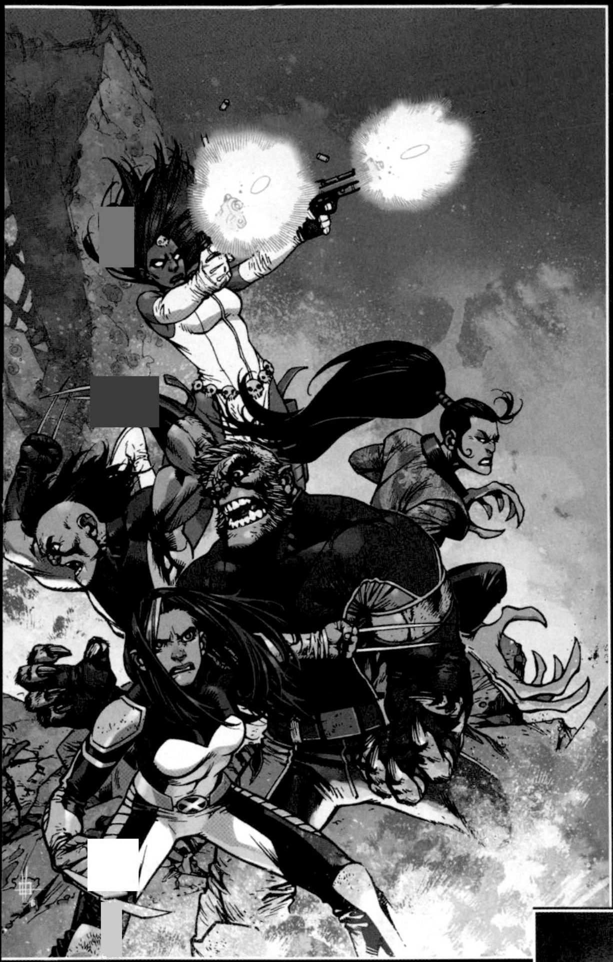

#1 VARIANT
BY ZACH HOWARD &
NELSON DANIEL

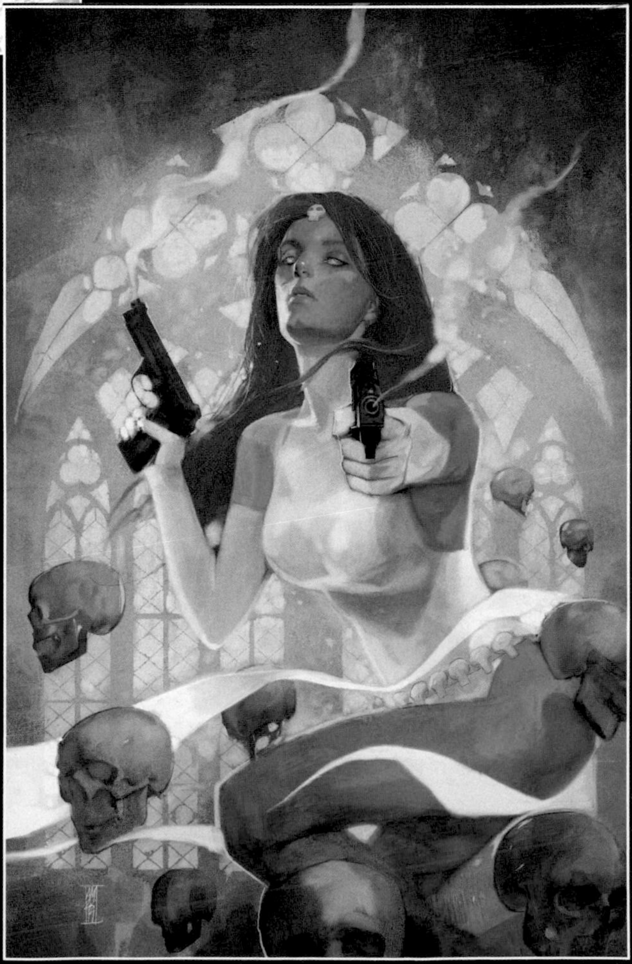

#2 VARIANT
BY ALEX MALEEV

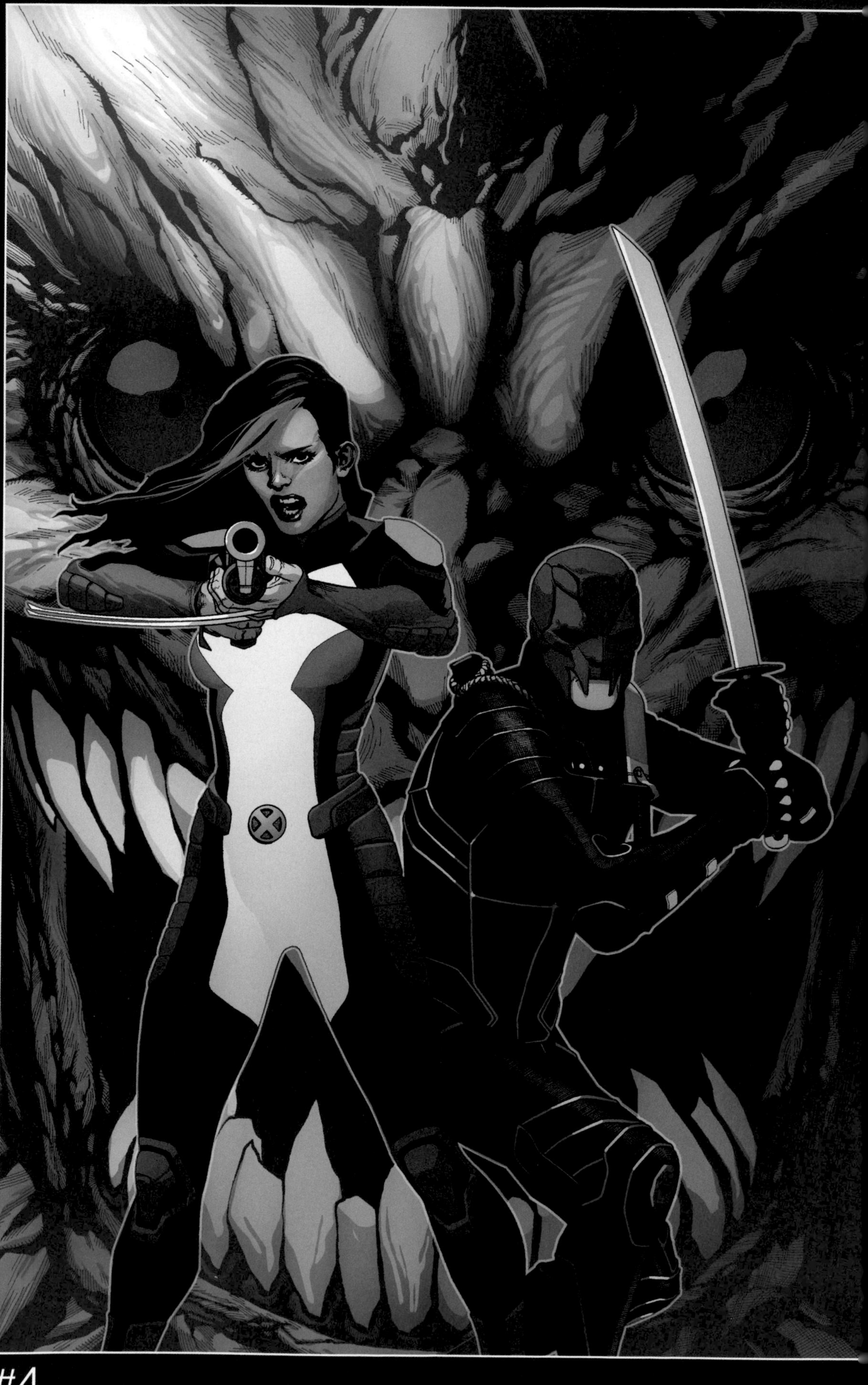

#4

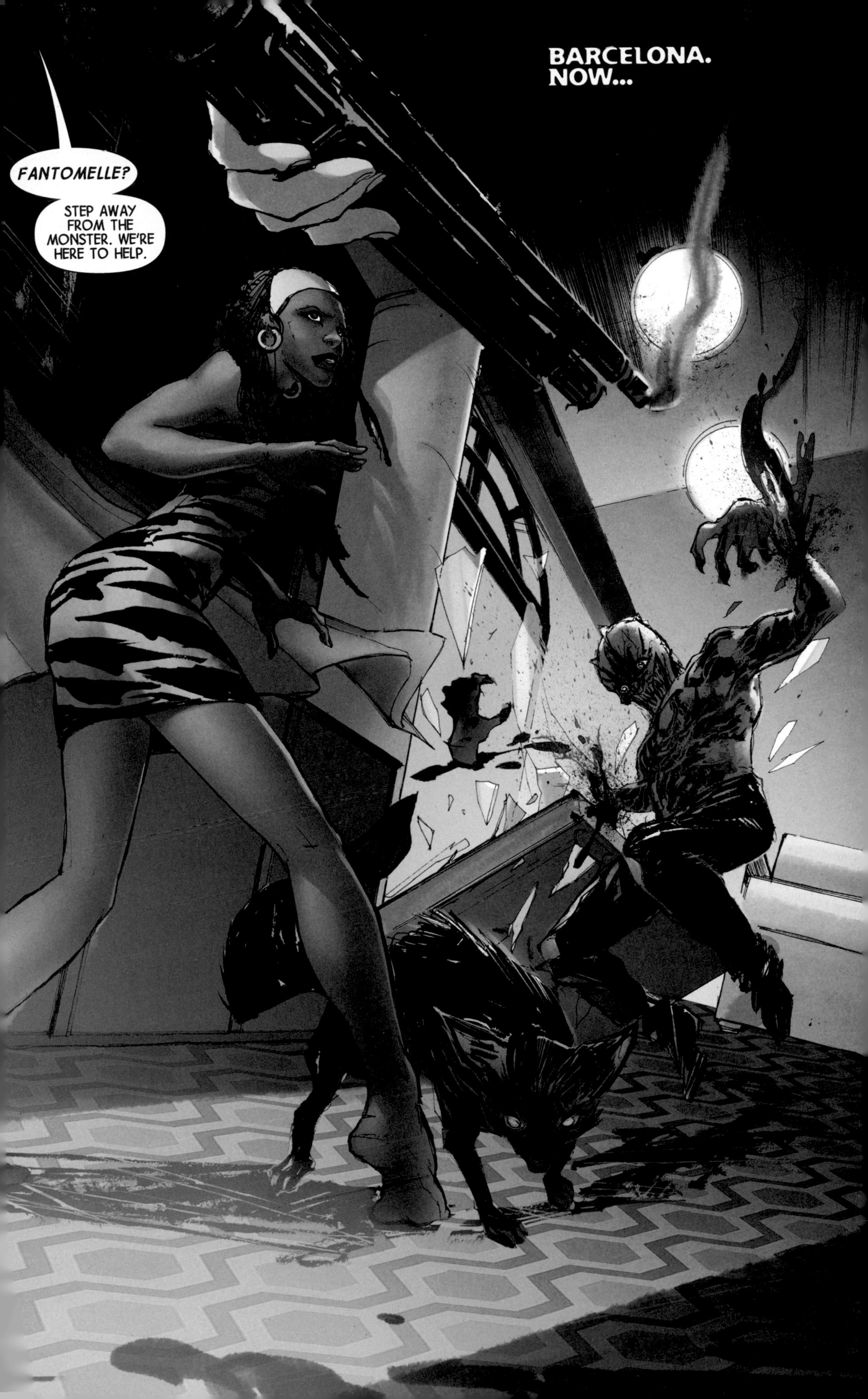
BARCELONA.
NOW...
FANTOMELLE?
STEP AWAY FROM THE MONSTER. WE'RE HERE TO HELP.

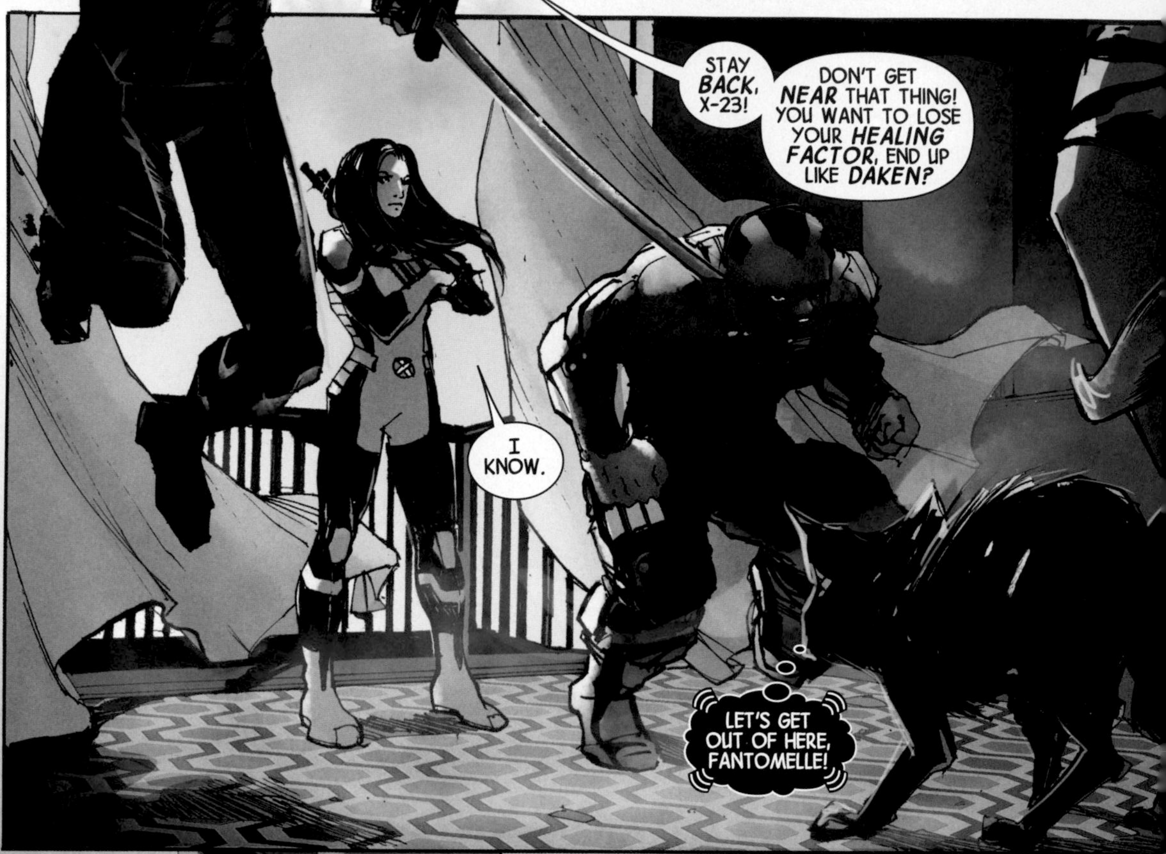
STAY BACK, X-23!
DON'T GET NEAR THAT THING! YOU WANT TO LOSE YOUR HEALING FACTOR, END UP LIKE DAKEN?
I KNOW.
LET'S GET OUT OF HERE, FANTOMELLE!

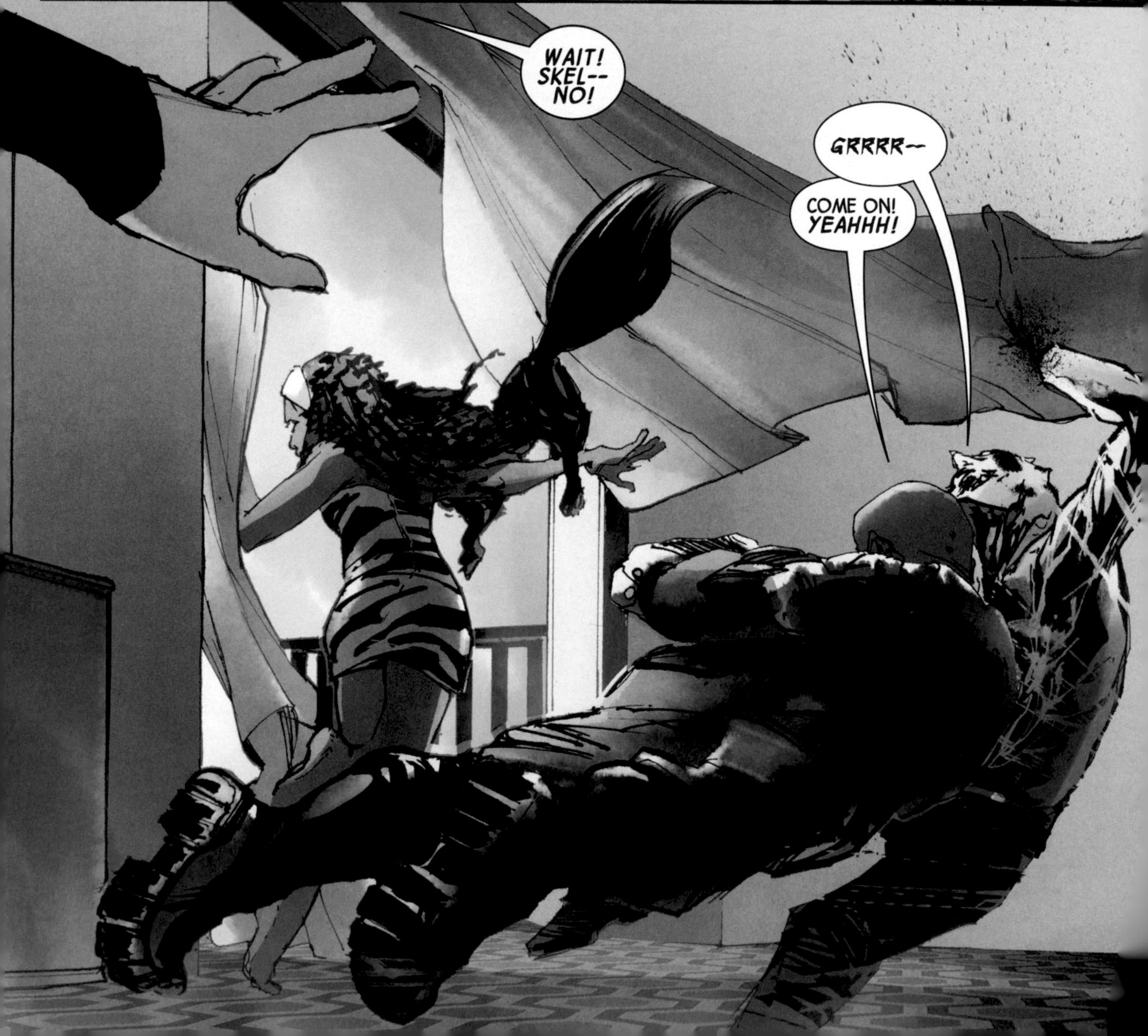
WAIT! SKEL-- NO!
GRRRR--
COME ON! YEAHHH!

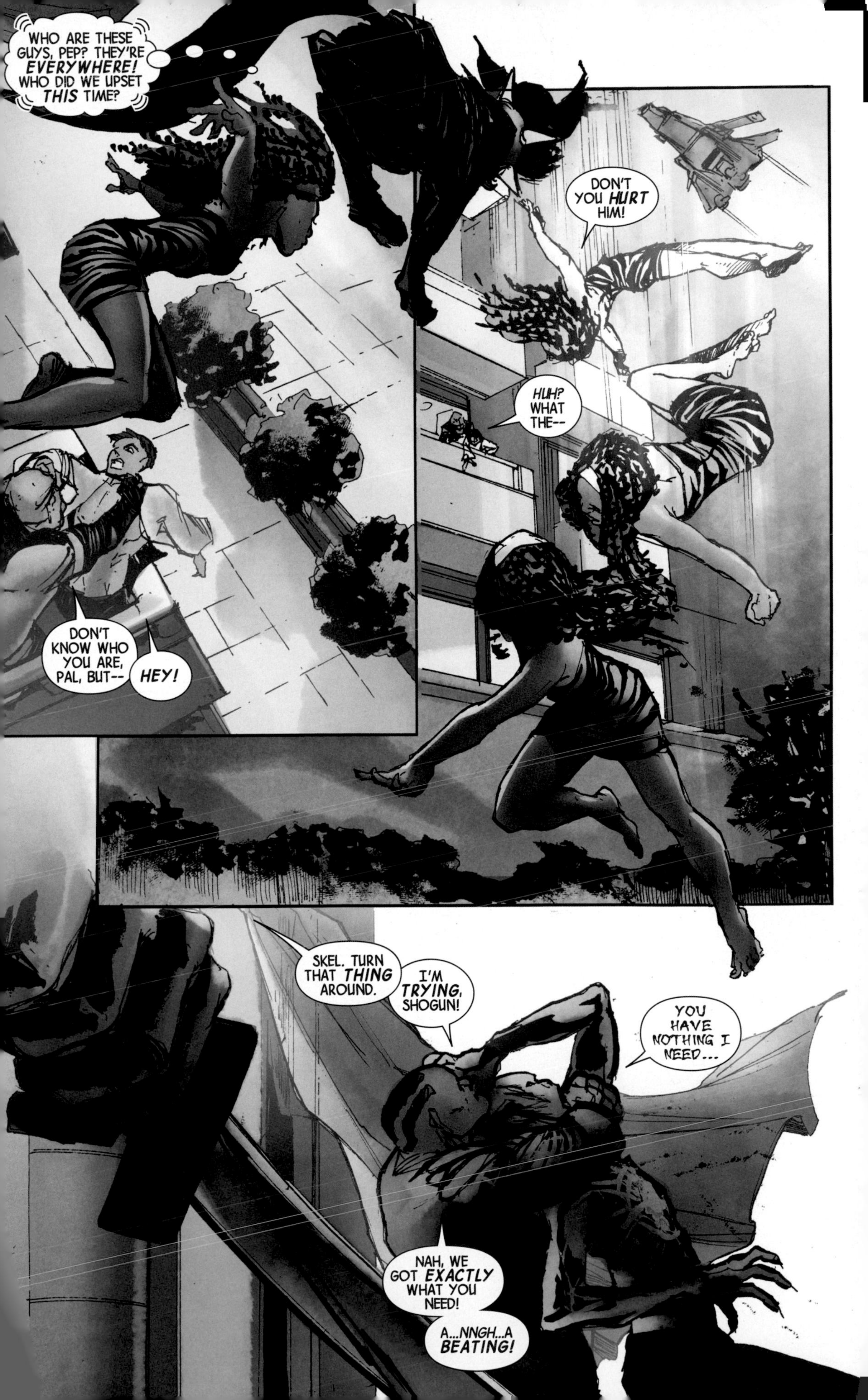
WHO ARE THESE GUYS, PEP? THEY'RE EVERYWHERE! WHO DID WE UPSET THIS TIME?
DON'T YOU HURT HIM!
HUH? WHAT THE--
DON'T KNOW WHO YOU ARE, PAL, BUT--
HEY!
SKEL. TURN THAT THING AROUND.
I'M TRYING, SHOGUN!
YOU HAVE NOTHING I NEED...
NAH, WE GOT EXACTLY WHAT YOU NEED!
A...NNGH...A BEATING!

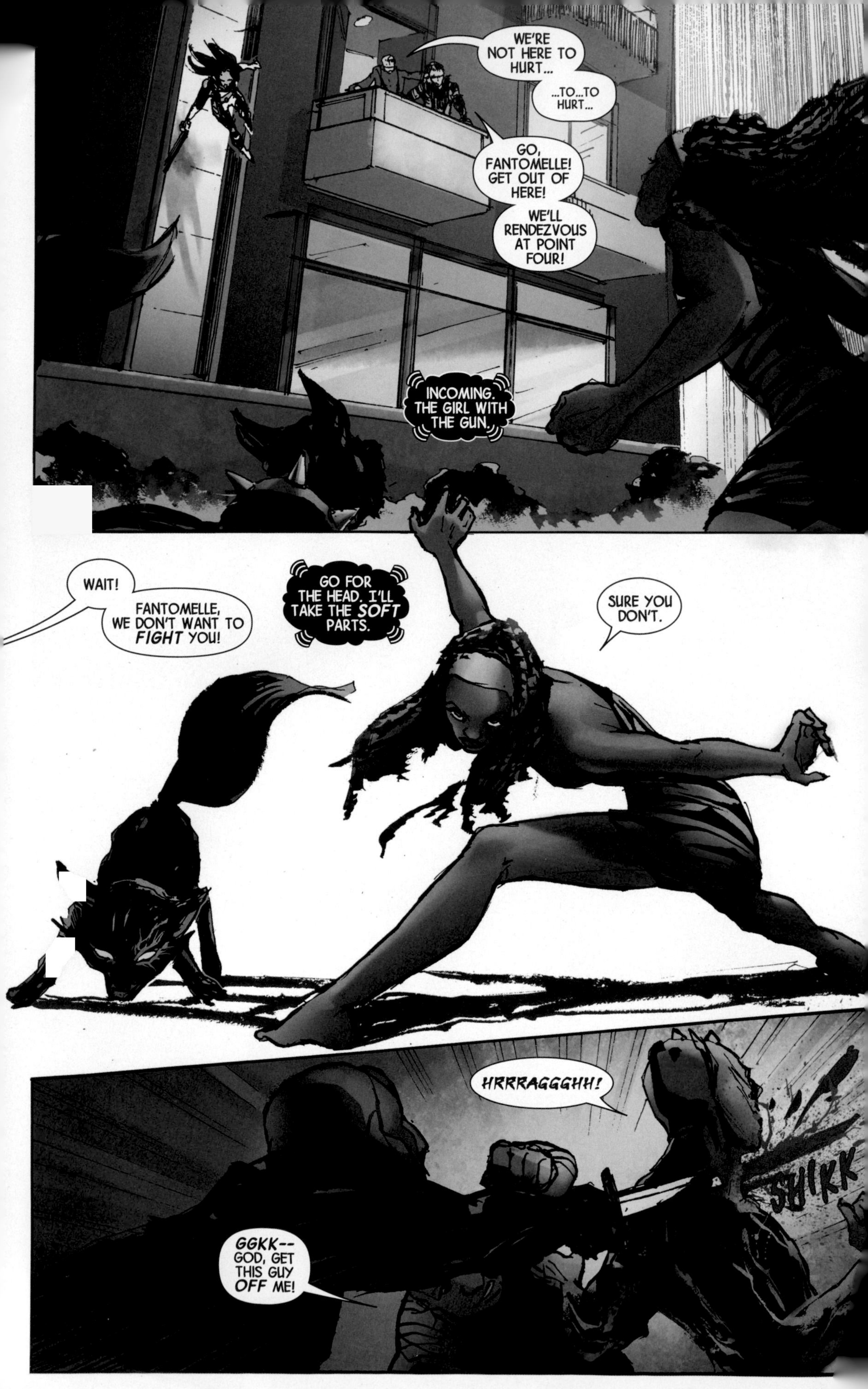
WE'RE NOT HERE TO HURT...
...TO...TO HURT...
GO, FANTOMELLE! GET OUT OF HERE!
WE'LL RENDEZVOUS AT POINT FOUR!
INCOMING. THE GIRL WITH THE GUN.
WAIT!
FANTOMELLE, WE DON'T WANT TO FIGHT YOU!
GO FOR THE HEAD. I'LL TAKE THE SOFT PARTS.
SURE YOU DON'T.
HRRRAGGGHH!
SHIKK
GGKK-- GOD, GET THIS GUY OFF ME!

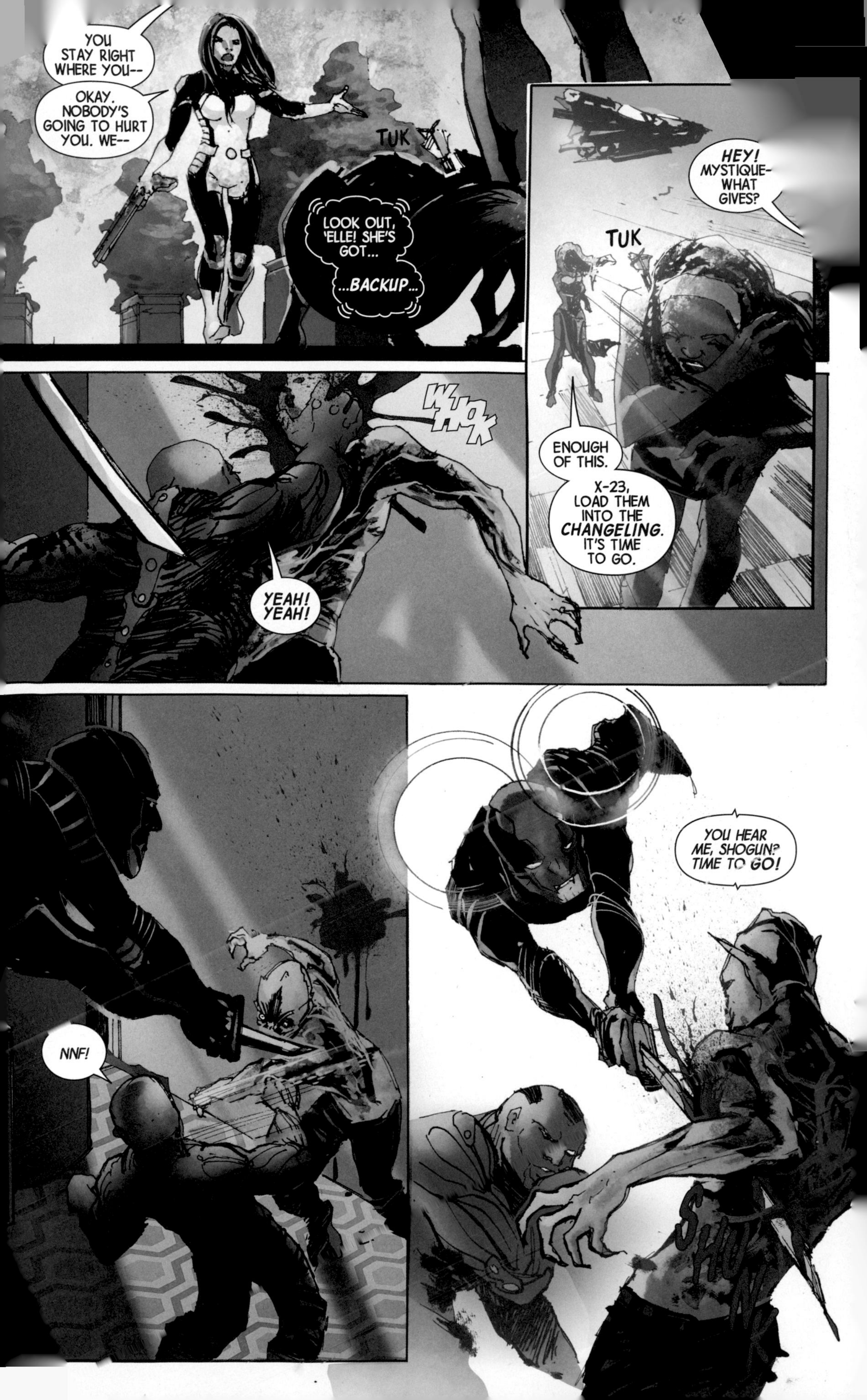
YOU STAY RIGHT WHERE YOU--
OKAY. NOBODY'S GOING TO HURT YOU. WE--
TUK
LOOK OUT, 'ELLE! SHE'S GOT...
...BACKUP...
HEY! MYSTIQUE-WHAT GIVES?
TUK
WHOK
YEAH! YEAH!
ENOUGH OF THIS.
X-23, LOAD THEM INTO THE CHANGELING. IT'S TIME TO GO.
NNF!
YOU HEAR ME, SHOGUN? TIME TO GO!
SHUNK

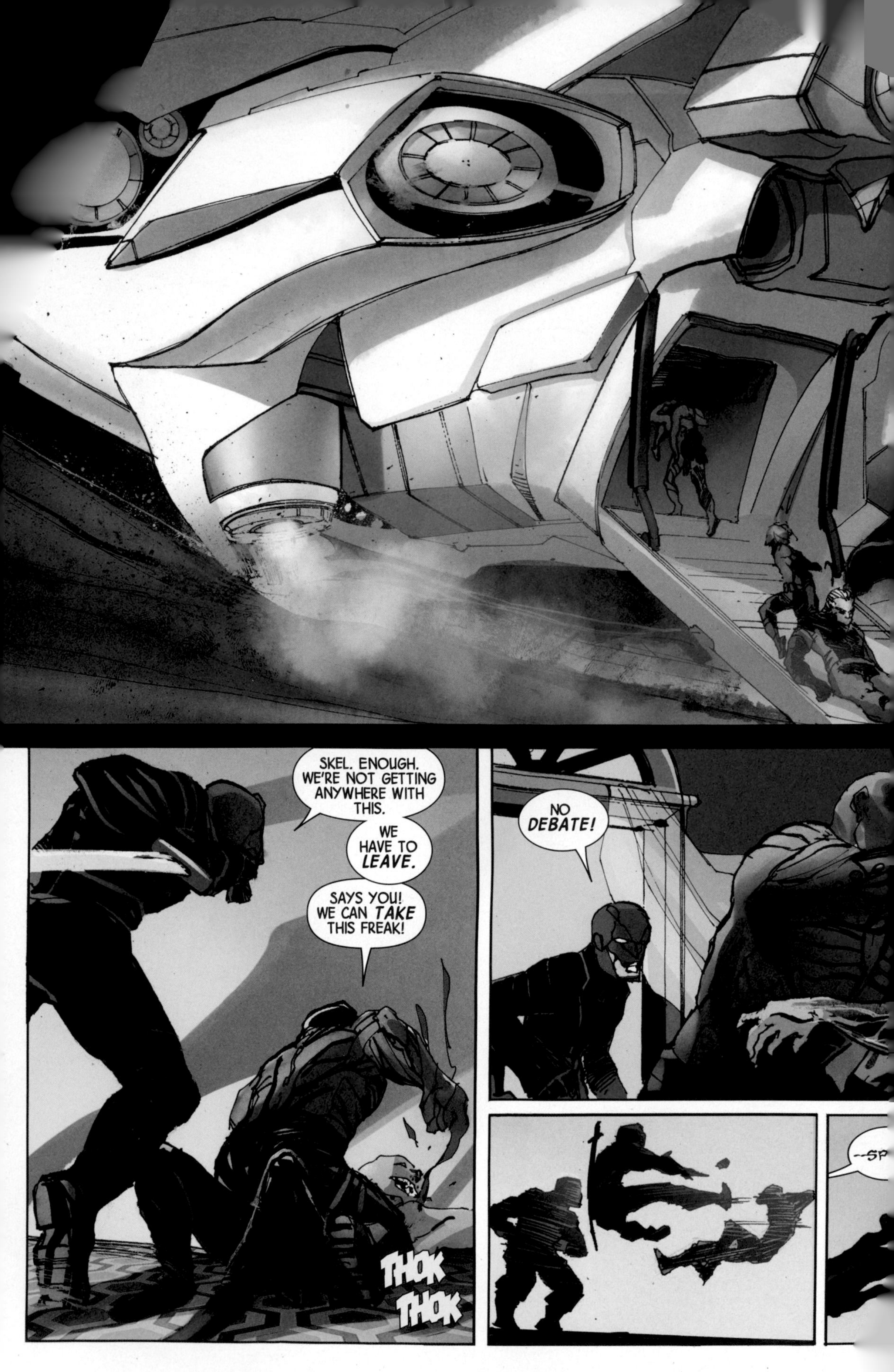
SKEL. ENOUGH. WE'RE NOT GETTING ANYWHERE WITH THIS.
WE HAVE TO LEAVE.
SAYS YOU! WE CAN TAKE THIS FREAK!
THOK THOK
NO DEBATE!
--SP

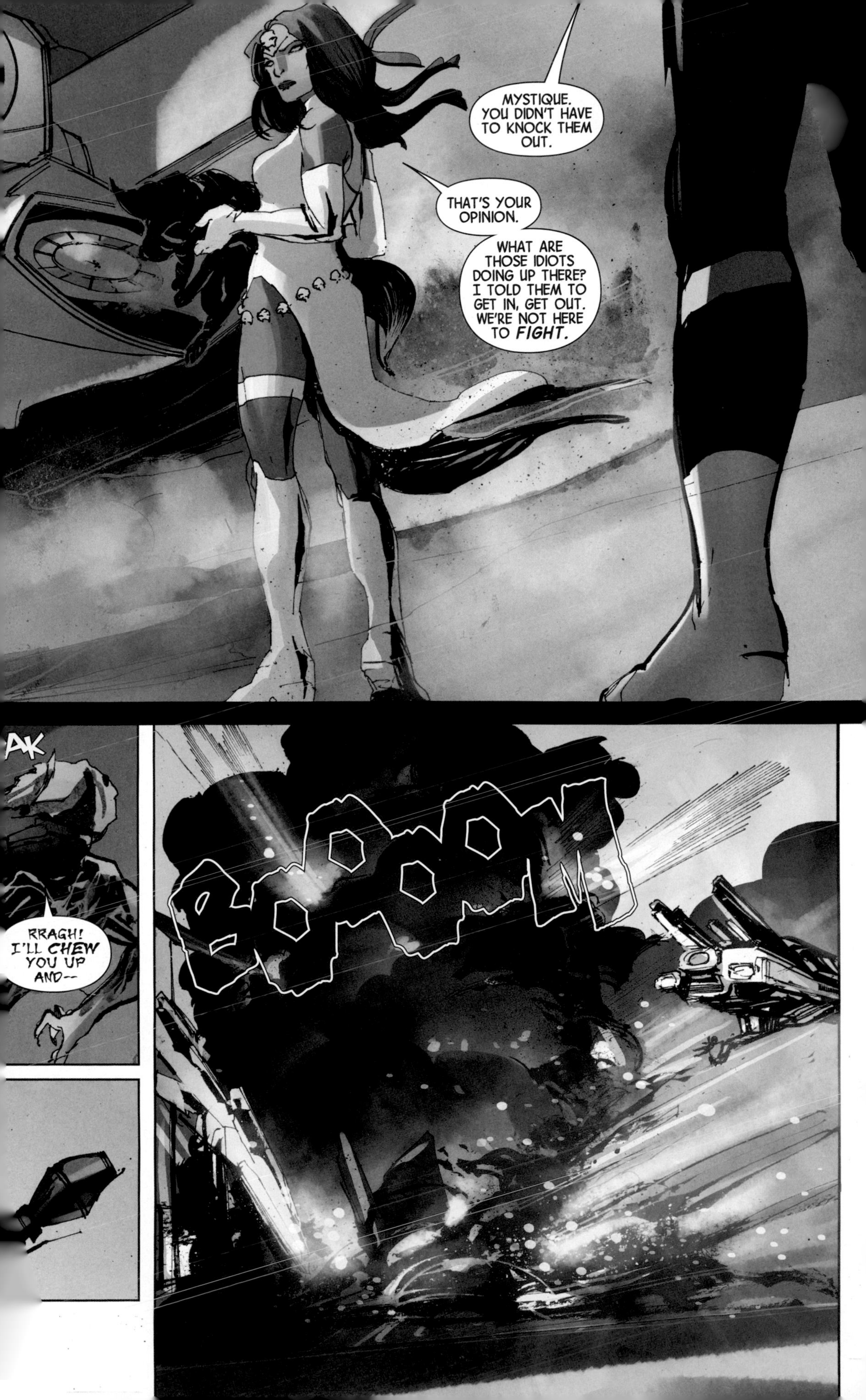
MYSTIQUE. YOU DIDN'T HAVE TO KNOCK THEM OUT.
THAT'S YOUR OPINION.
WHAT ARE THOSE IDIOTS DOING UP THERE? I TOLD THEM TO GET IN, GET OUT. WE'RE NOT HERE TO FIGHT.
AK
RRAGH! I'LL CHEW YOU UP AND--
BOOOOM

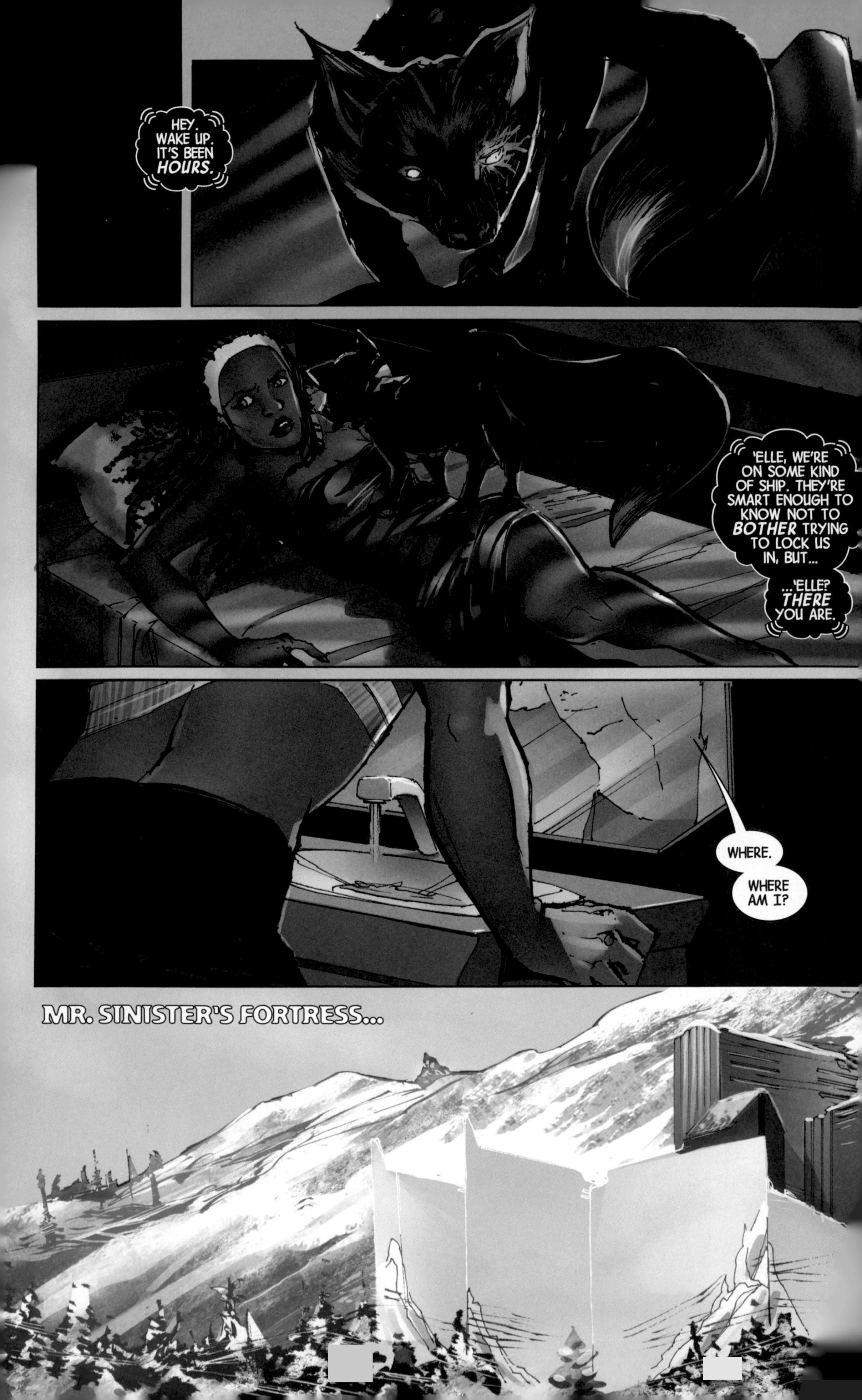
HEY. WAKE UP. IT'S BEEN HOURS.
'ELLE, WE'RE ON SOME KIND OF SHIP. THEY'RE SMART ENOUGH TO KNOW NOT TO BOTHER TRYING TO LOCK US IN, BUT...
...'ELLE? THERE YOU ARE.
WHERE.
WHERE AM I?
MR. SINISTER'S FORTRESS...

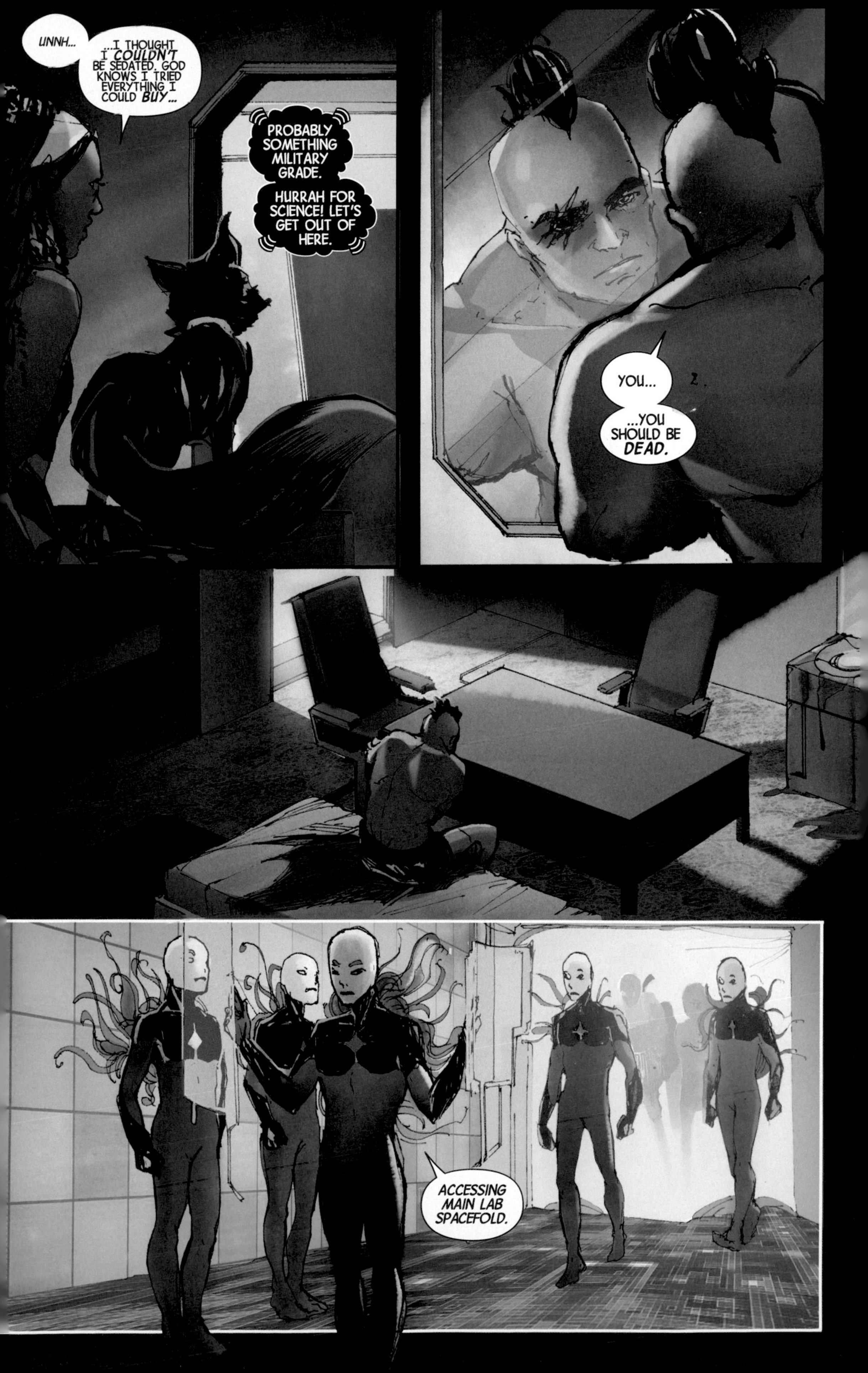
UNNH...
...I THOUGHT I COULDN'T BE SEDATED. GOD KNOWS I TRIED EVERYTHING I COULD BUY...
PROBABLY SOMETHING MILITARY GRADE.
HURRAH FOR SCIENCE! LET'S GET OUT OF HERE.
YOU...
...YOU SHOULD BE DEAD.
ACCESSING MAIN LAB SPACEFOLD.

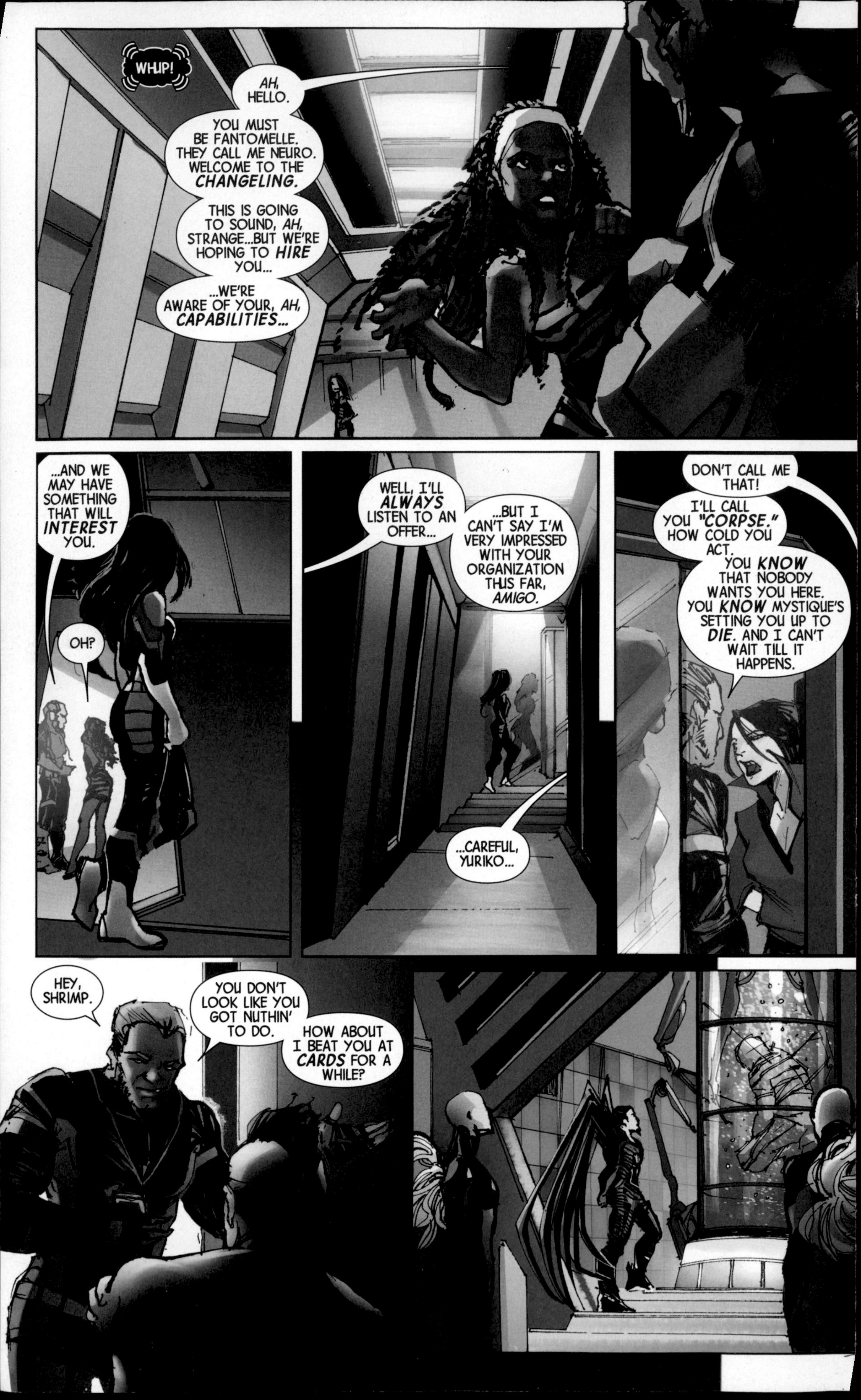
WHUP!
AH, HELLO.
YOU MUST BE FANTOMELLE. THEY CALL ME NEURO. WELCOME TO THE CHANGELING.
THIS IS GOING TO SOUND, AH, STRANGE...BUT WE'RE HOPING TO HIRE YOU...
...WE'RE AWARE OF YOUR, AH, CAPABILITIES...
...AND WE MAY HAVE SOMETHING THAT WILL INTEREST YOU.
OH?
WELL, I'LL ALWAYS LISTEN TO AN OFFER...
...BUT I CAN'T SAY I'M VERY IMPRESSED WITH YOUR ORGANIZATION THUS FAR, AMIGO.
...CAREFUL, YURIKO...
DON'T CALL ME THAT!
I'LL CALL YOU "CORPSE." HOW COLD YOU ACT.
YOU KNOW THAT NOBODY WANTS YOU HERE. YOU KNOW MYSTIQUE'S SETTING YOU UP TO DIE. AND I CAN'T WAIT TILL IT HAPPENS.
HEY, SHRIMP.
YOU DON'T LOOK LIKE YOU GOT NUTHIN' TO DO.
HOW ABOUT I BEAT YOU AT CARDS FOR A WHILE?

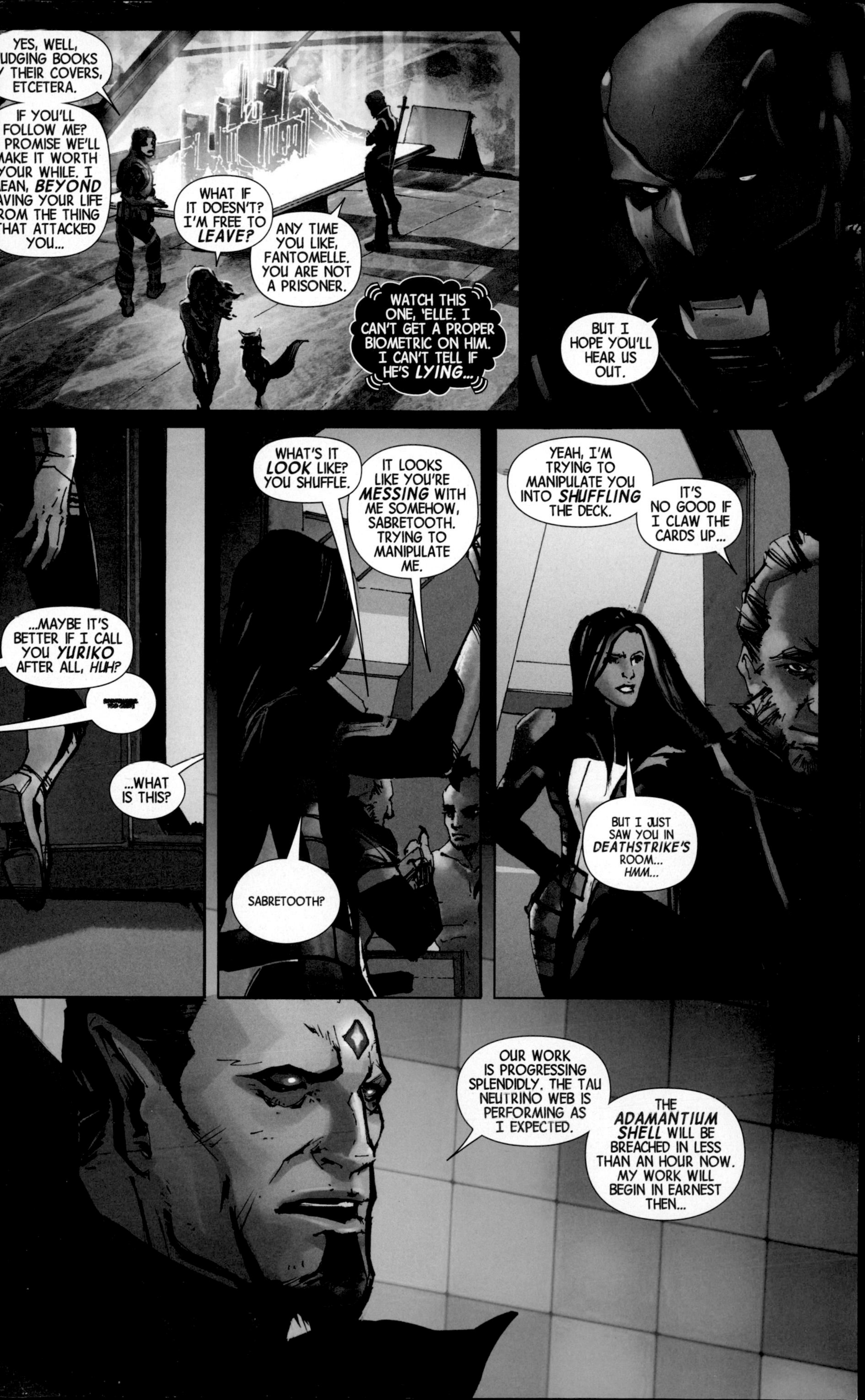
YES, WELL, UDGING BOOKS Y THEIR COVERS, ETCETERA.
IF YOU'LL FOLLOW ME? PROMISE WE'LL MAKE IT WORTH YOUR WHILE. I EAN, BEYOND AVING YOUR LIFE ROM THE THING THAT ATTACKED YOU...
WHAT IF IT DOESN'T? I'M FREE TO LEAVE?
ANY TIME YOU LIKE, FANTOMELLE. YOU ARE NOT A PRISONER.
WATCH THIS ONE, 'ELLE. I CAN'T GET A PROPER BIOMETRIC ON HIM. I CAN'T TELL IF HE'S LYING...
BUT I HOPE YOU'LL HEAR US OUT.
...MAYBE IT'S BETTER IF I CALL YOU YURIKO AFTER ALL, HUH?
...WHAT IS THIS?
WHAT'S IT LOOK LIKE? YOU SHUFFLE.
IT LOOKS LIKE YOU'RE MESSING WITH ME SOMEHOW, SABRETOOTH. TRYING TO MANIPULATE ME.
SABRETOOTH?
YEAH, I'M TRYING TO MANIPULATE YOU INTO SHUFFLING THE DECK.
IT'S NO GOOD IF I CLAW THE CARDS UP...
BUT I JUST SAW YOU IN DEATHSTRIKE'S ROOM... HMM...
OUR WORK IS PROGRESSING SPLENDIDLY. THE TAU NEUTRINO WEB IS PERFORMING AS I EXPECTED.
THE ADAMANTIUM SHELL WILL BE BREACHED IN LESS THAN AN HOUR NOW. MY WORK WILL BEGIN IN EARNEST THEN...

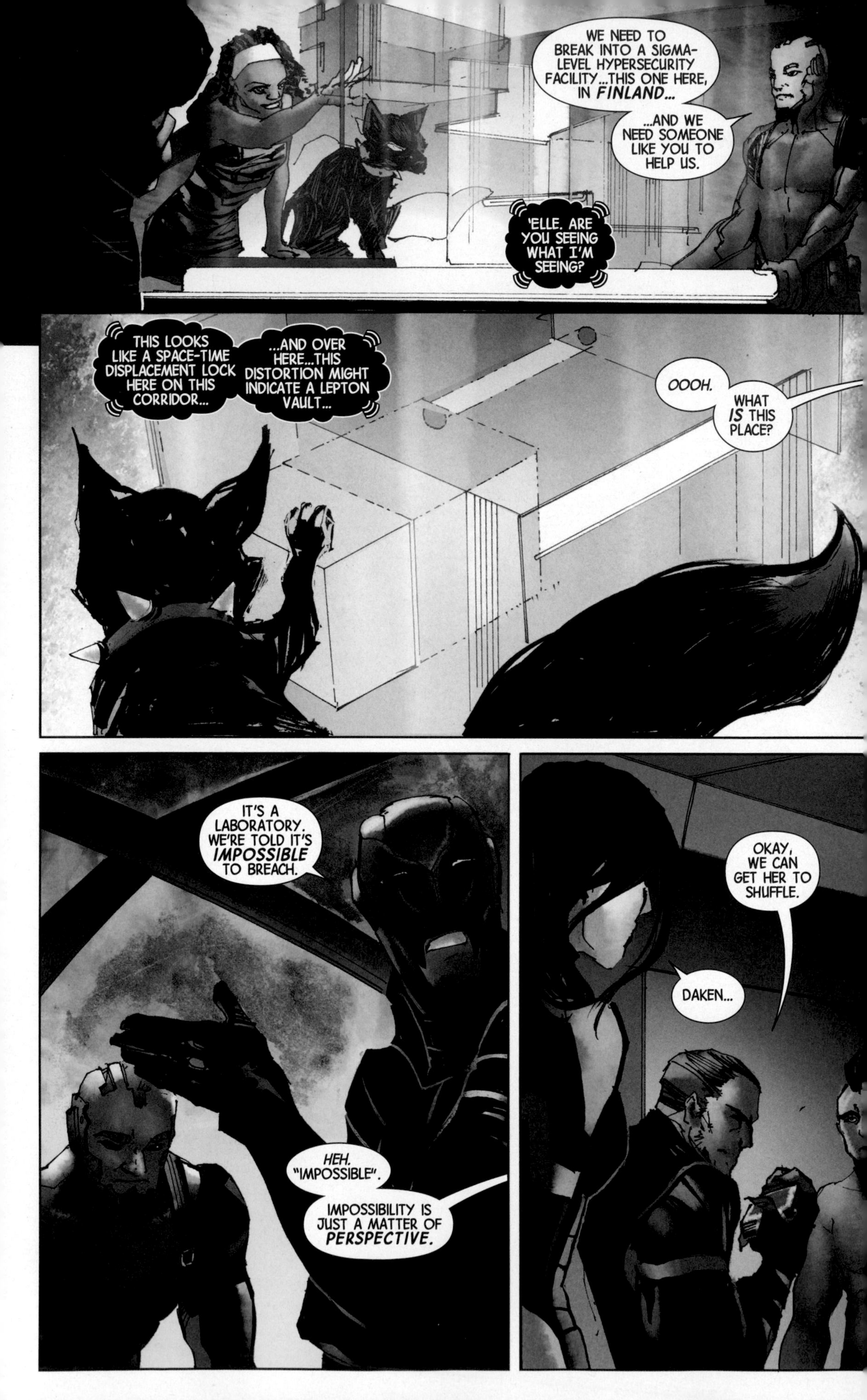
WE NEED TO BREAK INTO A SIGMA-LEVEL HYPERSECURITY FACILITY...THIS ONE HERE, IN FINLAND...
...AND WE NEED SOMEONE LIKE YOU TO HELP US.
'ELLE. ARE YOU SEEING WHAT I'M SEEING?
THIS LOOKS LIKE A SPACE-TIME DISPLACEMENT LOCK HERE ON THIS CORRIDOR...
...AND OVER HERE...THIS DISTORTION MIGHT INDICATE A LEPTON VAULT...
OOOH.
WHAT IS THIS PLACE?
IT'S A LABORATORY. WE'RE TOLD IT'S IMPOSSIBLE TO BREACH.
HEH. "IMPOSSIBLE".
IMPOSSIBILITY IS JUST A MATTER OF PERSPECTIVE.
OKAY, WE CAN GET HER TO SHUFFLE.
DAKEN...

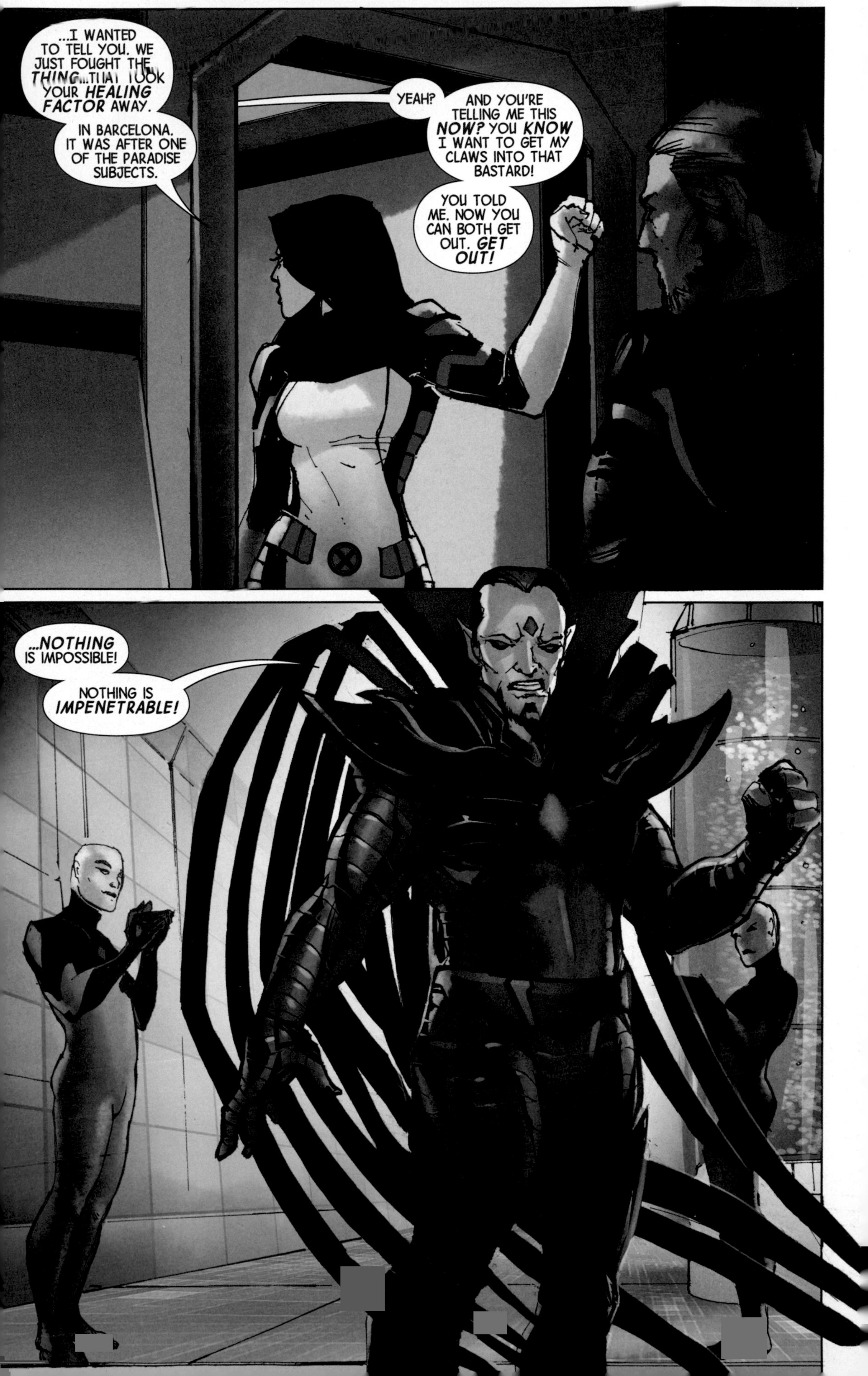
...I WANTED TO TELL YOU. WE JUST FOUGHT THE *THING*...THAT TOOK YOUR *HEALING FACTOR* AWAY.
IN BARCELONA. IT WAS AFTER ONE OF THE PARADISE SUBJECTS.
YEAH?
AND YOU'RE TELLING ME THIS *NOW?* YOU *KNOW* I WANT TO GET MY CLAWS INTO THAT BASTARD!
YOU TOLD ME. NOW YOU CAN BOTH GET OUT. *GET OUT!*
...*NOTHING* IS IMPOSSIBLE!
NOTHING IS *IMPENETRABLE!*

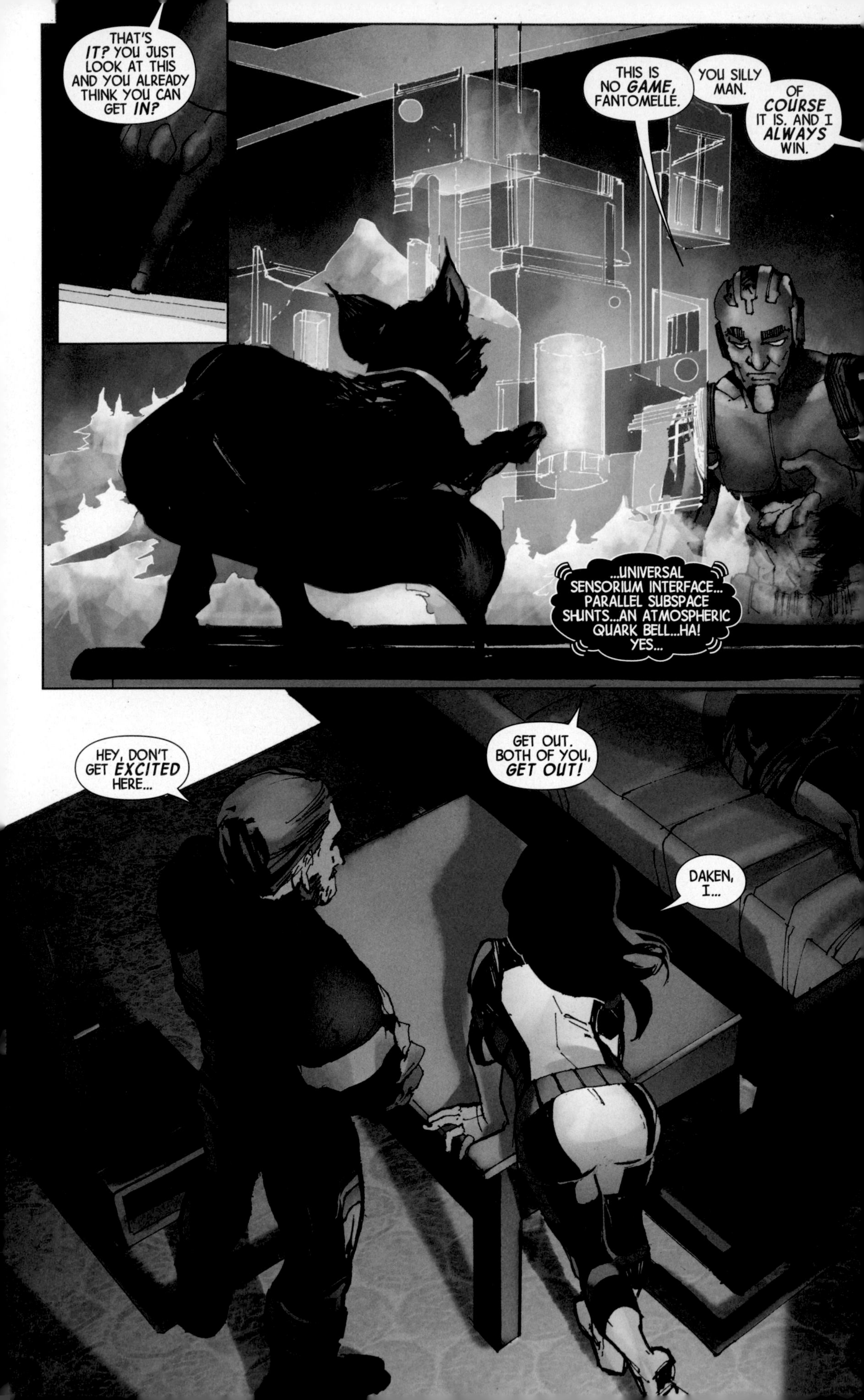
THAT'S IT? YOU JUST LOOK AT THIS AND YOU ALREADY THINK YOU CAN GET IN?
THIS IS NO GAME, FANTOMELLE.
YOU SILLY MAN.
OF COURSE IT IS. AND I ALWAYS WIN.
...UNIVERSAL SENSORIUM INTERFACE... PARALLEL SUBSPACE SHUNTS...AN ATMOSPHERIC QUARK BELL...HA! YES...
HEY, DON'T GET EXCITED HERE...
GET OUT. BOTH OF YOU, GET OUT!
DAKEN, I...

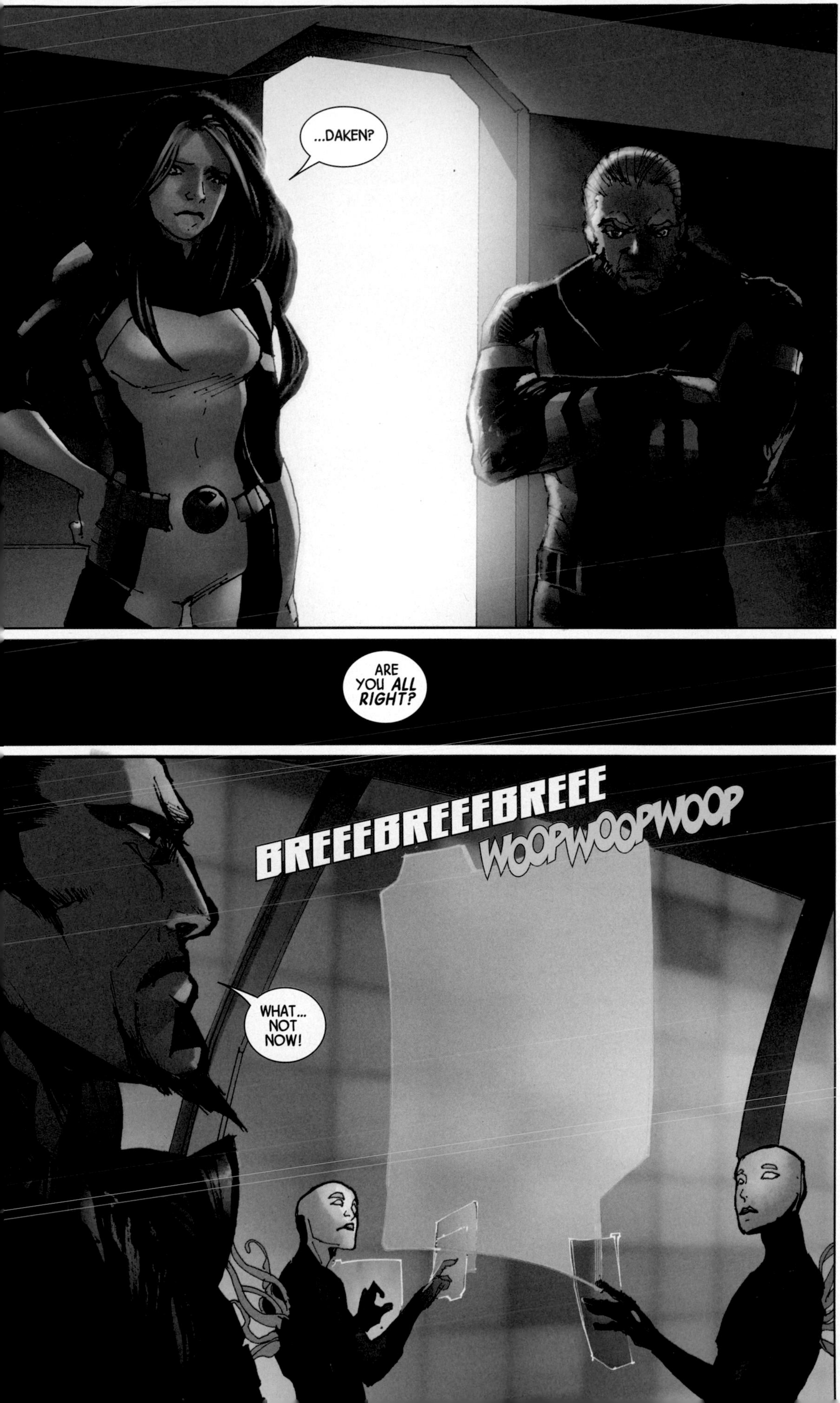
...DAKEN?
ARE YOU ALL RIGHT?
BREEEBREEEBREEE
WOOPWOOPWOOP
WHAT... NOT NOW!

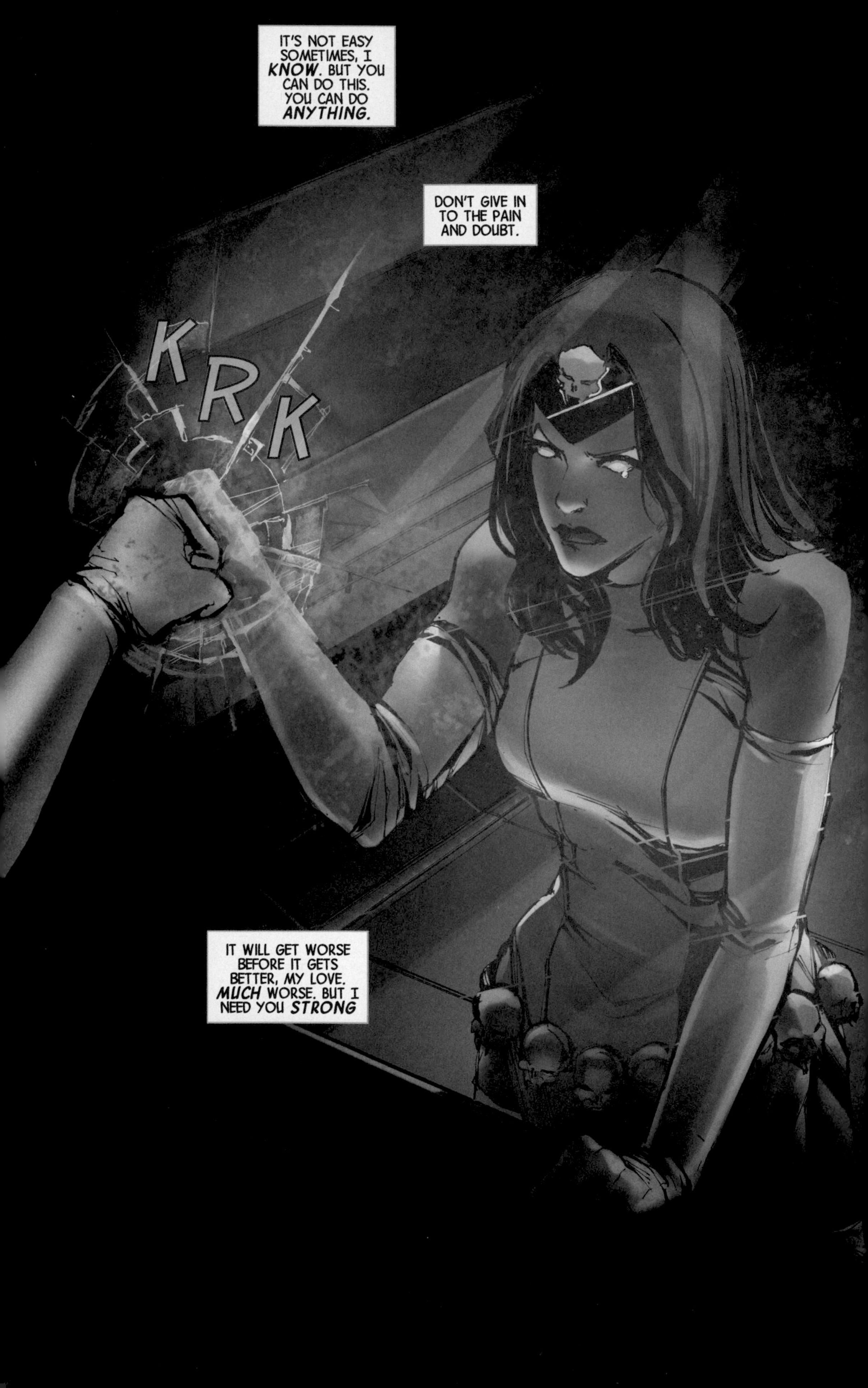
IT'S NOT EASY SOMETIMES, I KNOW. BUT YOU CAN DO THIS. YOU CAN DO ANYTHING.
DON'T GIVE IN TO THE PAIN AND DOUBT.
KRK
IT WILL GET WORSE BEFORE IT GETS BETTER, MY LOVE. MUCH WORSE. BUT I NEED YOU STRONG

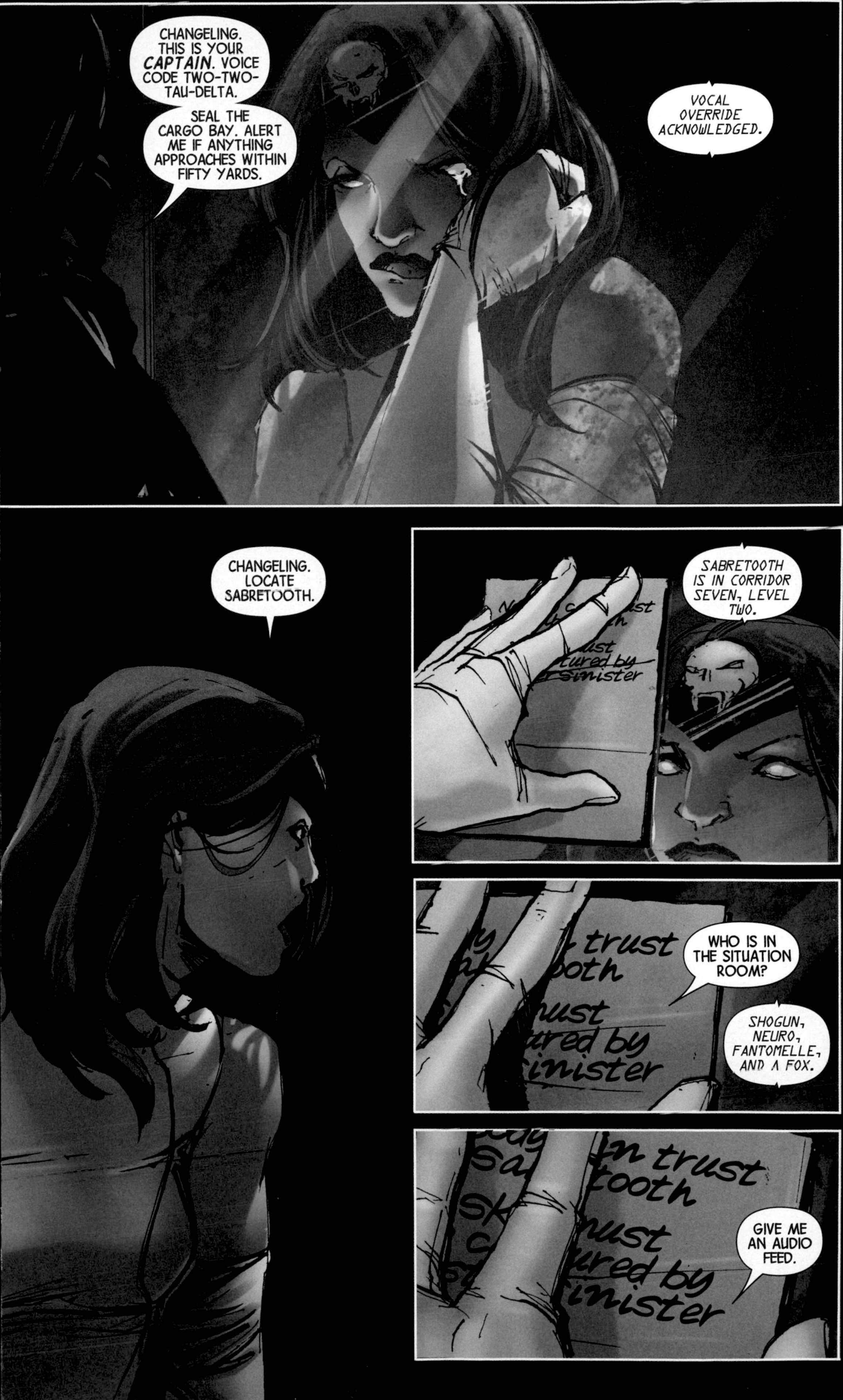
CHANGELING. THIS IS YOUR CAPTAIN. VOICE CODE TWO-TWO-TAU-DELTA.
SEAL THE CARGO BAY. ALERT ME IF ANYTHING APPROACHES WITHIN FIFTY YARDS.
VOCAL OVERRIDE ACKNOWLEDGED.
CHANGELING. LOCATE SABRETOOTH.
SABRETOOTH IS IN CORRIDOR SEVEN, LEVEL TWO.
WHO IS IN THE SITUATION ROOM?
SHOGUN, NEURO, FANTOMELLE, AND A FOX.
GIVE ME AN AUDIO FEED.

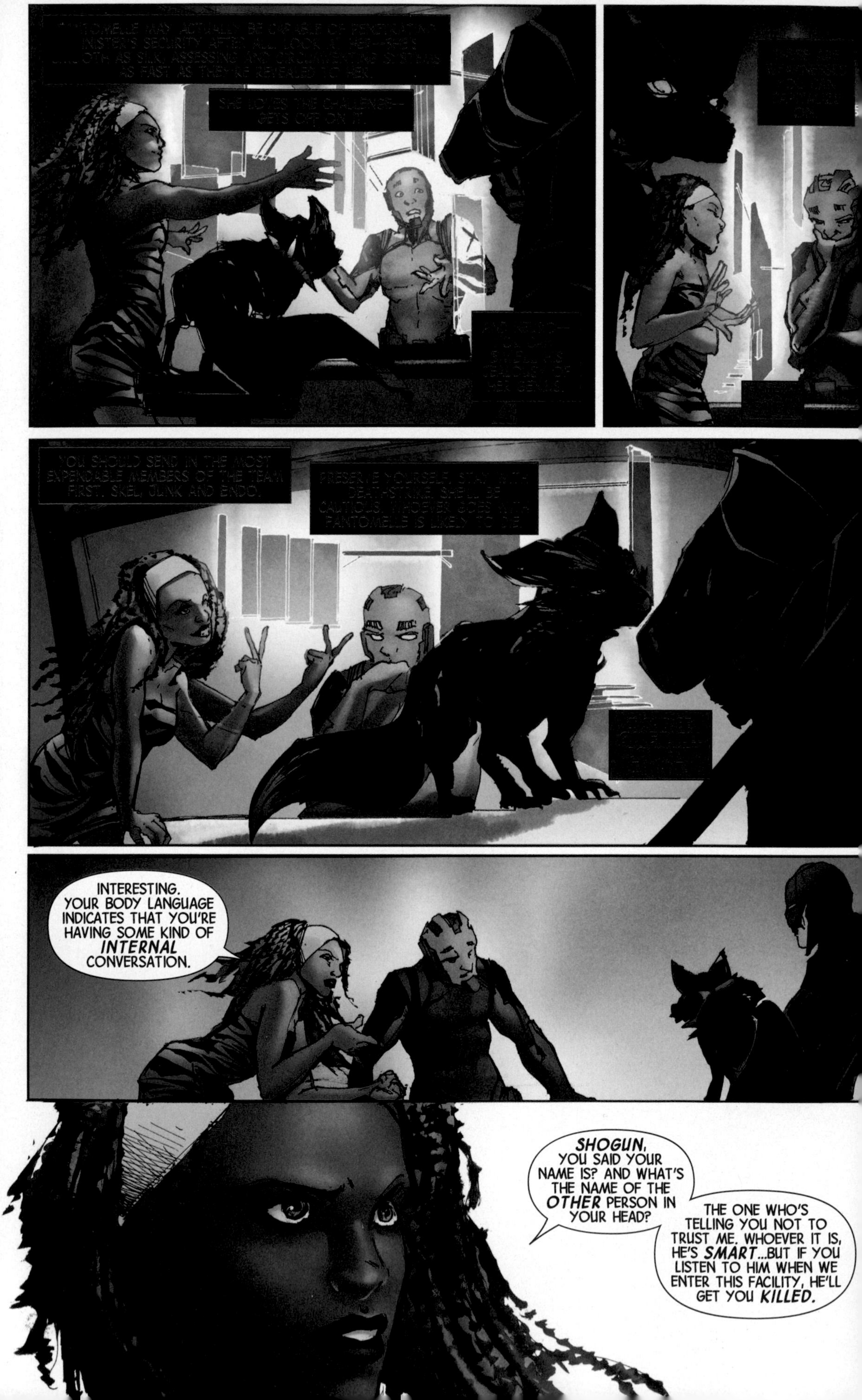
SHE LOVES THE CHALLENGE--
GETS OFF ON IT.
YOU SHOULD SEND IN THE MOST EXPENDABLE MEMBERS OF THE TEAM FIRST. SKEL, JUNK AND ENDO.
PRESERVE YOURSELF. STAY WITH DEATHSTRIKE. SHE'LL BE CAUTIOUS. WHOEVER GOES WITH PANTOMELLE IS LIKELY TO DIE.
INTERESTING. YOUR BODY LANGUAGE INDICATES THAT YOU'RE HAVING SOME KIND OF INTERNAL CONVERSATION.
SHOGUN, YOU SAID YOUR NAME IS? AND WHAT'S THE NAME OF THE OTHER PERSON IN YOUR HEAD?
THE ONE WHO'S TELLING YOU NOT TO TRUST ME. WHOEVER IT IS, HE'S SMART...BUT IF YOU LISTEN TO HIM WHEN WE ENTER THIS FACILITY, HE'LL GET YOU KILLED.

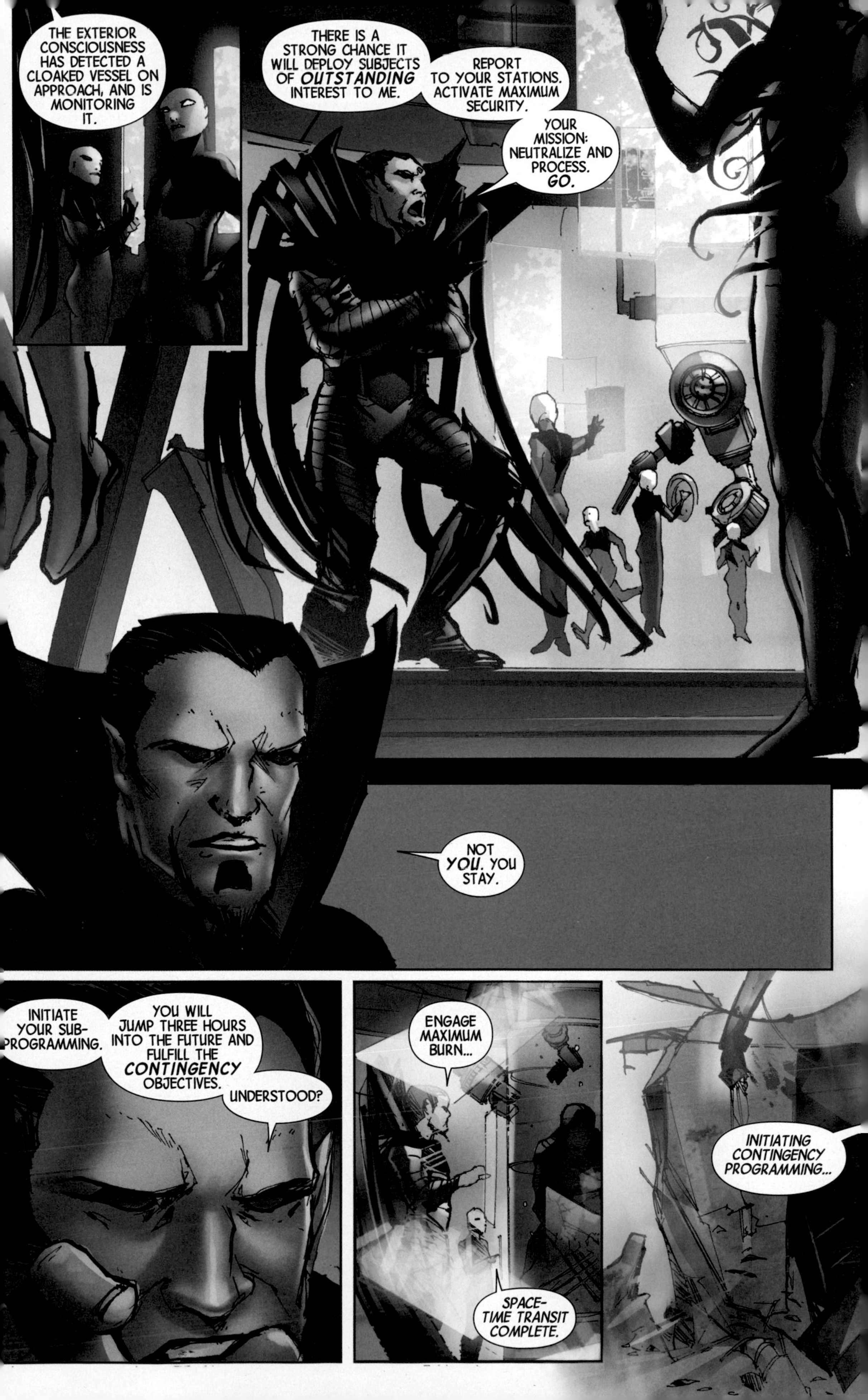
THE EXTERIOR CONSCIOUSNESS HAS DETECTED A CLOAKED VESSEL ON APPROACH, AND IS MONITORING IT.
THERE IS A STRONG CHANCE IT WILL DEPLOY SUBJECTS OF OUTSTANDING INTEREST TO ME.
REPORT TO YOUR STATIONS. ACTIVATE MAXIMUM SECURITY.
YOUR MISSION: NEUTRALIZE AND PROCESS. GO.
NOT YOU. YOU STAY.
INITIATE YOUR SUB-PROGRAMMING.
YOU WILL JUMP THREE HOURS INTO THE FUTURE AND FULFILL THE CONTINGENCY OBJECTIVES.
UNDERSTOOD?
ENGAGE MAXIMUM BURN...
SPACE-TIME TRANSIT COMPLETE.
INITIATING CONTINGENCY PROGRAMMING...

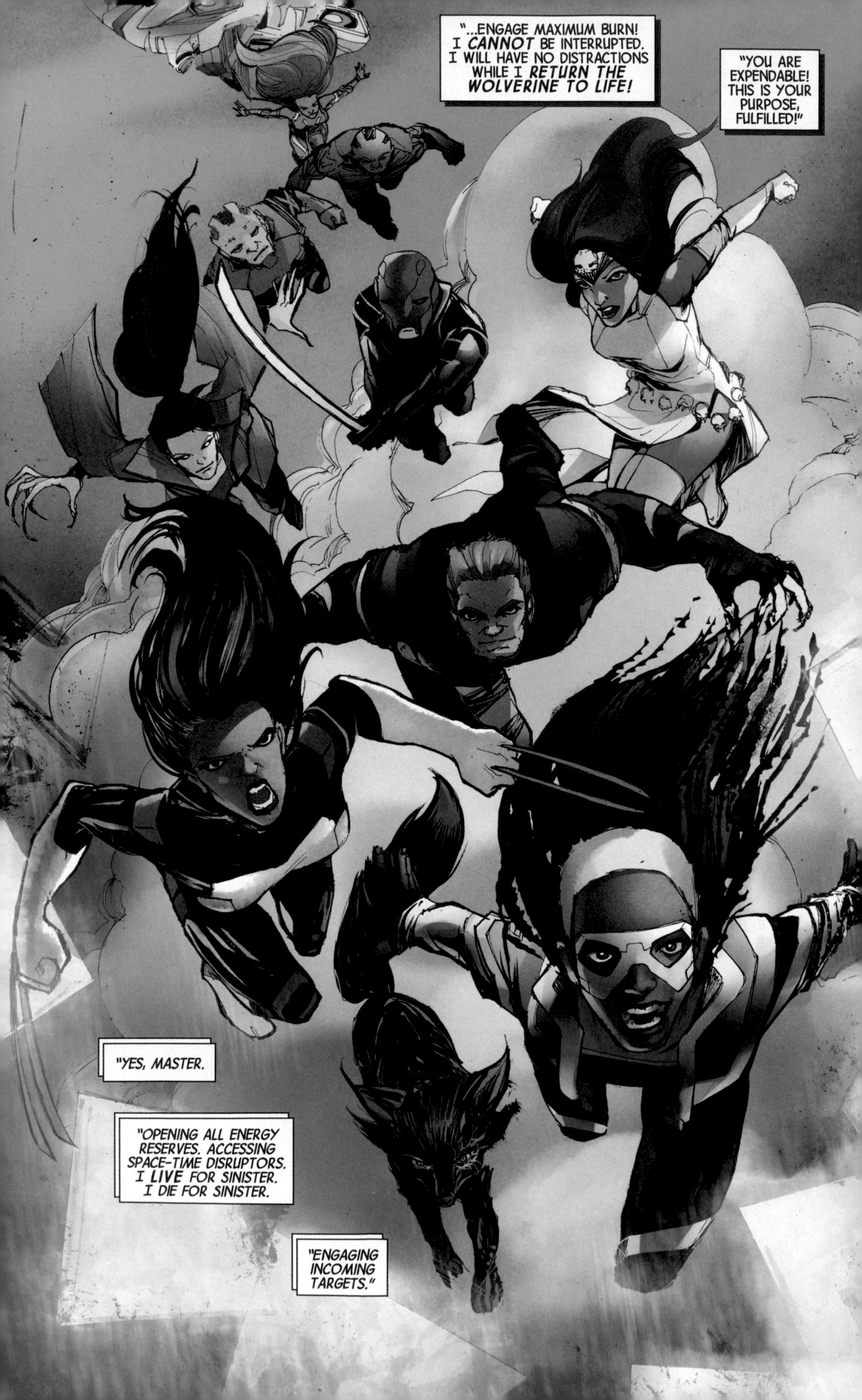
"...ENGAGE MAXIMUM BURN! I CANNOT BE INTERRUPTED. I WILL HAVE NO DISTRACTIONS WHILE I RETURN THE WOLVERINE TO LIFE!
"YOU ARE EXPENDABLE! THIS IS YOUR PURPOSE, FULFILLED!"
"YES, MASTER.
"OPENING ALL ENERGY RESERVES. ACCESSING SPACE-TIME DISRUPTORS. I LIVE FOR SINISTER. I DIE FOR SINISTER.
"ENGAGING INCOMING TARGETS."

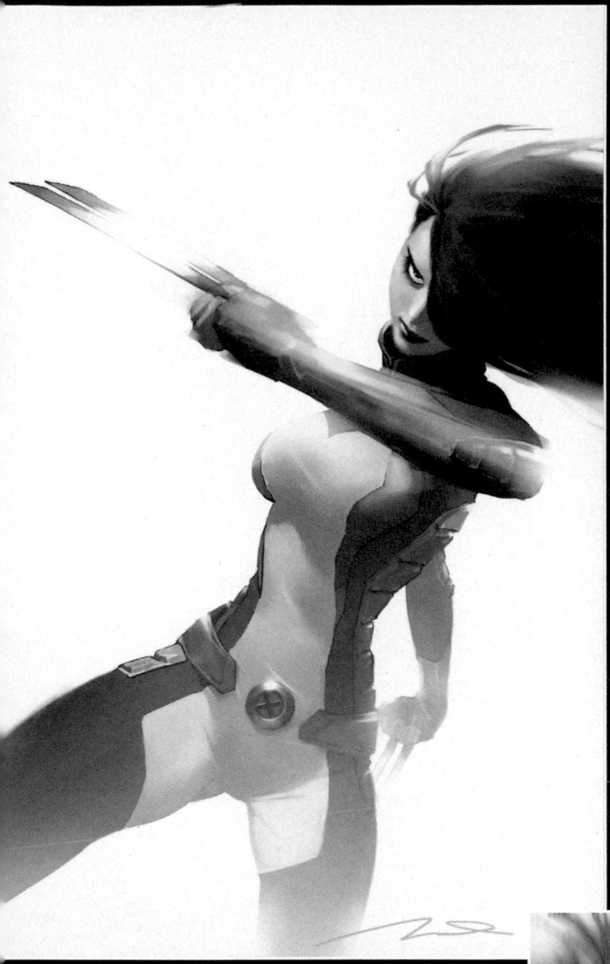

#3 VARIANT
BY GERALD PAREL

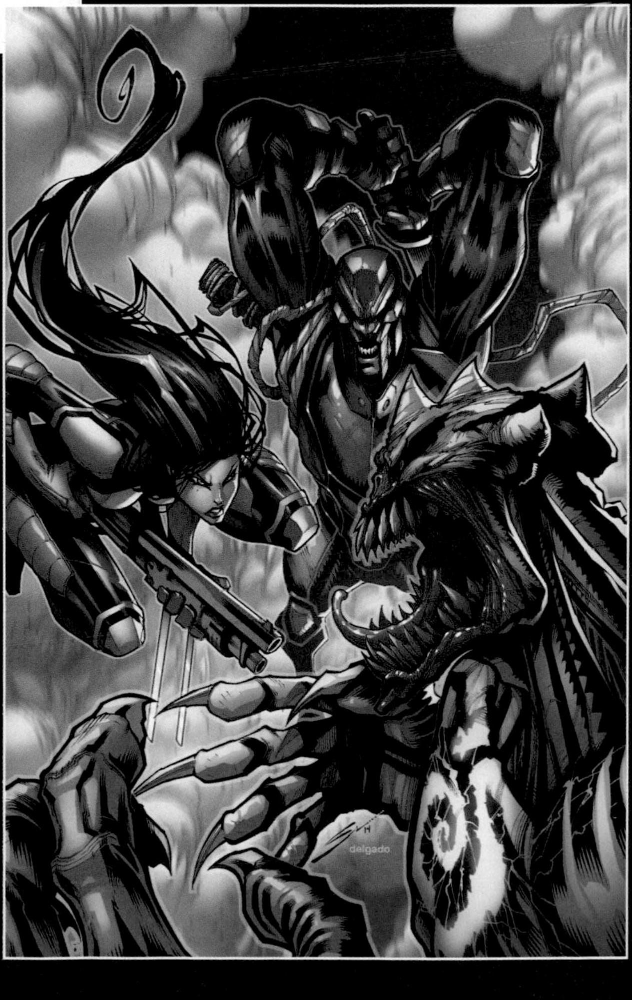

#4 VARIANT
BY GERARDO SANDOVAL &
EDGAR DELGADO

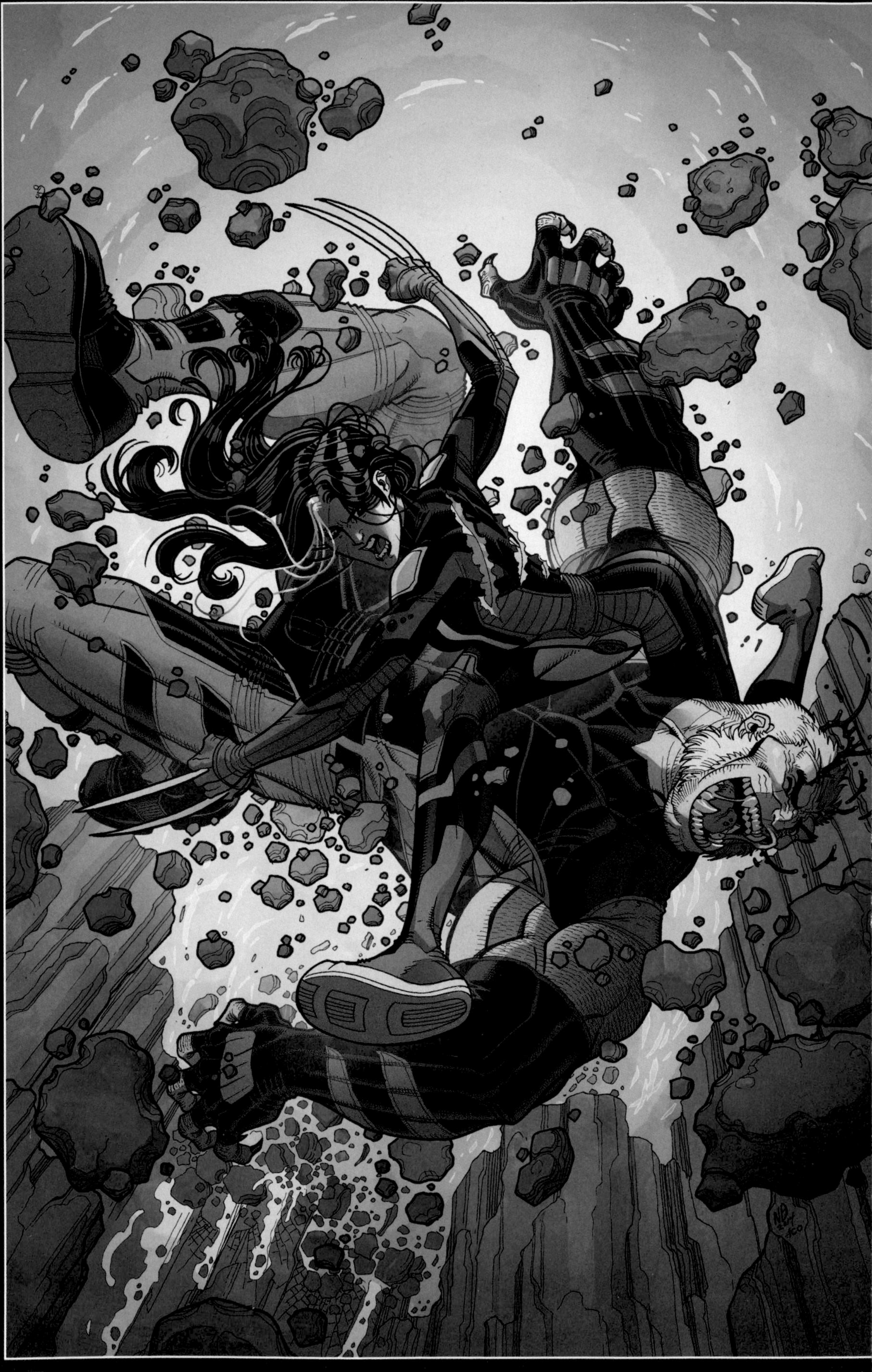

#5

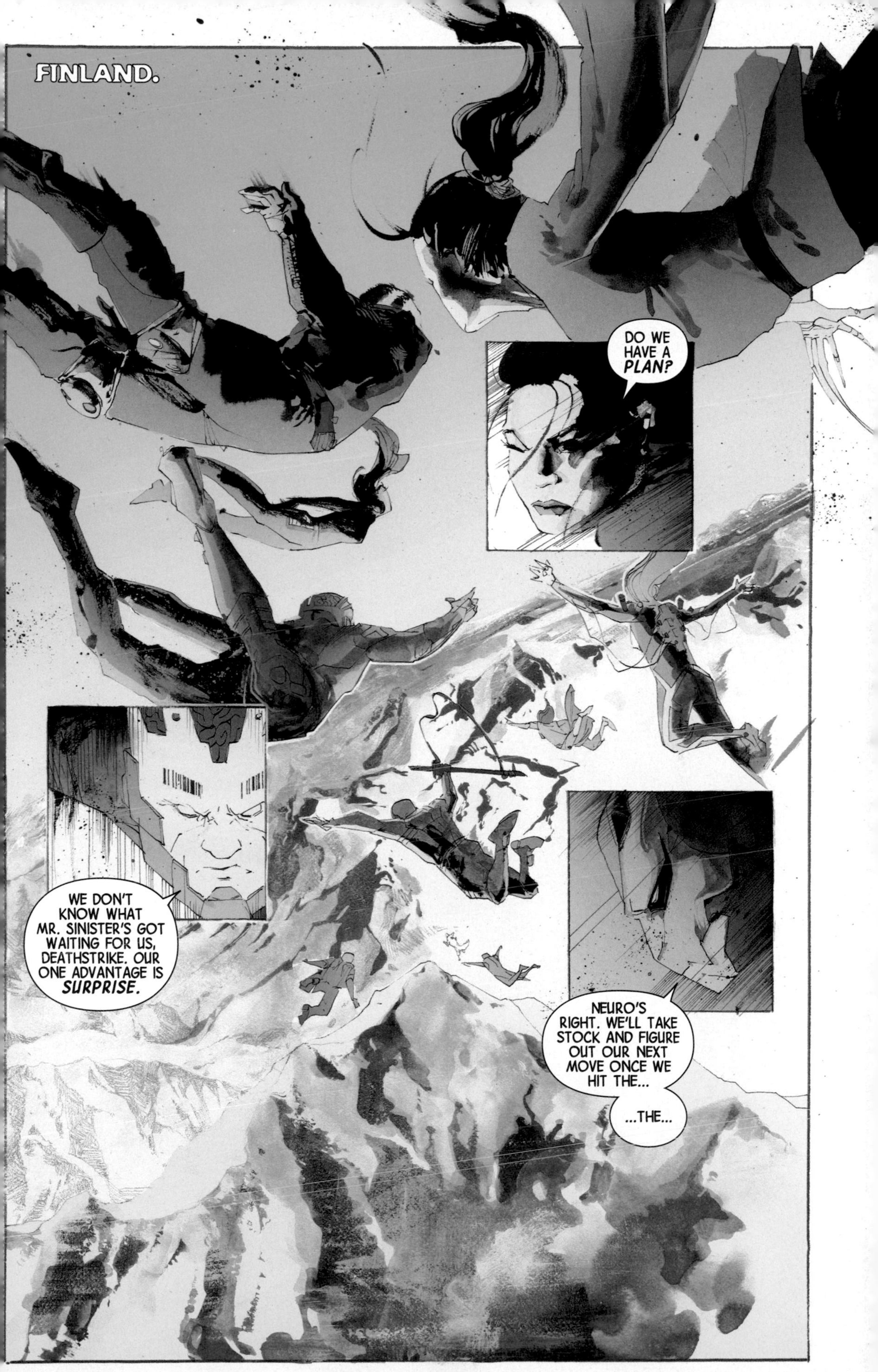
FINLAND.
DO WE HAVE A PLAN?
WE DON'T KNOW WHAT MR. SINISTER'S GOT WAITING FOR US, DEATHSTRIKE. OUR ONE ADVANTAGE IS SURPRISE.
NEURO'S RIGHT. WE'LL TAKE STOCK AND FIGURE OUT OUR NEXT MOVE ONCE WE HIT THE...
...THE...

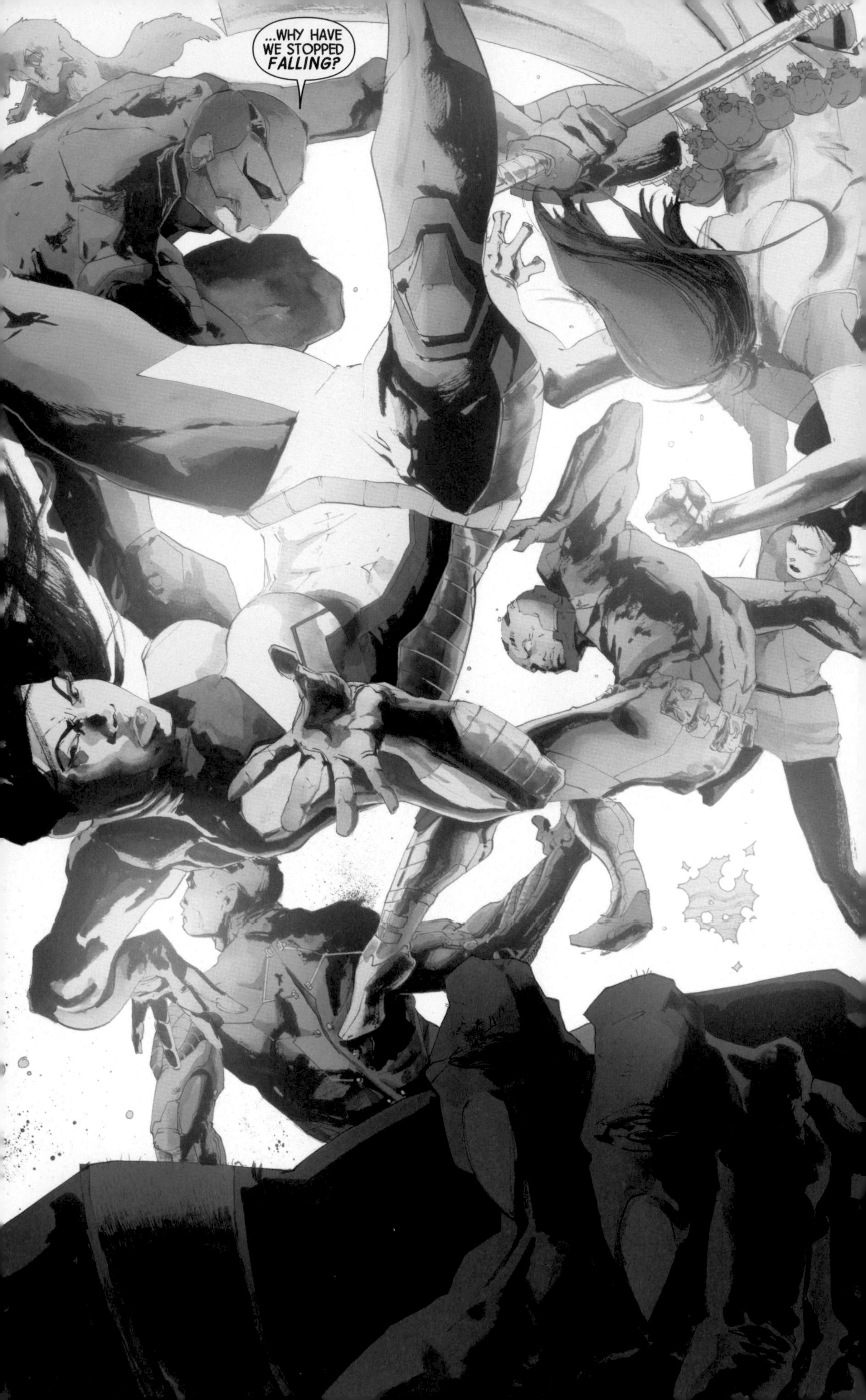
...WHY HAVE WE STOPPED FALLING?

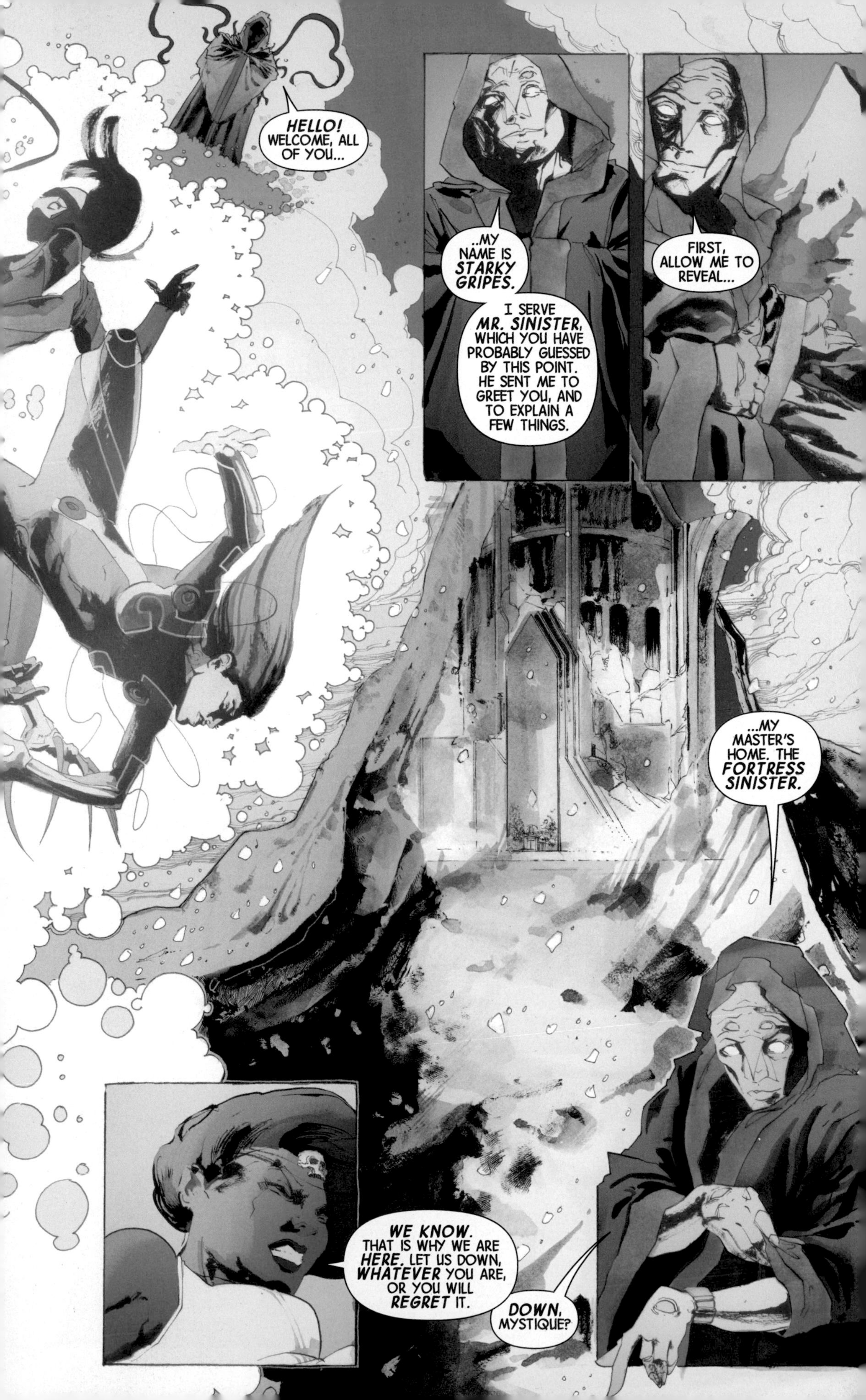
HELLO! WELCOME, ALL OF YOU...
..MY NAME IS STARKY GRIPES.
I SERVE MR. SINISTER, WHICH YOU HAVE PROBABLY GUESSED BY THIS POINT. HE SENT ME TO GREET YOU, AND TO EXPLAIN A FEW THINGS.
FIRST, ALLOW ME TO REVEAL...
...MY MASTER'S HOME. THE FORTRESS SINISTER.
WE KNOW. THAT IS WHY WE ARE HERE. LET US DOWN, WHATEVER YOU ARE, OR YOU WILL REGRET IT.
DOWN, MYSTIQUE?

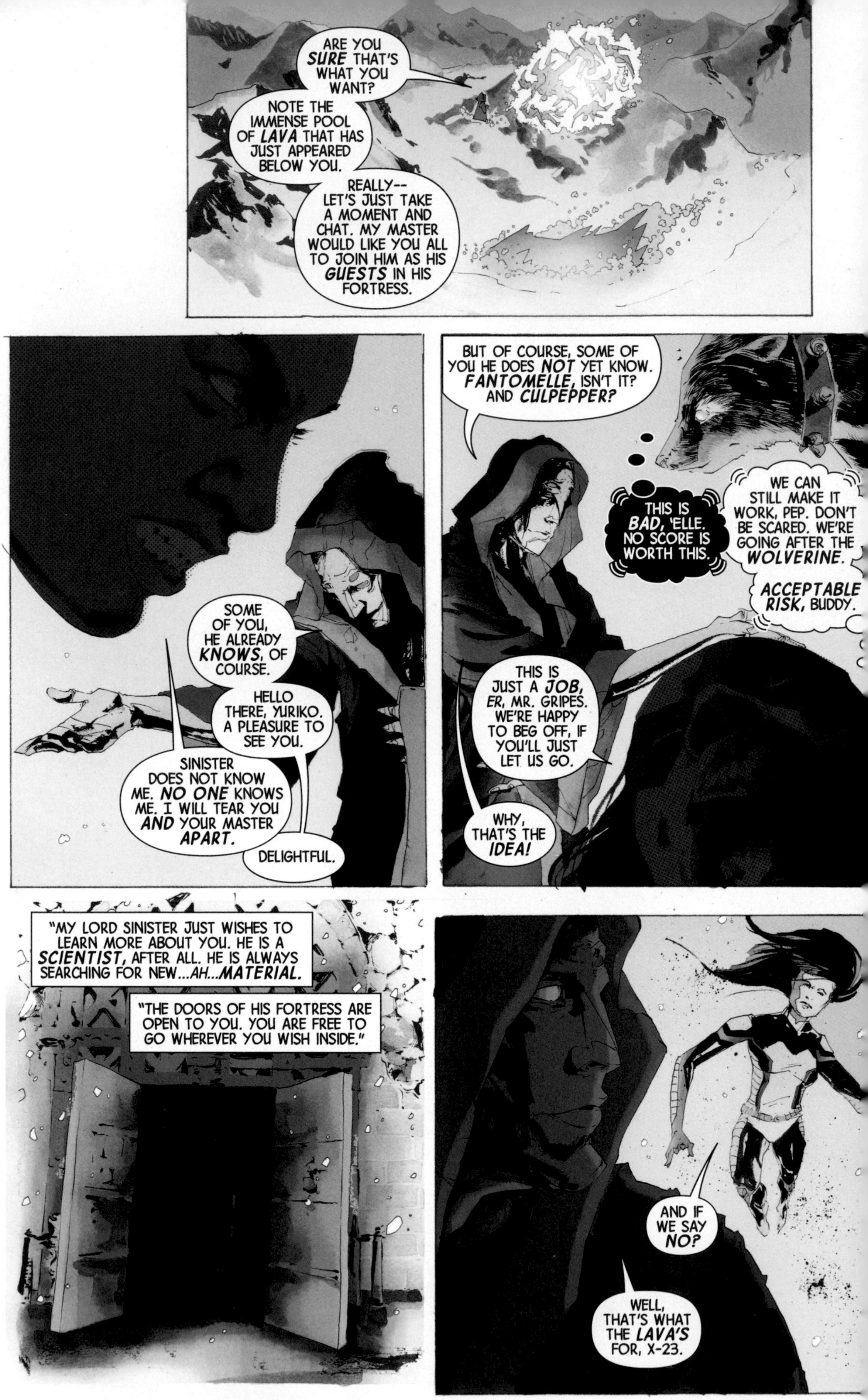
ARE YOU SURE THAT'S WHAT YOU WANT?
NOTE THE IMMENSE POOL OF LAVA THAT HAS JUST APPEARED BELOW YOU.
REALLY-- LET'S JUST TAKE A MOMENT AND CHAT. MY MASTER WOULD LIKE YOU ALL TO JOIN HIM AS HIS GUESTS IN HIS FORTRESS.
SOME OF YOU, HE ALREADY KNOWS, OF COURSE.
HELLO THERE, YURIKO. A PLEASURE TO SEE YOU.
SINISTER DOES NOT KNOW ME. NO ONE KNOWS ME. I WILL TEAR YOU AND YOUR MASTER APART.
DELIGHTFUL.
BUT OF COURSE, SOME OF YOU HE DOES NOT YET KNOW. FANTOMELLE, ISN'T IT? AND CULPEPPER?
THIS IS BAD, 'ELLE. NO SCORE IS WORTH THIS.
WE CAN STILL MAKE IT WORK, PEP. DON'T BE SCARED. WE'RE GOING AFTER THE WOLVERINE.
ACCEPTABLE RISK, BUDDY.
THIS IS JUST A JOB, ER, MR. GRIPES. WE'RE HAPPY TO BEG OFF, IF YOU'LL JUST LET US GO.
WHY, THAT'S THE IDEA!
"MY LORD SINISTER JUST WISHES TO LEARN MORE ABOUT YOU. HE IS A SCIENTIST, AFTER ALL. HE IS ALWAYS SEARCHING FOR NEW...AH...MATERIAL.
"THE DOORS OF HIS FORTRESS ARE OPEN TO YOU. YOU ARE FREE TO GO WHEREVER YOU WISH INSIDE."
AND IF WE SAY NO?
WELL, THAT'S WHAT THE LAVA'S FOR, X-23.

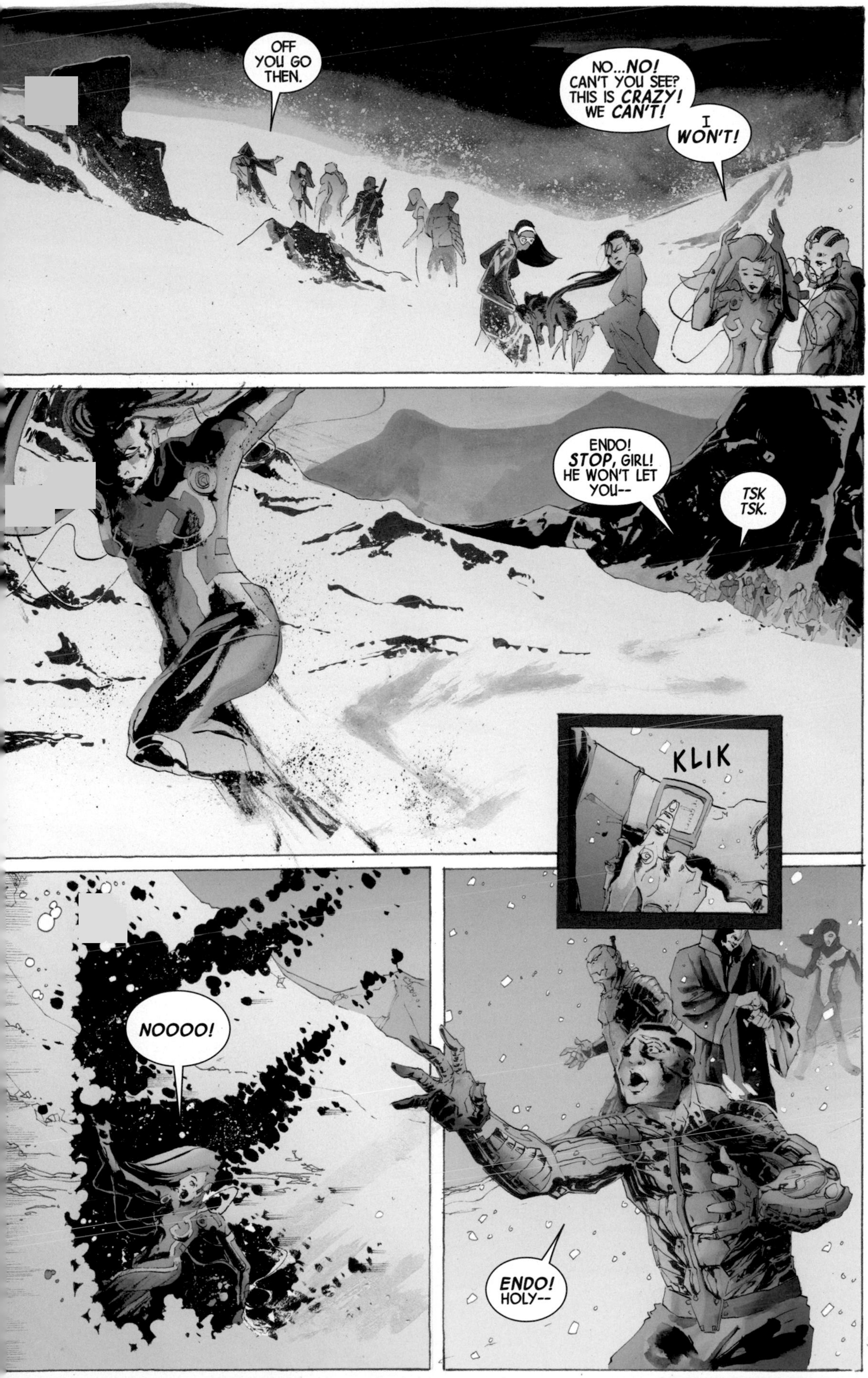
OFF YOU GO THEN.
NO...NO! CAN'T YOU SEE? THIS IS CRAZY! WE CAN'T!
I WON'T!
ENDO! STOP, GIRL! HE WON'T LET YOU--
TSK TSK.
KLIK
NOOOO!
ENDO! HOLY--

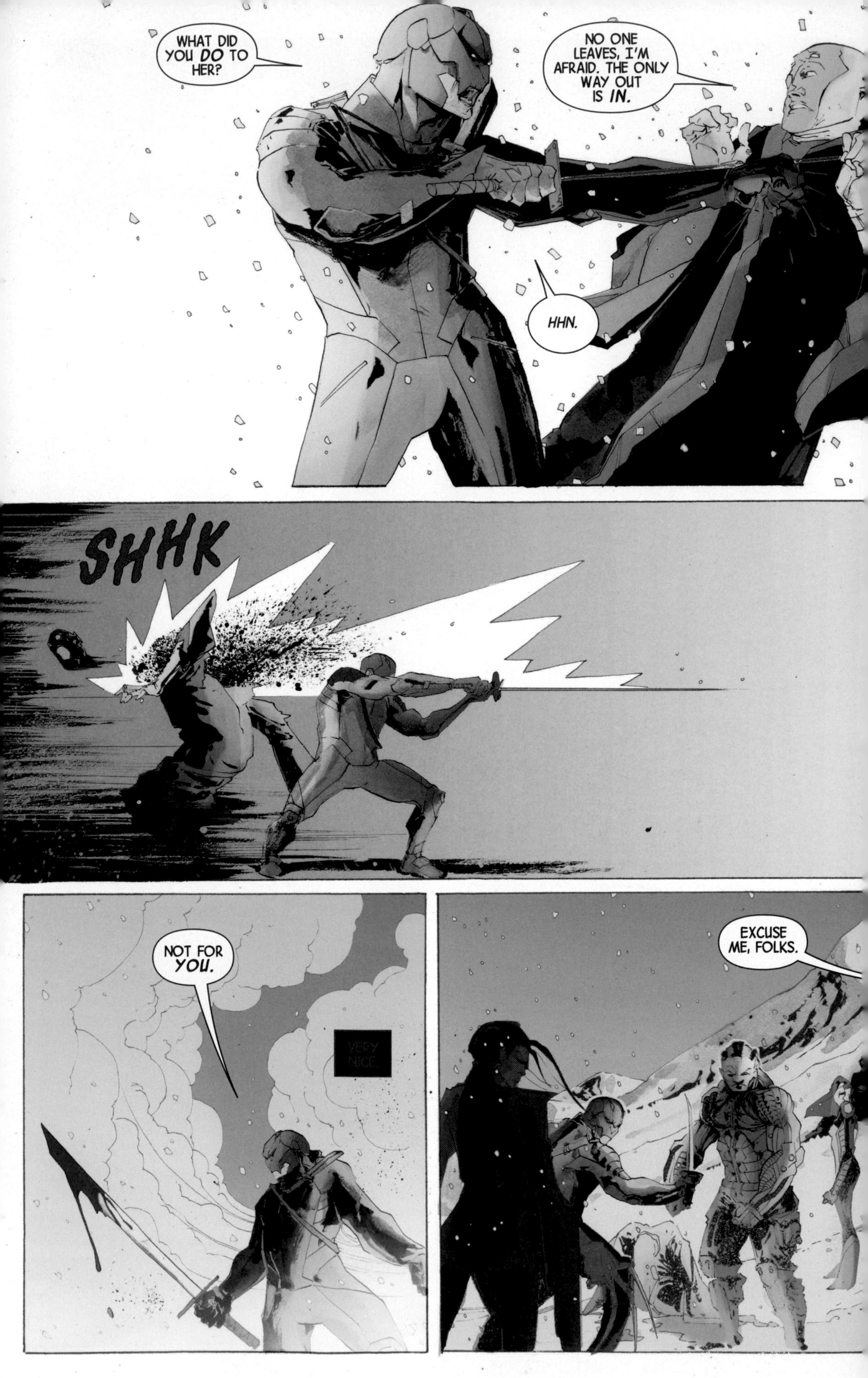
WHAT DID YOU DO TO HER?
NO ONE LEAVES, I'M AFRAID. THE ONLY WAY OUT IS IN.
HHN.
SHHK
NOT FOR YOU.
VERY NICE.
EXCUSE ME, FOLKS.

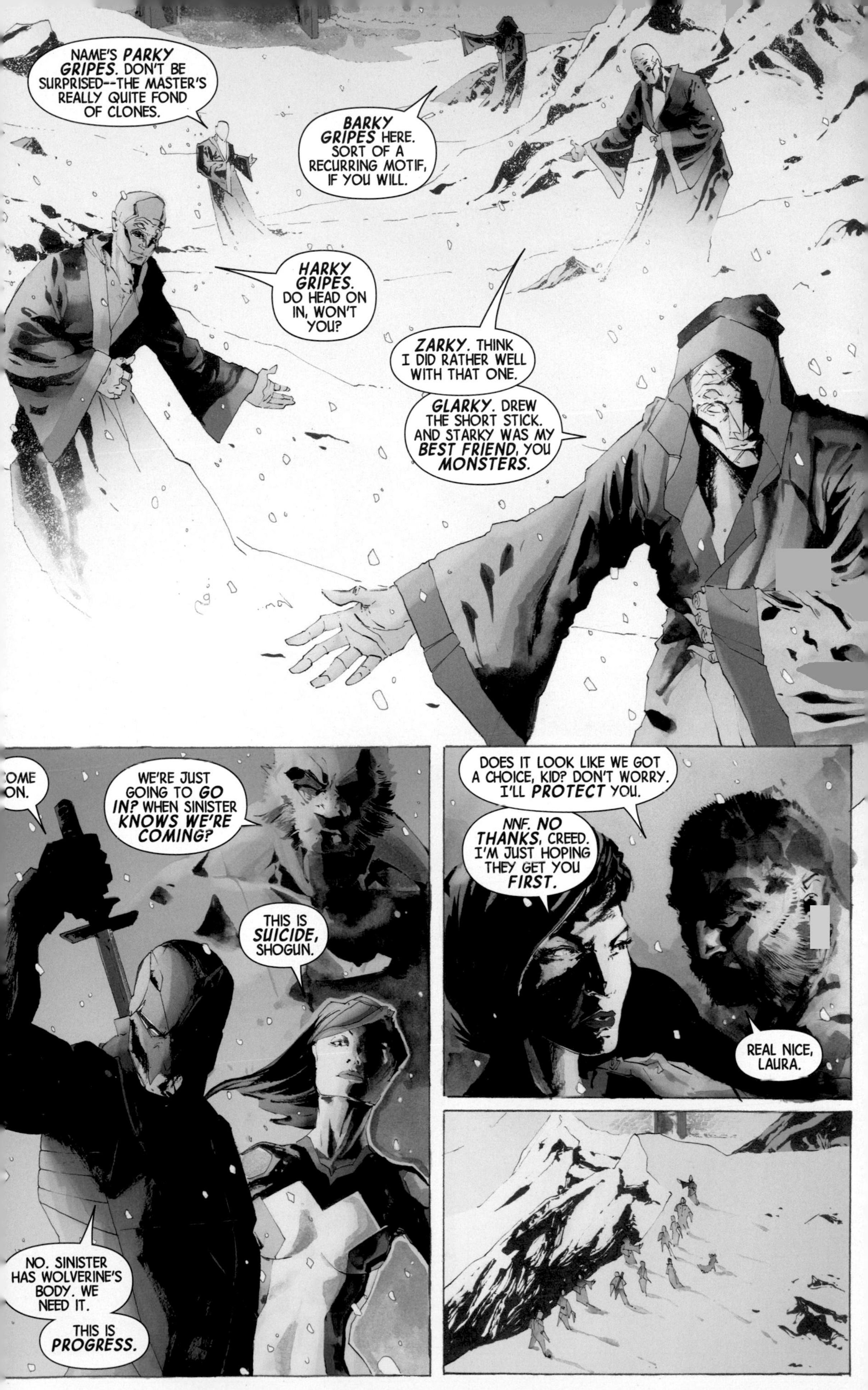
NAME'S PARKY GRIPES. DON'T BE SURPRISED--THE MASTER'S REALLY QUITE FOND OF CLONES.
BARKY GRIPES HERE. SORT OF A RECURRING MOTIF, IF YOU WILL.
HARKY GRIPES. DO HEAD ON IN, WON'T YOU?
ZARKY. THINK I DID RATHER WELL WITH THAT ONE.
GLARKY. DREW THE SHORT STICK. AND STARKY WAS MY BEST FRIEND, YOU MONSTERS.
WE'RE JUST GOING TO GO IN? WHEN SINISTER KNOWS WE'RE COMING?
THIS IS SUICIDE, SHOGUN.
NO. SINISTER HAS WOLVERINE'S BODY. WE NEED IT.
THIS IS PROGRESS.
DOES IT LOOK LIKE WE GOT A CHOICE, KID? DON'T WORRY. I'LL PROTECT YOU.
NNF. NO THANKS, CREED. I'M JUST HOPING THEY GET YOU FIRST.
REAL NICE, LAURA.

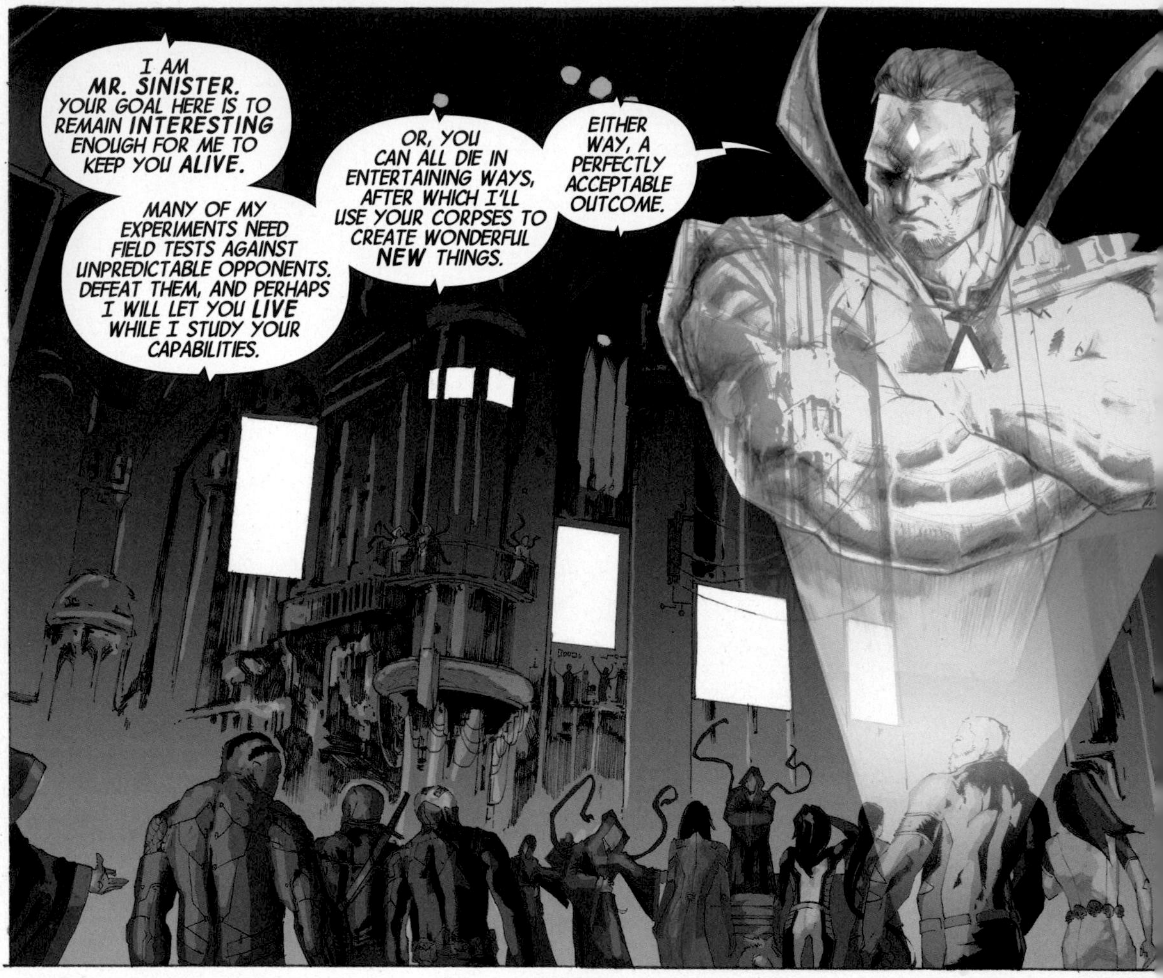
I AM MR. SINISTER. YOUR GOAL HERE IS TO REMAIN INTERESTING ENOUGH FOR ME TO KEEP YOU ALIVE.
MANY OF MY EXPERIMENTS NEED FIELD TESTS AGAINST UNPREDICTABLE OPPONENTS. DEFEAT THEM, AND PERHAPS I WILL LET YOU LIVE WHILE I STUDY YOUR CAPABILITIES.
OR, YOU CAN ALL DIE IN ENTERTAINING WAYS, AFTER WHICH I'LL USE YOUR CORPSES TO CREATE WONDERFUL NEW THINGS.
EITHER WAY, A PERFECTLY ACCEPTABLE OUTCOME.

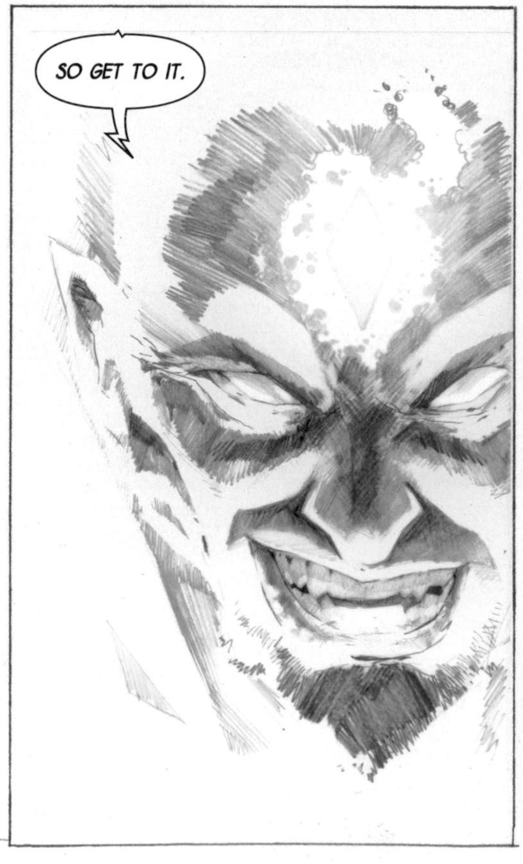
SO GET TO IT.

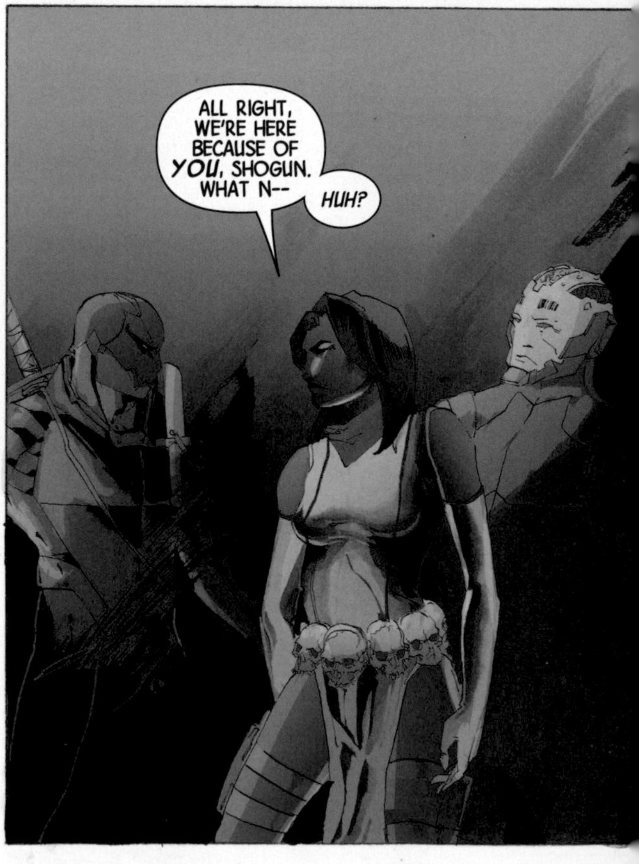
ALL RIGHT, WE'RE HERE BECAUSE OF YOU, SHOGUN. WHAT N--
HUH?

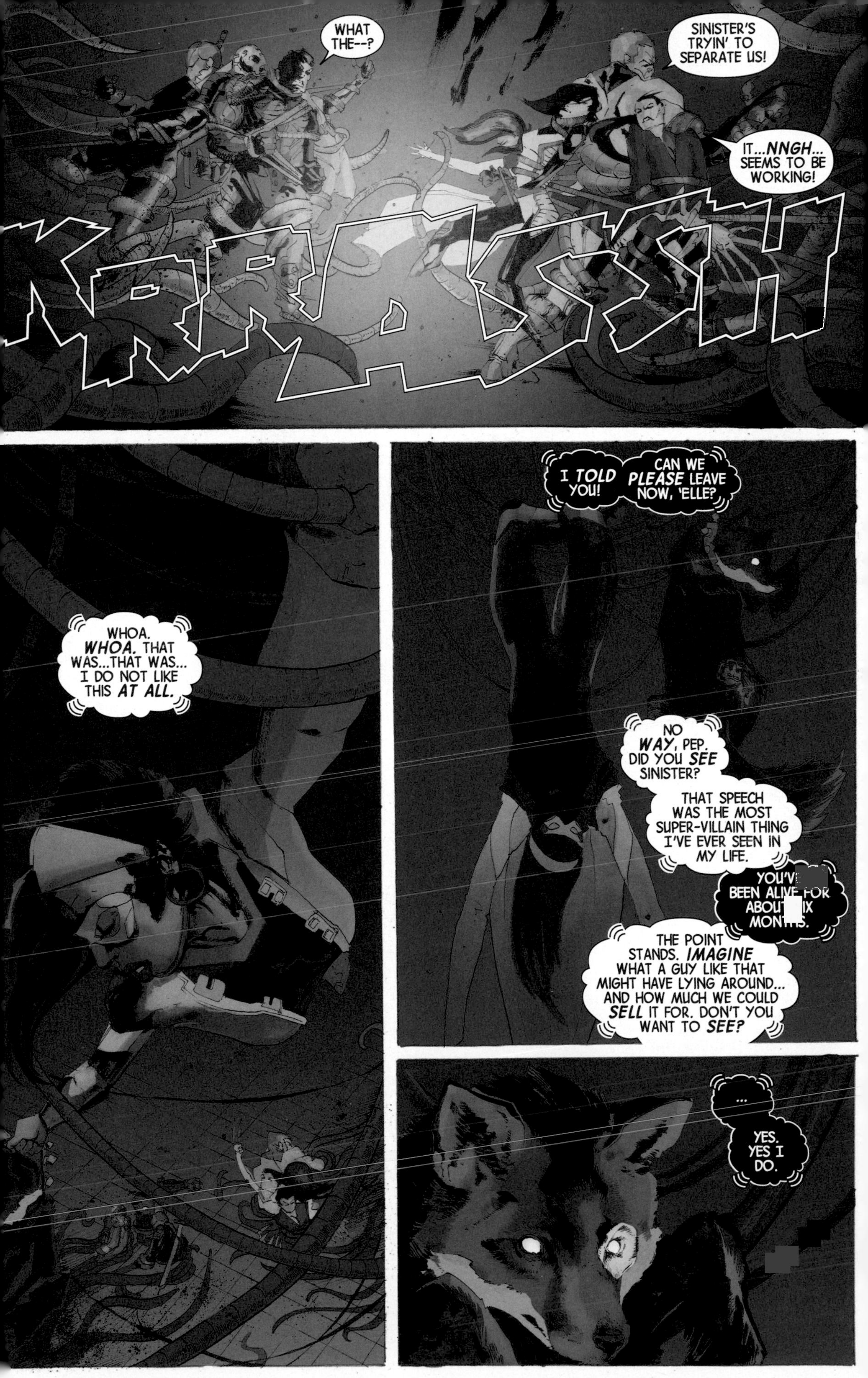
WHAT THE--?
SINISTER'S TRYIN' TO SEPARATE US!
IT...NNGH... SEEMS TO BE WORKING!
KRRASSH
WHOA. WHOA. THAT WAS...THAT WAS... I DO NOT LIKE THIS AT ALL.
I TOLD YOU!
CAN WE PLEASE LEAVE NOW, 'ELLE?
NO WAY, PEP. DID YOU SEE SINISTER?
THAT SPEECH WAS THE MOST SUPER-VILLAIN THING I'VE EVER SEEN IN MY LIFE.
YOU'VE BEEN ALIVE FOR ABOUT SIX MONTHS.
THE POINT STANDS. IMAGINE WHAT A GUY LIKE THAT MIGHT HAVE LYING AROUND... AND HOW MUCH WE COULD SELL IT FOR. DON'T YOU WANT TO SEE?
...
YES. YES I DO.

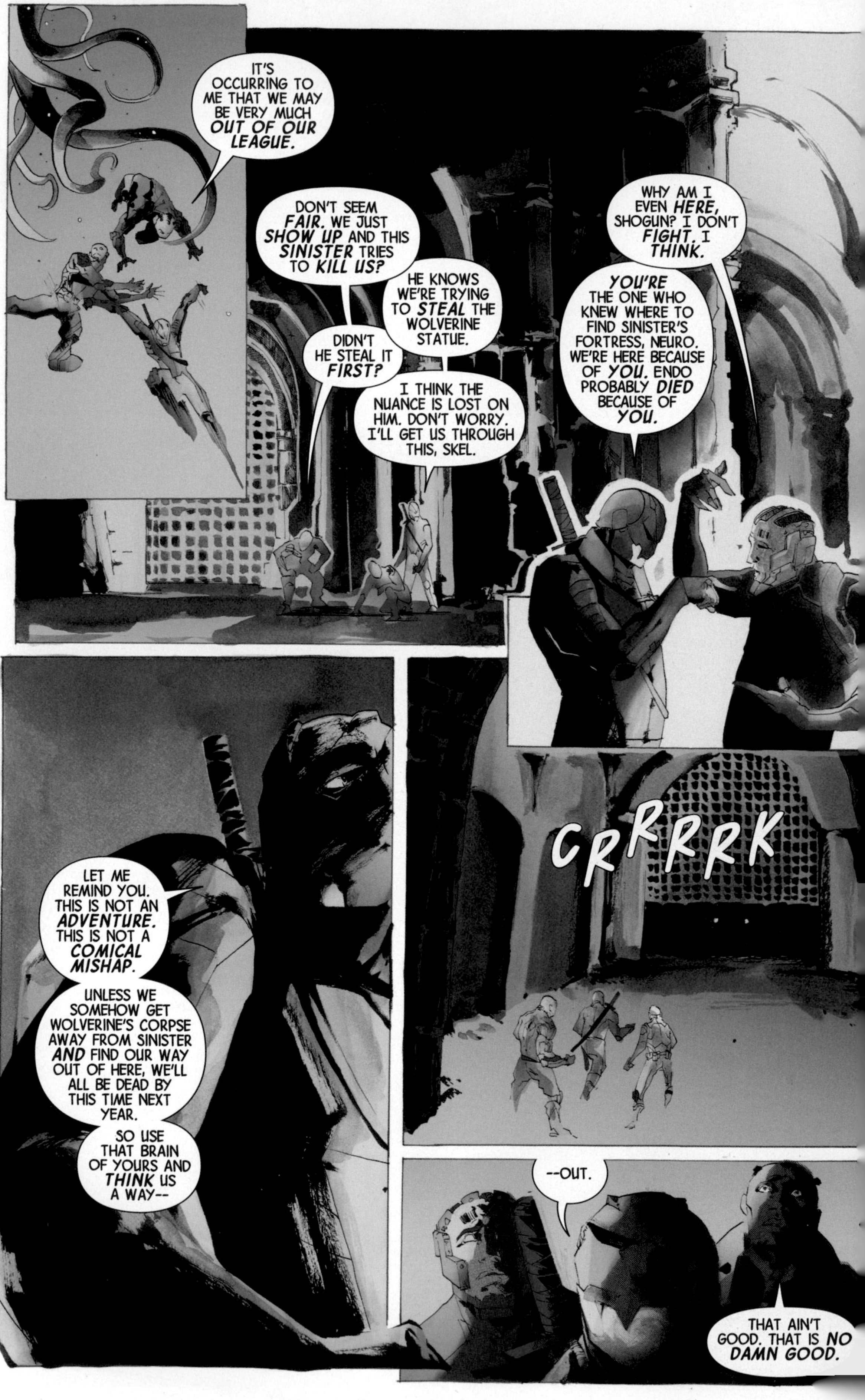
IT'S OCCURRING TO ME THAT WE MAY BE VERY MUCH OUT OF OUR LEAGUE.
DON'T SEEM FAIR. WE JUST SHOW UP AND THIS SINISTER TRIES TO KILL US?
HE KNOWS WE'RE TRYING TO STEAL THE WOLVERINE STATUE.
DIDN'T HE STEAL IT FIRST?
I THINK THE NUANCE IS LOST ON HIM. DON'T WORRY. I'LL GET US THROUGH THIS, SKEL.
WHY AM I EVEN HERE, SHOGUN? I DON'T FIGHT. I THINK.
YOU'RE THE ONE WHO KNEW WHERE TO FIND SINISTER'S FORTRESS, NEURO. WE'RE HERE BECAUSE OF YOU. ENDO PROBABLY DIED BECAUSE OF YOU.
LET ME REMIND YOU. THIS IS NOT AN ADVENTURE. THIS IS NOT A COMICAL MISHAP.
UNLESS WE SOMEHOW GET WOLVERINE'S CORPSE AWAY FROM SINISTER AND FIND OUR WAY OUT OF HERE, WE'LL ALL BE DEAD BY THIS TIME NEXT YEAR.
SO USE THAT BRAIN OF YOURS AND THINK US A WAY--
CRRRRK
--OUT.
THAT AIN'T GOOD. THAT IS NO DAMN GOOD.

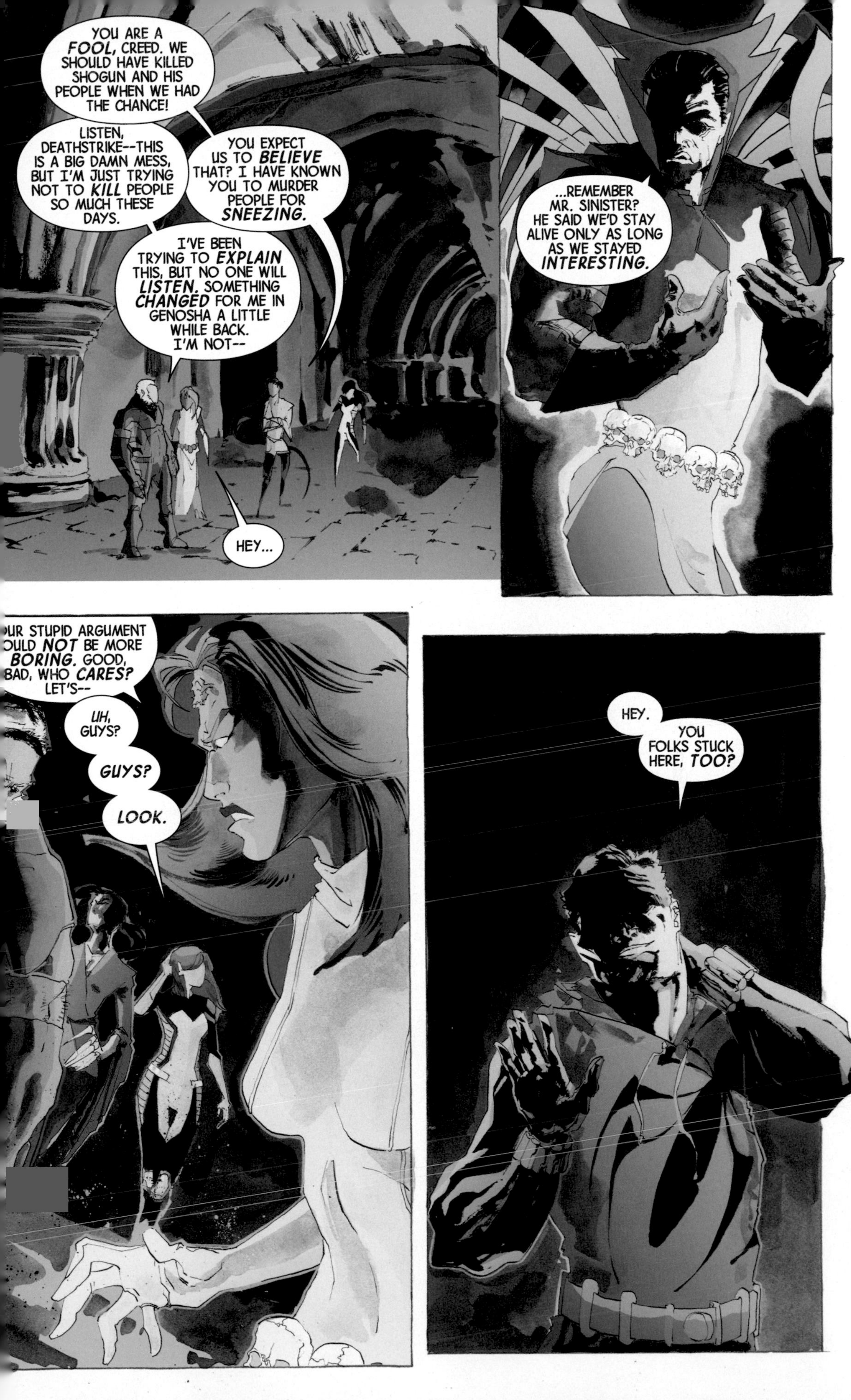
YOU ARE A FOOL, CREED. WE SHOULD HAVE KILLED SHOGUN AND HIS PEOPLE WHEN WE HAD THE CHANCE!
LISTEN, DEATHSTRIKE--THIS IS A BIG DAMN MESS, BUT I'M JUST TRYING NOT TO KILL PEOPLE SO MUCH THESE DAYS.
YOU EXPECT US TO BELIEVE THAT? I HAVE KNOWN YOU TO MURDER PEOPLE FOR SNEEZING.
I'VE BEEN TRYING TO EXPLAIN THIS, BUT NO ONE WILL LISTEN. SOMETHING CHANGED FOR ME IN GENOSHA A LITTLE WHILE BACK. I'M NOT--
HEY...
...REMEMBER MR. SINISTER? HE SAID WE'D STAY ALIVE ONLY AS LONG AS WE STAYED INTERESTING.
OUR STUPID ARGUMENT OULD NOT BE MORE BORING. GOOD, BAD, WHO CARES? LET'S--
UH, GUYS?
GUYS?
LOOK.
HEY.
YOU FOLKS STUCK HERE, TOO?

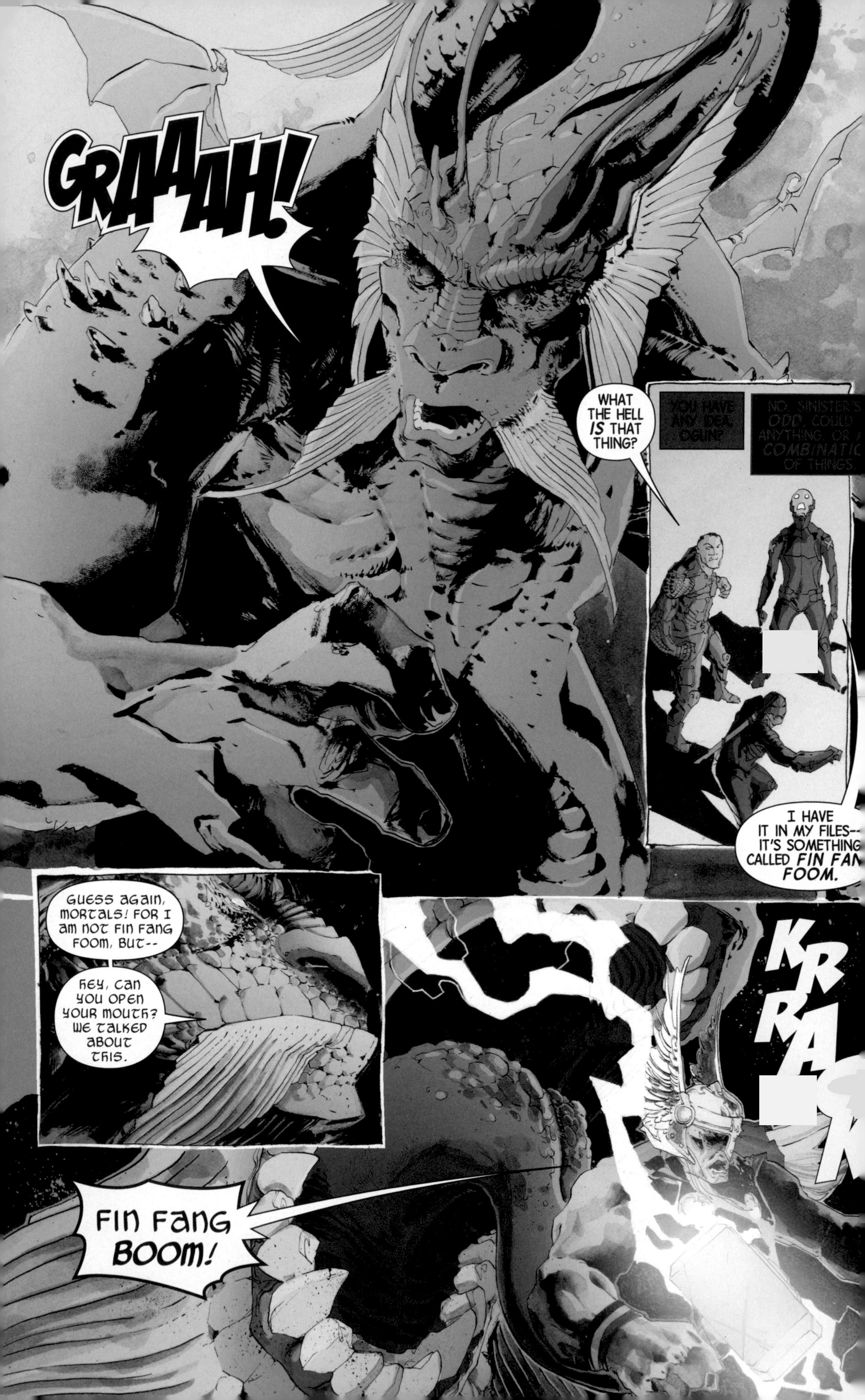
GRAAAH!
WHAT THE HELL IS THAT THING?
YOU HAVE ANY IDEA, OGUN?
NO. SINISTER'S ODD. COULD ANYTHING. OR COMBINATI OF THINGS.
I HAVE IT IN MY FILES-- IT'S SOMETHING CALLED FIN FAN FOOM.
GUESS AGAIN, MORTALS! FOR I AM NOT FIN FANG FOOM, BUT--
HEY, CAN YOU OPEN YOUR MOUTH? WE TALKED ABOUT THIS.
FIN FANG BOOM!
KRA K

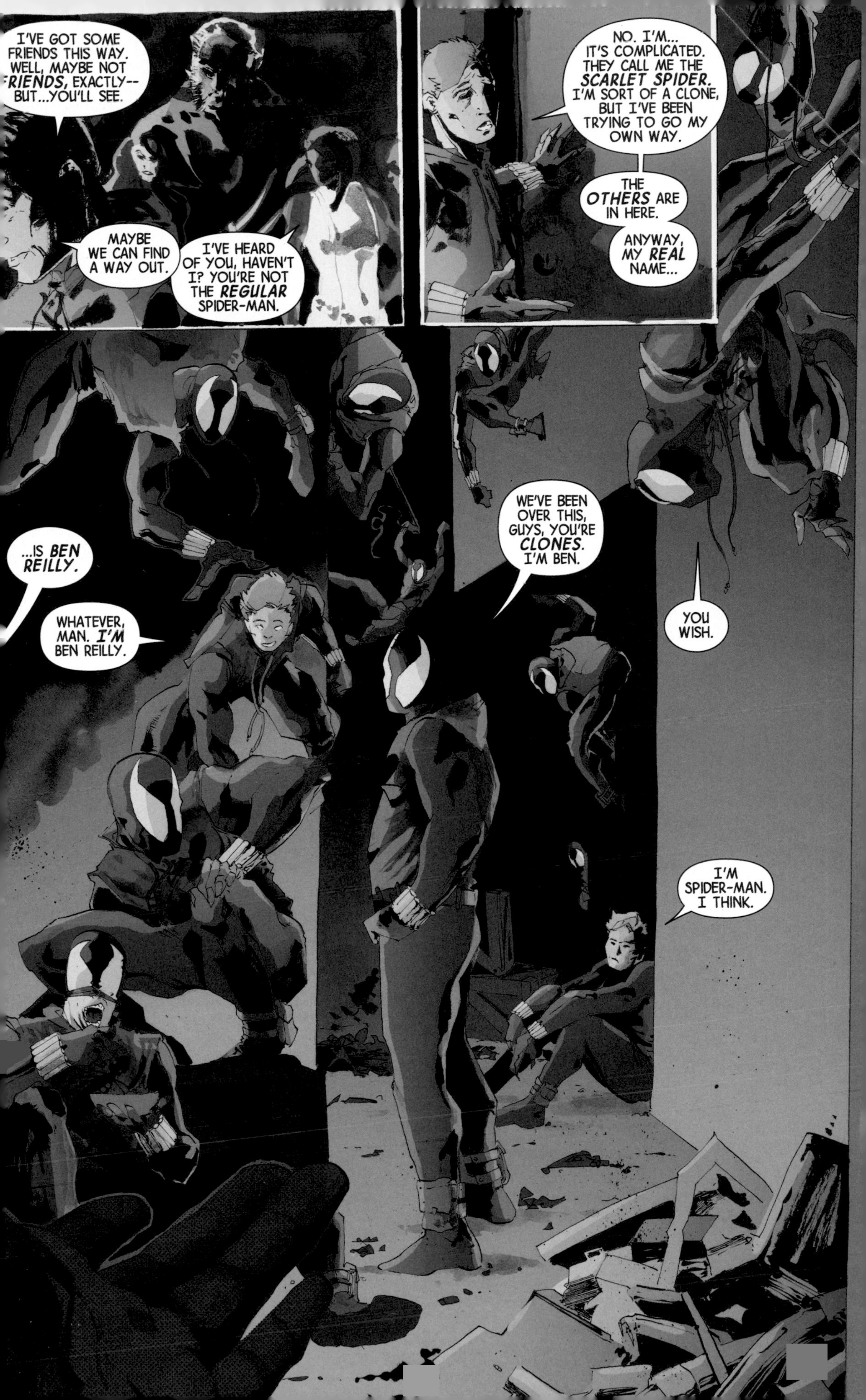
I'VE GOT SOME FRIENDS THIS WAY. WELL, MAYBE NOT FRIENDS, EXACTLY-- BUT...YOU'LL SEE.
MAYBE WE CAN FIND A WAY OUT.
I'VE HEARD OF YOU, HAVEN'T I? YOU'RE NOT THE REGULAR SPIDER-MAN.
NO. I'M... IT'S COMPLICATED. THEY CALL ME THE SCARLET SPIDER. I'M SORT OF A CLONE, BUT I'VE BEEN TRYING TO GO MY OWN WAY.
THE OTHERS ARE IN HERE.
ANYWAY, MY REAL NAME...
...IS BEN REILLY.
WHATEVER, MAN. I'M BEN REILLY.
WE'VE BEEN OVER THIS, GUYS, YOU'RE CLONES. I'M BEN.
YOU WISH.
I'M SPIDER-MAN. I THINK.

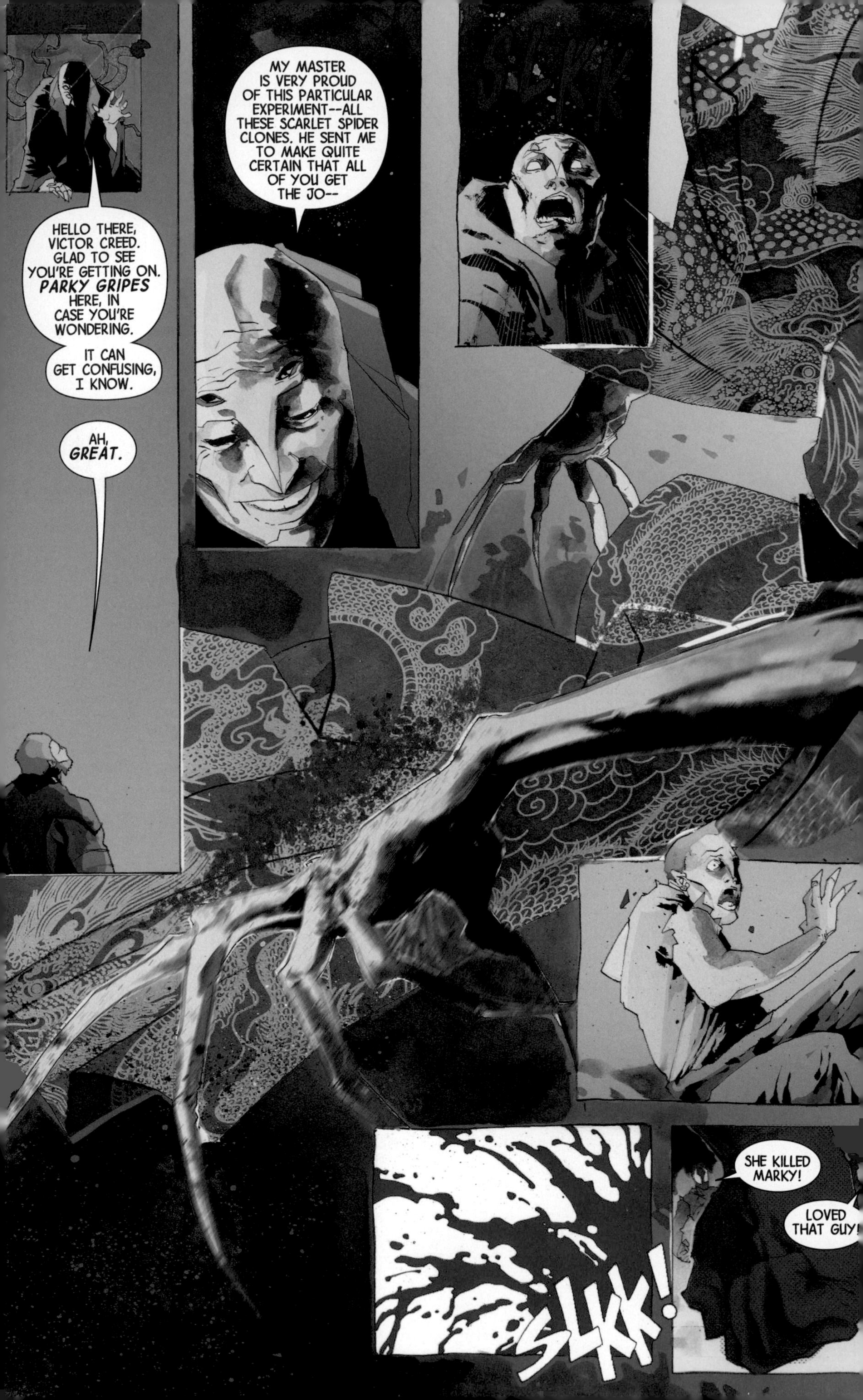
MY MASTER IS VERY PROUD OF THIS PARTICULAR EXPERIMENT--ALL THESE SCARLET SPIDER CLONES. HE SENT ME TO MAKE QUITE CERTAIN THAT ALL OF YOU GET THE JO--
HELLO THERE, VICTOR CREED. GLAD TO SEE YOU'RE GETTING ON. PARKY GRIPES HERE, IN CASE YOU'RE WONDERING.
IT CAN GET CONFUSING, I KNOW.
AH, GREAT.
SLKK!
SHE KILLED MARKY!
LOVED THAT GUY!

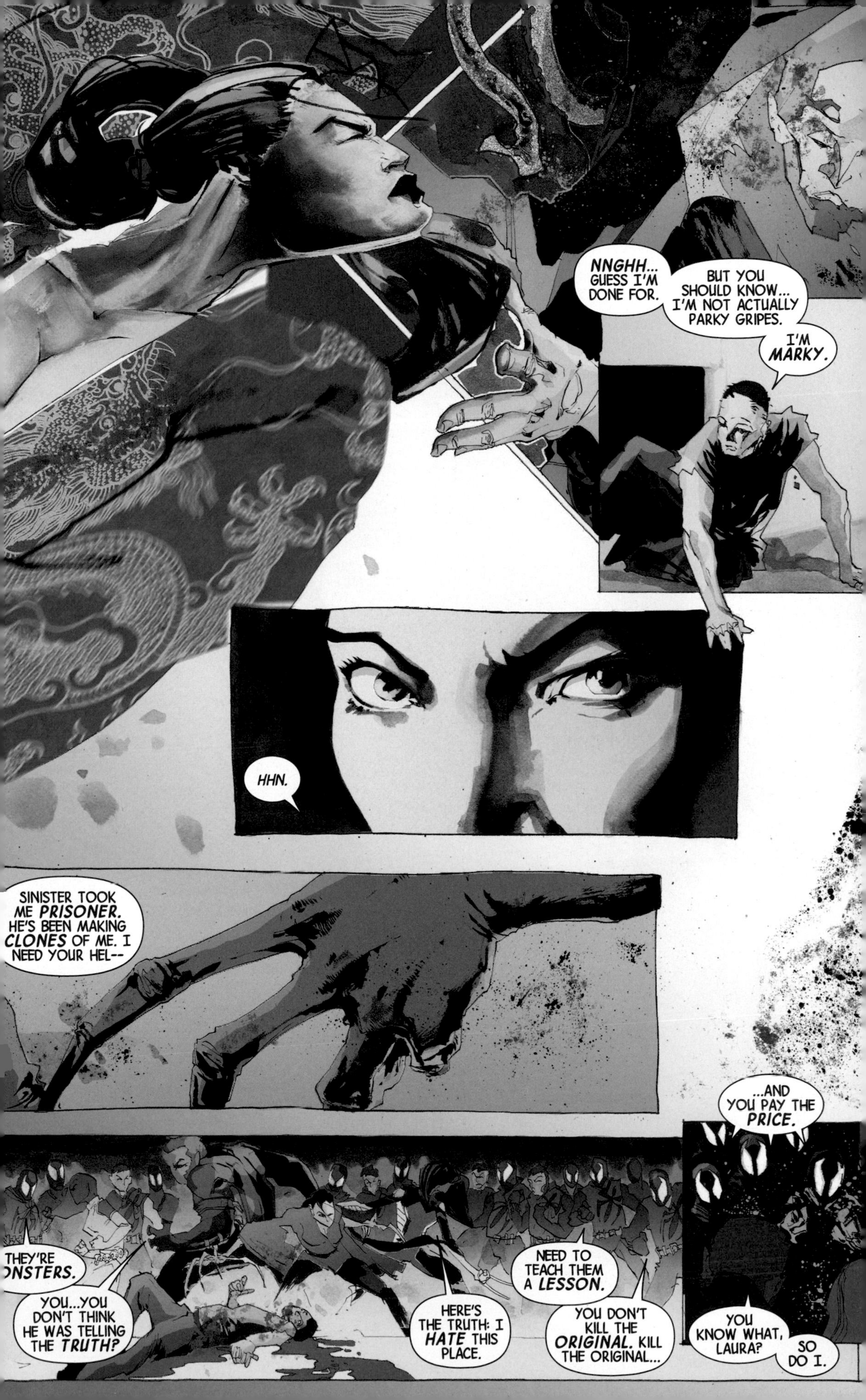

NNGHH... GUESS I'M DONE FOR.
BUT YOU SHOULD KNOW... I'M NOT ACTUALLY PARKY GRIPES.
I'M MARKY.
HHN.
SINISTER TOOK ME PRISONER. HE'S BEEN MAKING CLONES OF ME. I NEED YOUR HEL--
THEY'RE
NSTERS.
YOU...YOU DON'T THINK HE WAS TELLING THE TRUTH?
HERE'S THE TRUTH: I HATE THIS PLACE.
NEED TO TEACH THEM A LESSON.
YOU DON'T KILL THE ORIGINAL. KILL THE ORIGINAL...
...AND YOU PAY THE PRICE.
YOU KNOW WHAT, LAURA?
SO DO I.

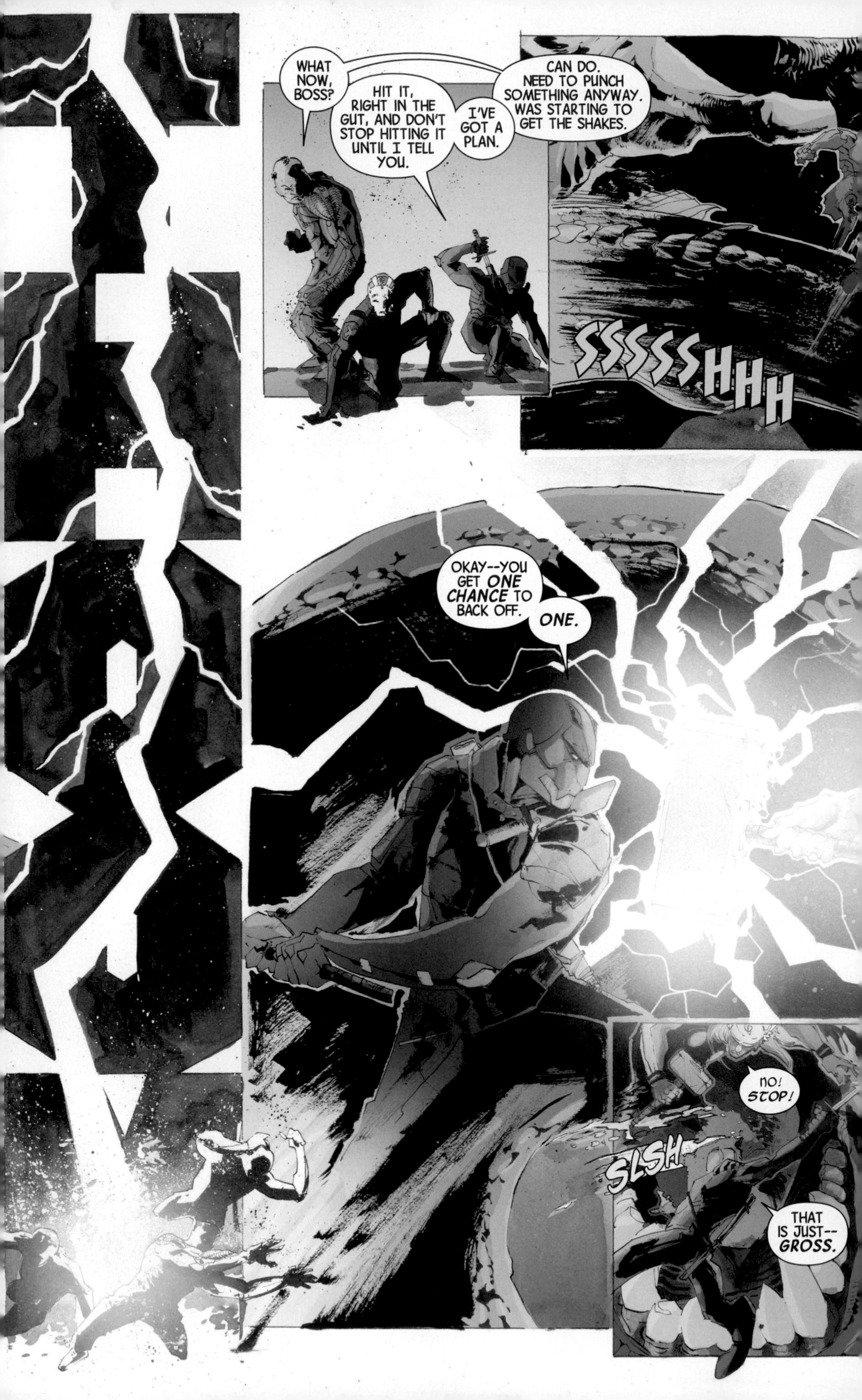
WHAT NOW, BOSS?
HIT IT, RIGHT IN THE GUT, AND DON'T STOP HITTING IT UNTIL I TELL YOU.
I'VE GOT A PLAN.
CAN DO. NEED TO PUNCH SOMETHING ANYWAY. WAS STARTING TO GET THE SHAKES.
SSSSSHHHH
OKAY--YOU GET ONE CHANCE TO BACK OFF.
ONE.
NO! STOP!
SLSH
THAT IS JUST--GROSS.

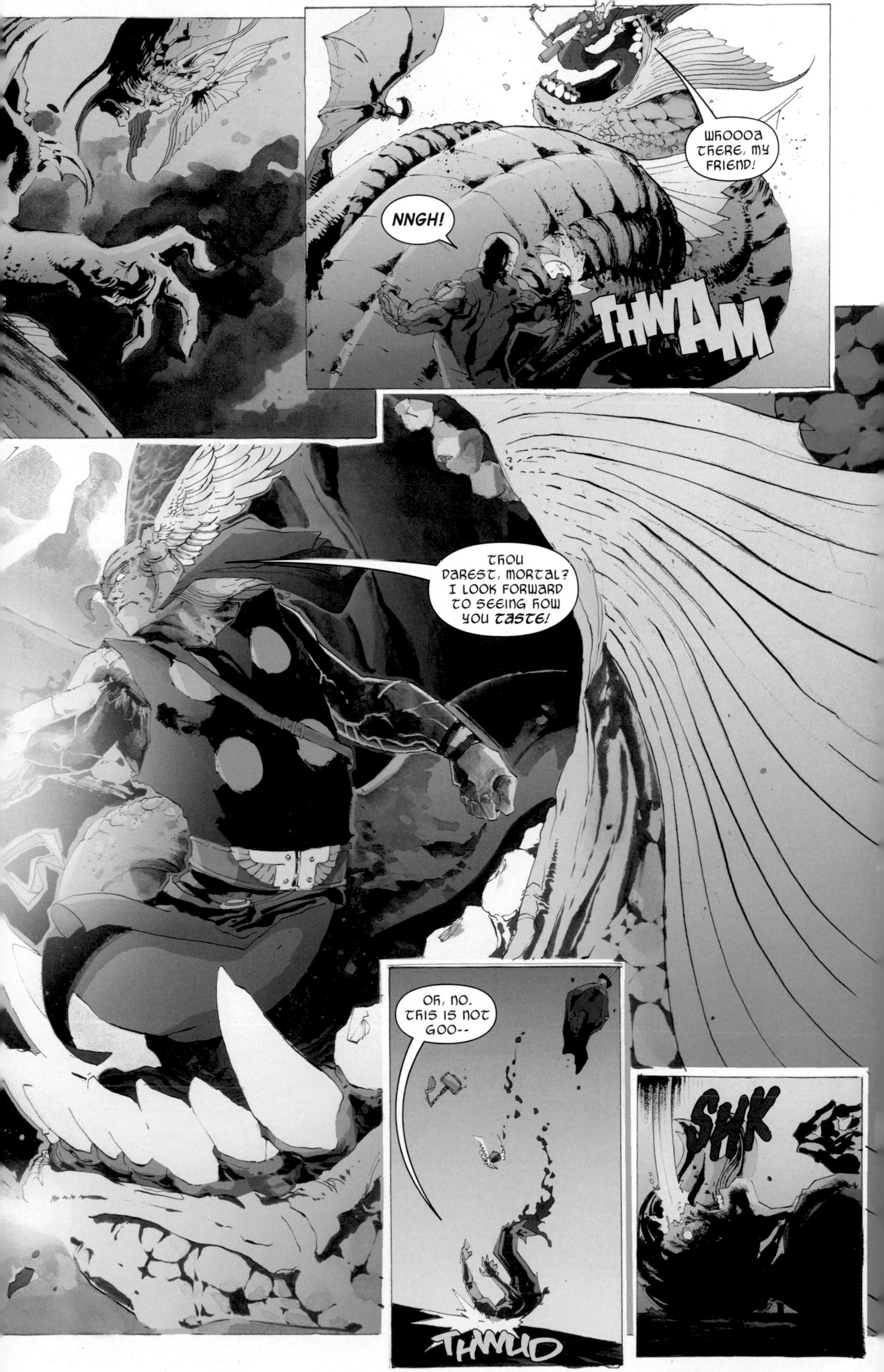
WHOOOA THERE, MY FRIEND!
NNGH!
THWAM
THOU DAREST, MORTAL? I LOOK FORWARD TO SEEING HOW YOU TASTE!
OH, NO. THIS IS NOT GOO--
THWUD
SHK

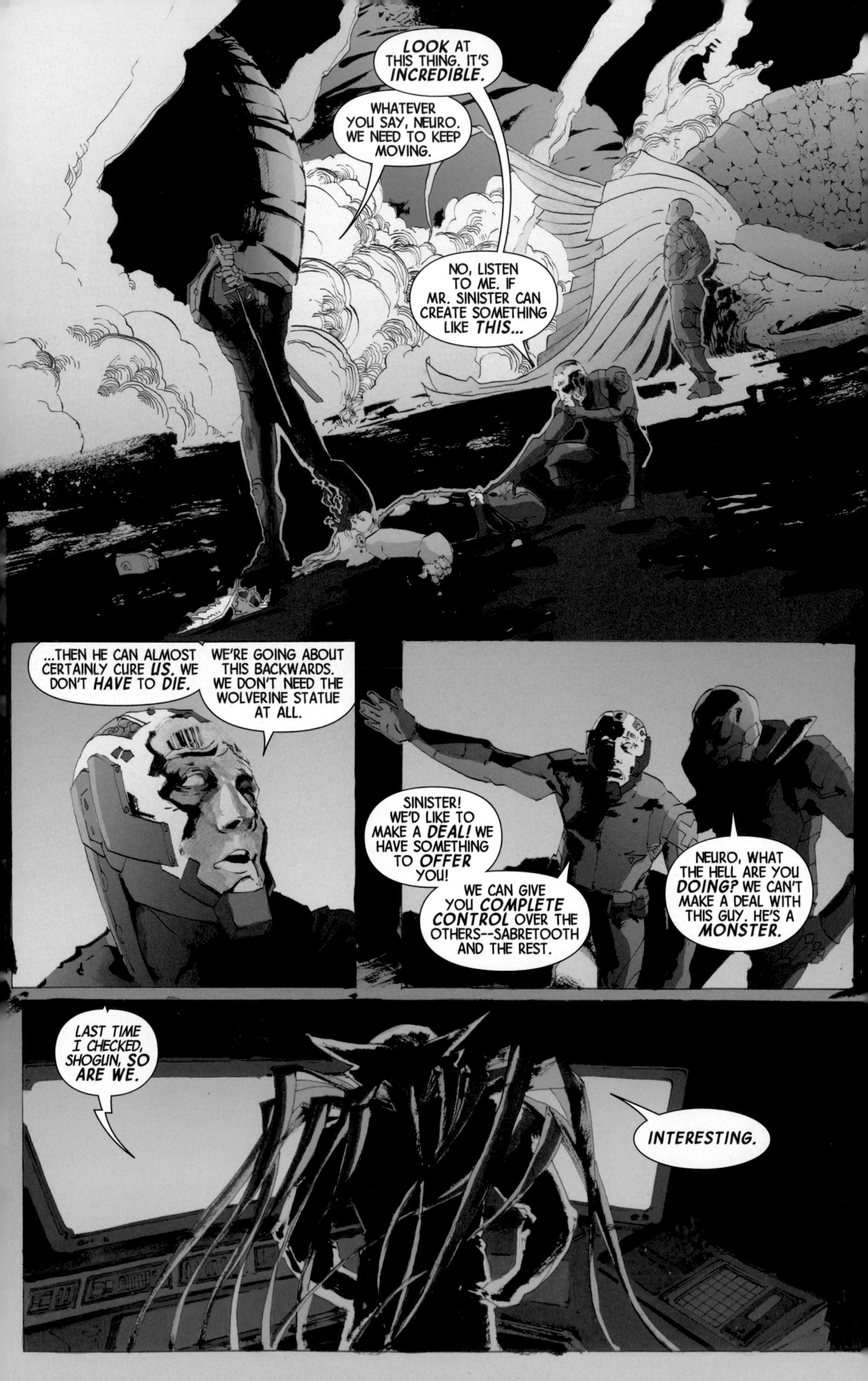
LOOK AT THIS THING. IT'S INCREDIBLE.
WHATEVER YOU SAY, NEURO. WE NEED TO KEEP MOVING.
NO, LISTEN TO ME. IF MR. SINISTER CAN CREATE SOMETHING LIKE THIS...
...THEN HE CAN ALMOST CERTAINLY CURE US. WE DON'T HAVE TO DIE.
WE'RE GOING ABOUT THIS BACKWARDS. WE DON'T NEED THE WOLVERINE STATUE AT ALL.
SINISTER! WE'D LIKE TO MAKE A DEAL! WE HAVE SOMETHING TO OFFER YOU!
WE CAN GIVE YOU COMPLETE CONTROL OVER THE OTHERS--SABRETOOTH AND THE REST.
NEURO, WHAT THE HELL ARE YOU DOING? WE CAN'T MAKE A DEAL WITH THIS GUY. HE'S A MONSTER.
LAST TIME I CHECKED, SHOGUN, SO ARE WE.
INTERESTING.

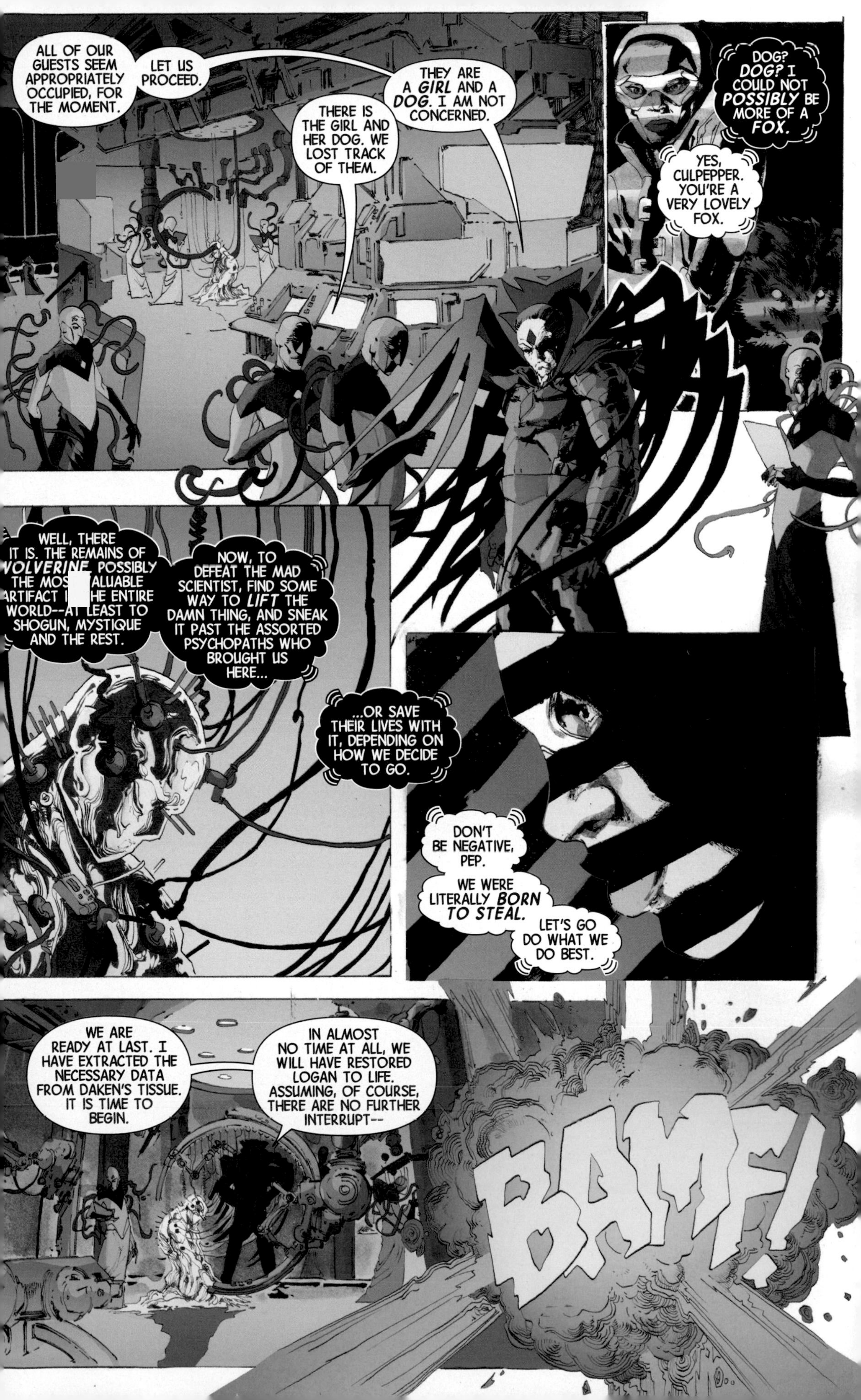

ALL OF OUR GUESTS SEEM APPROPRIATELY OCCUPIED, FOR THE MOMENT.
LET US PROCEED.
THERE IS THE GIRL AND HER DOG. WE LOST TRACK OF THEM.
THEY ARE A GIRL AND A DOG. I AM NOT CONCERNED.
DOG? DOG? I COULD NOT POSSIBLY BE MORE OF A FOX.
YES, CULPEPPER. YOU'RE A VERY LOVELY FOX.
WELL, THERE IT IS. THE REMAINS OF VOLVERINE, POSSIBLY THE MOS ALUABLE ARTIFACT I HE ENTIRE WORLD--AT LEAST TO SHOGUN, MYSTIQUE AND THE REST.
NOW, TO DEFEAT THE MAD SCIENTIST, FIND SOME WAY TO LIFT THE DAMN THING, AND SNEAK IT PAST THE ASSORTED PSYCHOPATHS WHO BROUGHT US HERE...
...OR SAVE THEIR LIVES WITH IT, DEPENDING ON HOW WE DECIDE TO GO.
DON'T BE NEGATIVE, PEP.
WE WERE LITERALLY BORN TO STEAL.
LET'S GO DO WHAT WE DO BEST.
WE ARE READY AT LAST. I HAVE EXTRACTED THE NECESSARY DATA FROM DAKEN'S TISSUE. IT IS TIME TO BEGIN.
IN ALMOST NO TIME AT ALL, WE WILL HAVE RESTORED LOGAN TO LIFE. ASSUMING, OF COURSE, THERE ARE NO FURTHER INTERRUPT--
BAMF!

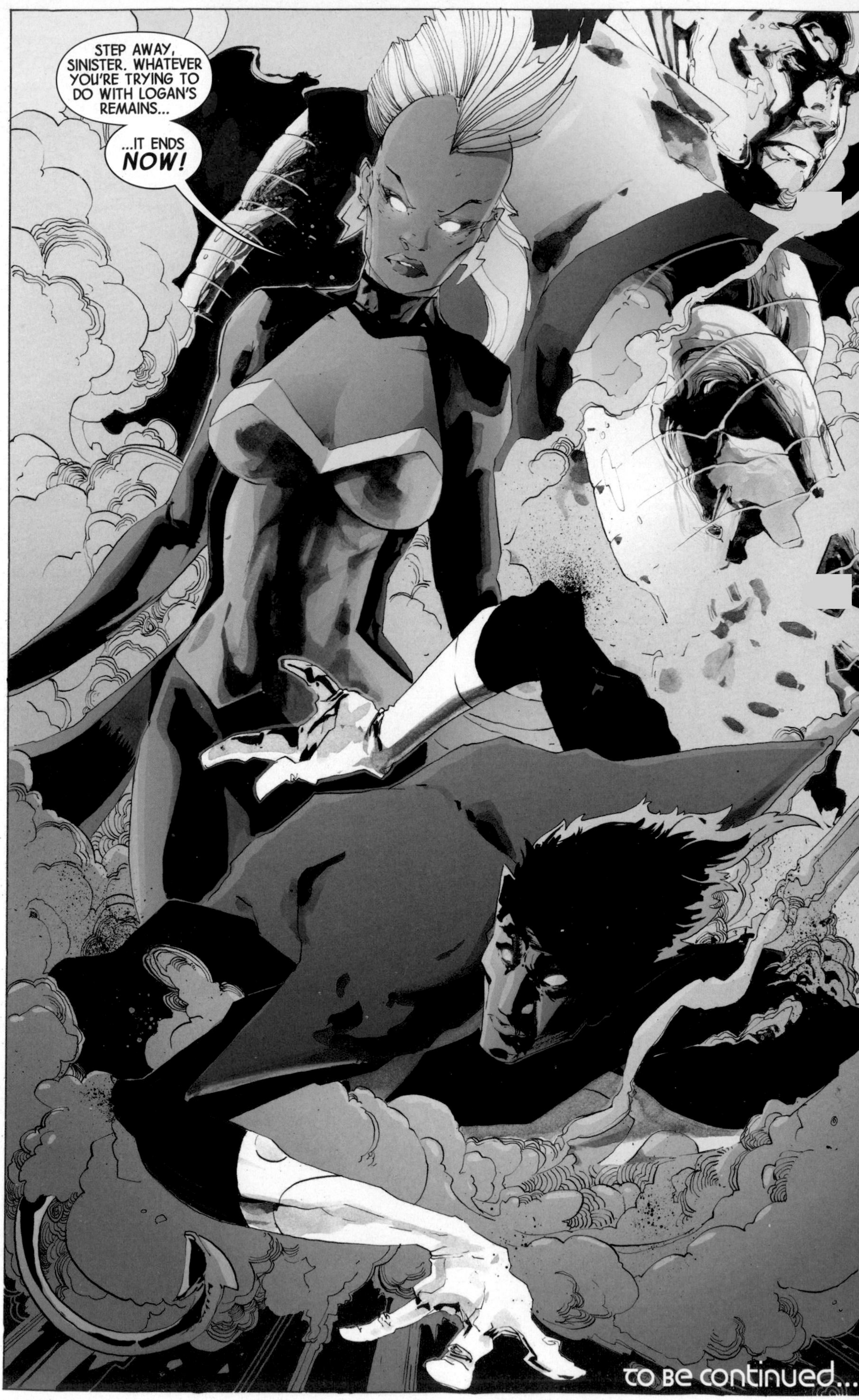
STEP AWAY, SINISTER. WHATEVER YOU'RE TRYING TO DO WITH LOGAN'S REMAINS...
...IT ENDS NOW!
TO BE CONTINUED...